Managing Equal Opportunities in Higher Education

A Guide to Understanding and Action

Diana Woodward and Karen Ross
with John Bird and Graham Upton

The Society for Research into Higher Education
& Open University Press

Published by SRHE and
Open University Press
Celtic Court
22 Ballmoor
Buckingham
MK18 1XW

email: enquiries@openup.co.uk
world wide web: http://www.openup.co.uk

and
325 Chestnut Street
Philadelphia, PA 19106, USA

First Published 2000

ISBN 0 335 19560 1 (pb) 0 335 19561 X (hb)

A catalogue record of this book is available from the British Library

Library of Congress Cataloging-in-Publication Data
Woodward, Diana, 1948–
    Managing equal opportunities in higher education: guide to understanding and action /
    Diana Woodward and Karen Ross with John Bird and Graham Upton.
      p.   cm.
    Includes bibliographical references and index.
    0 335 19561 X (hbk)   0 335 19560 1 (pbk)
    1. Educational equalization–Great Britain. 2. Discrimination in higher education–Great
  Britain. 3. Minorities–Education (Higher)–Great Britain. 1. Ross, Karen, 1957– II. Title
  1.C213.3.G7 W66 2000
  379.2'6–dc21   99-050128

Copy-edited and typeset by The Running Head Limited, www.therunninghead.com
Printed in Great Britain by St Edmundsbury Press, Bury St Edmunds, Suffolk

Managing Equal Opportunities in Higher Education

SRHE and Open University Press Imprint
General Editor: Heather Eggins

Current titles include:

Contents

Acknowledgements

As first-generation university students, both of us owe our present careers to the expansion of higher education that occurred in the UK from the mid-1960s. However, we have also sometimes had to struggle as unwelcome interlopers into the boys' club. We have both encountered prejudice within academia in our time as students and later as researchers, lecturers and now managers within higher education, arising from sexism, racism and homophobia. No doubt these experiences were partly responsible for our research interests in issues of gender, 'race' and disability, and our enduring commitment to feminism. However, we have also enjoyed strong, mutually supportive friendships with colleagues which have made the bad days bearable and the good days even better. To these people we say 'You know who you are'.

Without the support of our families we would not have reached first base. Without the tolerance and patience of our present 'significant others' this book would not have been completed. A former colleague once remarked disparagingly that in his view sociologists tended to have 'irregular private lives'. We are no exception and we would like to thank our families, who believed in us; and Celia and Barry, for being there and not complaining too much when we needed to work instead of play. Diana would particularly like to express her gratitude to her sons for still being happy to spend time with her, and to say 'thank you' to her wonderful research students for the intellectual challenges and stimulation which they have provided. Karen would like to thank all the good women with whom she has broken bread over the past few years and from whom she has drawn strength and courage to go onwards and upwards. May our children have different struggles from our own.

Diana Woodward and Karen Ross

Acronyms and Websites

A-level	Advanced-level examinations (success in which has traditionally determined school-leavers' access to popular universities and courses of study)
AUT	Association of University Teachers (principal lecturers' trade union in pre-1992 universities)
CVCP	Committee of Vice-Chancellors and Principals of the Universities of the United Kingdom
DDA	Disability Discrimination Act (1995)
EO	equal opportunities
FE	further education
GCSE	General Certificate of Secondary Education
HE	higher education
HEFCE	Higher Education Funding Council for England
HEI	higher education institution
HESA	Higher Education Statistics Agency
HNC/HND	Higher National Certificate/Higher National Diploma (higher education awards at sub-degree level)
MBA	Master of Business Administration
NATFHE	National Association of Teachers in Further and Higher Education (principal lecturers' union in post-1992 universities and colleges of higher education. The Further and Higher Education Act (1992) permitted former polytechnics to be designated as universities, without having to meet any additional criteria.)
NCIHE	National Committee of Inquiry into Higher Education (Dearing Committee)
OU	Open University
PCAS	Polytechnics Central Admissions System (now defunct)
THES	*Times Higher Education Supplement*
UCAS	Universities and Colleges Admissions Service
UCCA	Universities Central Council on Admissions (now defunct)

CVCP	http://www.cvcp.ac.uk
DfEE	http://www.dfee.ac.uk
HEFCE	http://www.hefce.ac.uk
HESA	http://www.hesa.ac.uk
UCAS	http://www.ucas.ac.uk

Part 1

Overview

1

Introduction

Diana Woodward

A personal view

When in October 1966, aged almost 18, I set off for Leicester University, I was the first member of my extended family to leave home to pursue my education. At that time the gender mix at Leicester was more even than at many universities, with a 3:2 ratio in favour of male students. Barely aware then of the decades of struggle which it had taken to secure access to higher education for women and for people of both sexes from less advantaged backgrounds, I was delighted and proud to be at university. I was determined to make the most of this opportunity, which I saw as a personal reward for my years of study. It was only much later that I acquired the intellectual tools to analyse this situation in social structural terms, rather than as a purely personal matter. I came to see that the university system restricted access to the advantages conferred by higher education, notably opportunities to enter middle-class careers, to the elite few who had received an academic secondary education and who were disproportionately drawn from the middle and upper social strata. The inherent inequality of this situation, whereby the taxes of those who had not received the educational advantages I had had were funding my continuing acquisition of yet more advantage, did not preoccupy me greatly at that time, I am now ashamed to admit. As I discovered, statistics existed to chart the extent of elitism in access to higher education, which allowed an examination of social class in relation to selective secondary school education and independent schooling as the essential prerequisite to university entry. It was only some years later in my discipline, sociology, that the social processes underlying this selectivity came to be identified, not only in relation to social class but also to other variables such as gender and ethnicity.

After completing my first degree at Leicester, I went on to do a doctorate on the experiences of women students in male-dominated disciplines and their expectations for life after graduation, at the University of Cambridge, in the Management Studies Group, Department of Engineering. This came as a rude shock after the relative gender parity and easy social relationships between the students at Leicester. There were only three women's colleges at Cambridge then, compared with a couple of dozen for men, and so women students were outnumbered 9:1. Out of some 200 postgraduate students in the Engineering Department, only two others were female and I rarely saw either of them. The academic staff were all men, and the clerical and catering staff were all women. The prevailing assumption (which admittedly had some statistical validity) was that if you were young and female, you must be a secretary.

Feminism later provided the concepts and perspectives to enable me to understand why there were so few women academic staff in university departments, even in those where half or more of the students were women, and why those few marginalized individuals were excluded from the exercise of power and decision-making; why fewer women students than men were awarded first-class degrees; how male students benefited from the 'sponsorship' of senior male members of staff, which secured them postgraduate scholarships at prestigious universities through personal recommendation; and why the curriculum and the published research which we read dealt almost exclusively with men's lives, activities and concerns. At Leicester, as elsewhere, the social life of the university revolved around the bar, which was off limits to women for two evenings a week after rugby matches, unless we were willing to risk unwanted attention or public humiliation. Universities at that time were run by men, and in ways that advantaged men (see, for example, Roberts and Woodward, 1981), as many are still, although we then lacked the analytic tools to identify and challenge this situation. Also, I recall meeting very few black staff or students at either of the universities I attended, hardly any identifiably disabled staff or students, nor any overtly gay or lesbian staff or students, except one 'out' lesbian lecturer.

Thirty years on, there is now a healthy concern in many (but by no means all) universities and colleges to try to redress these and other kinds of inequality in the professed ethos of higher education institutions, in patterns of student recruitment and support, in the curriculum, and in the staffing profile. The notion has gained ground that higher education, because it is still predominantly funded by the state, therefore has an obligation to try to meet the needs of the wider society and not just of one elite stratum within it. If this 'moral' argument is insufficiently persuasive, then perhaps the 'business case' for equal opportunities might be more compelling. This argues that it represents a waste of the company's (or, in this case, the nation's) talent, to fail to develop the potential of all its capable members, with a consequent loss of competitive advantage. This was clearly expressed as the first principle in the terms of reference for the National Committee of Inquiry into Higher Education, led by Lord Dearing (commonly known and referred to as the Dearing Report). This Committee, the first major national investigation of higher education for a generation (the previous review being the Robbins Report of 1963) reported its findings in 1997. It made a clear declaration that:

> There should be maximum participation in initial higher education by young and mature students and in lifetime learning by adults, having

regard to the needs of individuals, the nation and the future labour market.

(National Committee of Inquiry into Higher Education, Report 5, 1997: 3)

The Dearing Committee was set up by the British Conservative government in order to address thorny issues about the supply and funding of higher education. By the time it reported, the complexion of the administration had changed. The election of a Labour government in the UK in 1997, after 18 years of Conservative rule, has once again made social engineering through education not only legitimate but indeed a national priority. Under the previous Conservative administration, the ideology of the pursuit of individual prosperity ruled supreme, in a late twentieth-century version of social Darwinism in which the fittest survive and prosper, and the state provision of welfare benefits is restricted, in favour of private provision. Universities explicitly became medium-sized or large businesses rather than extensions of central or local government. However, in practice, their funding continued to come mainly from the government, making them highly responsive to government policy and special initiatives, although with pressures to earn income from other sources. The expansion of higher education was encouraged – to boost the national pool of qualified labour – but without a significant shift in social policy towards recruitment from traditionally under-represented groups, other than part-time students. Total student numbers grew by 80 per cent in the decade 1983 to 1993, with over half of this expansion occurring in the early 1990s. The most notable increases were in full-time student numbers, in the former polytechnics and colleges, and in the numbers of students aged over 21 on entry (HEFCE, 1996). The 'unit of resource' (i.e. expenditure per student) fell as government funding slipped well behind this growth in student numbers: between 1990 and 1998, when the pace of expansion was at its height, public funding for higher education fell by 35 per cent in real terms (HEFCE, 1998b). Other initiatives introduced by the Conservative government that reflected its preference for private over state provision include the award of chartered status to the private University of Buckingham (which remains the country's only private university and which, after 20 years, still has fewer students than many state schools' A-level groups), and the Private Finance Initiative, which encouraged publicly-funded institutions such as universities and hospitals to raise capital sums through partnerships with private firms. Coupled with a steep decline in government funding for capital expenditure, this latter initiative represented a superficially attractive means of funding new buildings. However, these arrangements have not proved popular because of the difficulty and expense of setting up partnerships, and the much greater total cost incurred in financing construction in this way over the buildings' anticipated life.

Both the Labour and the Liberal Democrat parties used the 1997 election campaign to argue the national importance of investment in education. Since taking office the Labour government has put forward a series of initiatives, backed by some additional funding, which are intended to promote children's performance in school and access to higher education for members of under-represented groups, and (through these and other measures) to combat 'social exclusion'. Some, but by no means all, of the Dearing Committee's recom-mendations have been accepted, and the Labour government's own Green Paper, *The Learning Age* (1998), has proposed further strategic objectives for edu-cation. A number of the cuts imposed under the Conservative administration in the collection of national data of interest to social scientists have been restored, and projected questions for inclusion in the 2001 census will for the first time permit the detailed national mapping of various dimensions of inequality. Social scientists in higher education and 'think tanks' are now find-ing a ready audience in Whitehall for their ideas. The importance of research to inform policy has been acknowledged by the Chief Executive of the Higher Education Funding Council for England:

> In meeting these challenges [as identified in the Dearing Report and *The Learning Age*] there is an ever greater need to take strategic approaches to future policy development . . . Policies and practices need, however, to be underpinned by research and development studies, and we commission these whenever we consider they will add value to our deliberations.
>
> (HEFCE, 1998b: 3)

In the Labour government's first two years in office, initiatives have been or are being developed to reward universities and colleges for recruiting and retaining students from disadvantaged communities, students with disabilities and part-time (thus, almost by definition, mature) students. However, the sums made available to support these developments have not been generous, pro-viding nothing like comparable levels of support to those institutions with a strong commitment to widening access that others get from the same govern-ment sources to reward their research excellence. Taking as an example two nearby universities with roughly equal student numbers, University College London had 15,500 students in 1997–8 and received £102 million from HEFCE (comprising £44.6 million to support its teaching, £57 million to sup-port research and £660,000 in 'other allocations'). South Bank University, with 17,500 students, received £39 million in HEFCE funding (including £36.5 million for teaching, £1.7 million for research and £775,000 in 'other allocations'). In 1998–9, HEFCE distributed £2,694 million to support teach-ing and £829 million to reward research (based on the results of its 1996 UK-wide Research Assessment Exercise), but only £334 million for 'special funding' of all kinds, £16 million of which goes to support research collabor-ation. Out of this 'special funding' budget, £5 million was awarded to projects concerning students with disabilities and almost £4 million per year is funding 'widening participation' projects (HEFCE, 1998b). However, even these modest amounts represent a significant step in the direction of support for equal opportunities in higher education, reflecting the funding councils' new-found commitment. As the Chief Executive of HEFCE, Sir Brian Fender, recently wrote:

[E]nhancing teaching and learning and widening access [are] right at the heart of our agenda . . . We passionately believe that in the interests of both the individual and society we should try to make higher education available to as many as possible who can benefit. Universities and colleges collectively have an excellent record in encouraging students from nearly all the ethnic minority groups. Awareness of the needs of disabled students is also much greater than a few years ago. But there is more to be done to raise aspirations and to open up access routes, particularly for students from poorer backgrounds. One of the reasons the Council is encouraging regional partnerships is the potential for collaboration in widening access.

(HEFCE, 1998b: 3–4)

Since the early 1990s, the promotion of equal opportunities has become a major objective for some (but by no means all) British universities and colleges. Commitment has been greatest among the former polytechnics and colleges which achieved university status following the 1992 Further and Higher Education Act, whose planned expansion of student numbers has required renewed efforts to recruit and retain students from social groups with little history of entering higher education. Also, many had historic missions of bringing higher education to those capable of benefiting from it, dating back to their Victorian philanthropic foundations or their history as colleges for the part-time training of technicians and apprentices employed in local industries. Government initiatives to fund 'widening access', following the recommendations of the Dearing Report in July 1997 (NCIHE, 1997), provide financial encouragement for other institutions to espouse this commitment.

Many universities claim to be 'equal opportunities employers' and are eager to express a commitment to equal opportunities for students and staff in their mission statements. However, change is slow, and challenges to institutionalized power bases will only succeed where those in control perceive it as being in their interests to change. Partly because years of funding constraints have restricted new appointments and the associated influx of new ideas, there are still far too many departments (and not just within such traditionally male disciplines as engineering, the applied sciences and politics) where the almost exclusively white, male staff, many of them nearing retirement, are ignorant of or are bewildered by these pressures for change, and so are incapable of appropriate responses. Such staff do not understand what measures they can take to improve the recruitment of women to traditionally male subject-areas, nor how to deal with them other than with benign paternalism. Some universities have designated staff to support overseas students, but too few have seen any need to provide support for British students from minority ethnic groups, such as through actively seeking to modify the staffing profile, or through 'compacts' or mentoring schemes with secondary schools in racially mixed communities. Many institutions have been slow to grasp the benefits of actively recruiting locally based mature students, and too many prospectuses, particularly in the 'old' university sector, still appear to be designed to attract young, white, middle-class, heterosexual school-leavers leaving home to study, even though this group now comprises less than half of all students in higher education. Even where universities are seeking and securing government funding for widening access, their senior staff often seem unaware of the extent of cultural change required to retain 'new' kinds of student, once they have been recruited, and to enable them to thrive.

Far-sighted vice-chancellors correctly perceive student school-leavers to be a declining breed, particularly those whose families are able to afford the expense of residence away from home, often remote from opportunities for part-time employment during term-time to finance their studies. In the early aftermath of the introduction of students' fee payments and the replacement of student grants by loans, it appears that mature students' applications are running at about 10 per cent below the levels of recent years. Too many institutions fail to see that the active recruitment of disabled students ought to be their concern, and respond to those who do apply for a student place on a one-off basis by seeking to resolve their individual 'problems' rather than implementing general improvements in physical access and support systems that would benefit the whole academic community. Too few senior managers realize that the successful recruitment of a more diverse student body must be accompanied by a series of measures which ensure that students from all backgrounds feel that they are valued members of the academic community, with access to appropriate support systems.

Apart from strategies to increase the recruitment of students from formerly under-represented groups (such as partnerships based on mutual respect with local schools, colleges and other bodies), the infrastructural changes required to bring this about must include such measures as the recruitment, retention and promotion of a diverse body of staff; the provision of staff development and training for all staff to sensitize them to equal opportunities issues; and the embedding of monitoring and evaluation in relation to institutional targets within the institution's standard, routine systems. These measures involve challenges to the organizational culture, which cannot remain dominated by a white, male, ageing, middle-class elite if universities are to be open institutions which value the varied contributions of its socially diverse members. As a precursor to these changes, institutions need to establish their current position, using both quantitative and qualitative measures, to devise policies based on wide consultation and to set out corporate objectives with a schedule for progress towards achieving them.

The National Committee of Inquiry into Higher Education (the Dearing Report, 1997) commissioned a series of studies into differential patterns of participation in higher education between social groups. One of these studies concluded that one reason for the lower participation of students from lower socio-economic groups is their 'cultural alienation'.

Universities can appear unwelcoming to students from lower social class backgrounds (and to members of some minority ethnic groups and some students with a disability as well); universities promise a 'cultural apprenticeship' in 'other people's culture' by which the voice and experience of lower socio-economic groups is redefined and reinterpreted by professional academic tutors from higher socio-economic backgrounds (Metcalf, 1993). Yet Hogarth *et al.* (1997) report no differential in performance once entry has been achieved, although students from lower socio-economic groups are more likely to report a lack of personal confidence and family/peer support (NCIHE, Report 6, 1997: 56).

However, some of the cultural barriers which discourage potential students by making them feel that university is 'not for them' are still all too evident. On the day on which I am writing this, my newspaper carries a story about the University of Cambridge. Its council is being urged to change its regulation that members of its academic staff who hold degrees from other universities can only wear a plain black Cambridge Masters gown on formal occasions such as the award of honorary degrees, whereas those with Cambridge doctorates wear splendid mediaeval scarlet and black robes. The article quotes Dr Anthony Edwards, Reader in Biometry, 'who successfully led the opposition to the idea last time it was proposed, in 1979, and is set to challenge it again, [who] said: . . . These ceremonies could turn into Gilbertian pantomimes all too easily. With gowns of all sorts and hues I think they might fall through thin ice' (*The Guardian*, 17 February 1998). Leaving aside what kind of 'thin ice' Dr Edwards had in mind, and my own view that a diversity of flamboyant academic dress is actually a rather attractive feature of degree conferment ceremonies, this kind of exclusionary device symbolizes the extremes of difference between those universities that seek to remain bastions of exclusivity and privilege, buttressed by arcane practices, and those that seek to welcome students from a much wider cross-section of the community.

Of course, these critical comments do not apply to all universities; far from it. Indeed, the following chapters include case studies and examples of initiatives from a range of universities and colleges to show what kind of measures can be taken to address inequality in higher education, and the circumstances required for them to achieve their objectives. However, the government has endorsed the Dearing Report's call for all institutions to devise strategies for widening participation, while acknowledging the need to respect their varying character and mission by articulating this request in terms of the development of corporate plans, and emphasizing the responsibility of governing bodies to monitor and review achievements (HEFCE, 1998a). I hope that either a moral commitment, as expressed in mission statements, or enlightened self-interest will soon drive most universities towards more open recruitment policies for both students and staff, and to making all their members feel valued participants within their diverse academic communities. The Robbins Committee's rejection in 1963 of the elitist argument that there was a strictly limited pool of ability from which university students should be selected has been resoundingly endorsed in the light of experience (NCIHE, Report 5, 1997). As Richard Hoggart has put it, the recent massive expansion of higher education 'confirmed that there was far more talent in the country than we had guessed or were willing, out of class-and-culture meanness, to recognise' (Hoggart, 1996: 42). Thus the annual investment of some £4 billion of public funds can be justified, and the traditional role of higher education will be maintained as a force for both personal enlightenment and national prosperity.

For those readers whose political affiliations lead them to be suspicious of the language of 'equal opportunities' as merely an expression of so-called 'political correctness', perhaps substitution of other phrases might be helpful as they work their way through this book. They may find its content more to their liking if they replace any mention of equality of opportunity in relation to students with the terms 'customer care' or 'customer services', and any mention of staffing issues with 'good practice in relation to HRM' (human relations management). I cannot empathize with the notion that management in higher education entails nothing more than the application of principles and practices which have proved 'successful' in the private sector (where the main objectives are the profit motive and growth in market share, share prices and shareholders' returns), devoid of any concern with wider issues of social justice and the public good. However, even if these arguments of principle fail to persuade, I hope that this volume will nevertheless motivate readers to seek to improve the position of both students and staff from disadvantaged groups, even if the primary motivation for so doing is to be found in other reasons, such as the financial health of the institution and the maintenance of its market share (of student applications, research grant awards, or whatever).

Higher education in the UK today

Throughout the developed world the rapid expansion of tertiary education has become a national priority in order to maintain prosperity through upgrading the skills of the labour force. More than a third of the population of the 29 member countries of the Organization for Economic Co-operation and Development will enter university-level education at some point in their lives, if current trends are maintained (OECD, 1998 cited in *THES*, 27 November 1998). Already half the population enters university or college in the United States. In the UK, this figure is just over 40 per cent, but the lower withdrawal rates mean that the UK, Hungary and Japan are producing the highest proportions of graduates, with success rates of about 80 per cent, compared with 60 per cent in the States, and as low as 47 per cent in Austria and 35 per cent in Italy. Part of this difference is attributable to the shorter duration of the typical British undergraduate degree, lasting three or four years in comparison with the six or more years which are customary in Austria, Germany and Italy, but patterns of tertiary education vary widely between OECD countries, making comparisons problematic. So although in both Finland and Poland between 45 and 50 per cent of young people are educated to degree level, in Finland virtually all tertiary education is full-time whereas in Poland it is virtually all part-time.

During the 1990s, expenditure on higher education as a proportion of gross domestic product has generally increased in the OECD countries: in 1994 it was about 2.4 per cent in Canada, 1.7 per cent in the Netherlands and New

Zealand, 1.5 per cent in Australia, and about 1.3 per cent in the United Kingdom, Turkey, the United States and Ireland (HEFCE, 1999). Throughout the OECD countries private financing is supplementing public spending, mainly through higher tuition fees, and the expansion in student numbers has generally been accompanied by a reduction in expenditure per student. The British fall in expenditure per student of 20 per cent since 1990 for tertiary education (as defined by OECD) and 35 per cent for university-level education, as cited earlier, represents one of the sharpest declines within an OECD country. By the 1996–7 academic year, the 171 higher education institutions in the United Kingdom had a total of 1.7 million students studying at higher education level (Higher Education Statistics Agency, 1997a; HEFCE, 1999). They provided employment for some 100,000 full-time and over 14,000 part-time academic staff, and as many support and ancillary staff, comprising in all about 318,000 people, or 1.2 per cent of the UK workforce (HEFCE, 1999). The universities' combined income was over £11 billion (Higher Education Funding Agency, 1994; HESA, 1997b, 1997c; HEFCE, 1999). Higher education, in the UK as in other developed societies, is now very big business, and in the UK generates an annual contribution of some £40 billion to the economy (CVCP, 1997; HEFCE, 1999).

Governments are rightly concerned about the production of graduates as an aspect of their employment policy, to ensure an adequate supply of highly skilled labour capable of maintaining a national competitive edge in the global economy, and to generate sufficient wealth to fund pensions, education and health care for both those in paid work and the economically inactive. Graduates now comprise about a quarter of the British workforce, but they are unevenly distributed in geographical terms. Nearly one-third (32 per cent) of adult residents in one central London borough (Kensington and Chelsea) hold post-school qualifications, compared with 3.5 per cent (barely one-tenth as many) in another London borough (Barking and Dagenham), which is east of London (Local Base Statistics, based on 1991 census data). The rate of return on investment in higher education has been estimated as about 14 per cent, and there is a positive correlation (albeit an unexplained one) between the expansion of higher education since 1960 and economic growth for OECD countries (NCIHE, Report 8, 1997).

Also, the provision of higher education for substantial numbers of overseas students has itself become a valuable form of international commerce (for example, in the United States and Australia and, to a lesser extent, the UK) or an arm of overseas aid with strategic political objectives (such as in the case of the former Eastern bloc countries, which provided university education for students from Cuba and certain African states). About 200,000 students (11 per cent of the total student population) come to the UK's universities and colleges from overseas, 44 per cent of them from European Union countries (HESA, 1997a; HEFCE, 1999). The overseas income generated by the British university sector in 1995–6 was £1.78 billion, one-third of it from the fees paid by overseas students (from outside the European Union) and half from off-campus expenditure by those students and overseas visitors (HEFCE, 1999).

In many cities universities have become major local employers, compensating for the decline in traditional forms of employment such as mining, heavy industry and agriculture. They generate significant wealth and other benefits for the local economy in a variety of ways. These include expenditure by students and visitors on accommodation and services, and the purchasing power of universities and their staff, who spend a significant part of their salaries within the local economy. There is also the contribution made by universities to the development of local commerce and industry via the transfer of skills and research-based knowledge, as well as to the cultural capital of the locality. (See, for example, Harris 1997, for a recent study of this phenomenon, and CVCP 1997 and DfEE 1998 for overviews of the issue.) Areas with an under-provision of higher education places suffer from the permanent exodus of educated young people, as well as the 'invisible export' of their spending power during their studies. In Northern Ireland it is estimated that an additional 12,500 university places are required to sustain the production of graduates at a comparable rate to that in Scotland (NCIHE, Report 9, 1997) where a higher proportion of young people have traditionally proceeded to higher education than in the rest of the UK, although this difference has apparently narrowed in recent years (NCIHE, Report 6, 1997).

The stereotype of the typical student as a school-leaver from a middle-class home may have been true at the time of the Robbins Report in the early 1960s, when university education was avowedly elitist. It has already been noted that the number of students aged over 21 on entry to higher education (i.e. 'mature' students) now exceeds the number of 18- and 19-year-olds: 64 per cent of those pursuing a qualification in 1996–7 were mature students (HEFCE, 1998b). The age participation rate for school-leavers is itself now six times higher than in 1960, when 5.4 per cent of the 18+ age group entered higher education, compared with 19.3 per cent in 1990 and 32 per cent in 1995 (NCIHE, Report 6, 1997). However, the advantage conferred by high social class has remained stubbornly resistant to change. Young people from the most affluent neighbourhoods are up to 12 times more likely to enter higher education than those from the poorest areas (HEFCE, 1997, 1998a, 1998b). Just over half (54 per cent) of young people from professional and managerial homes now go on to higher education, compared with only 17 per cent of those from semi-skilled and unskilled family backgrounds.

This enduring inequality matters to the individuals concerned, to their communities and to the wider society. Individuals forgo the enhanced income which graduates can command, and their communities lose the economic multiplier benefits of this expenditure, as well as the 'cultural capital' represented by an educated workforce and group of citizens. The government, in partnership with providers of education including universities, further education colleges and schools, is implementing measures backed by funding worth £30 million which is intended to increase the participation of under-represented groups in higher education, and to ensure that such students succeed (HEFCE, 1998a, 1998c).

The rationale and structure of the book

Over the past fifteen years, the issue of equal opportunities in higher education has assumed growing significance for both senior managers and teaching staff. For some institutions this has been both a moral and a political imperative to widen access beyond the traditional, elite social groups, as a means of institutional survival, with the growth in student numbers generating a growth in income. The primary intention of this book is to persuade senior managers in universities and colleges of the case for promoting equality of opportunity for both students and staff, and to provide some case study examples and sources of further information to assist them to do so. An additional intended audience is those who are studying these issues within postgraduate courses in education management or management in public sector organizations. A handful of institutions also offer postgraduate courses or modules in equal opportunities. In recent years, the volume of literature on this topic has expanded rapidly with the publication of handbooks, analyses of good practice, reports and policy statements, many of which will be cited later. However, few of them cover the whole range of equal opportunities issues which affect the many groups within the population who have not traditionally enjoyed access to a university education or to professional employment in higher education. Fewer still seek to explain the present position in terms of its socio-historical context, as this one does.

The intention of the book is to draw attention to the many dimensions of inequality which exist within higher education, and to propose measures for identifying and addressing them. Some aspects of disadvantage have long been acknowledged, and a great deal has been written about them. The position of women as staff within higher education, especially academic staff, is a case in point. The transformational impact of the second wave of feminism from the 1970s on academic work in social science and the humanities enabled women academics to analyse their own disadvantage within the academy, in terms of recruitment and promotion, salaries, organizational cultures, historical position and linguistic discourses. The same women launched campaigns within the National Association of Teachers in Further and Higher Education (NATFHE) and the Association of University Teachers (AUT) to challenge inequality. British, European and international networks now exist to promote women's interests within higher education, and a voluminous literature of both scholarly and action-oriented texts is available on this topic. In contrast, sexual orientation is covered by a meagre literature and features far less frequently in mission statements, prospectuses and other statements of institutional aims and policy than many of the other forms of disadvantage addressed in this book. Other disadvantaged groups, such as students with disabilities and those from certain minority ethnic groups, occupy an intermediate position in terms of universities' responsiveness to political pressures exerted on their behalf and their capacity to implement effective strategies to promote their access to higher education.

This book addresses the management of equal opportunities in higher education in three parts. The first, which includes this introductory chapter, seeks to set these issues in a wider context. An appreciation of the historical, philosophical and theoretical backcloth to these issues will, it is hoped, enable the reader to understand better why the pressures for equality of opportunity have arisen and the wider understandings which its proponents bring with them to their mission. The inclusion of a vice-chancellor's perspective in this first section attempts to ground the rhetoric of equal opportunities in an empirical example of one university's strategy of developing an equal opportunities policy, actually making it happen and then monitoring its development.

The second part of the book is divided into chapters based on specific forms of inequality, such as gender, ethnicity, social class, sexual orientation and disability, supported by case study examples and useful additional sources. However, readers should be aware that these various forms of inequality are neither homogeneous nor exclusive: a student with a disability may also be a middle-aged Asian woman from a socially disadvantaged family who is a lesbian. In addition, the position of students and of staff in relation to each of these 'categories of disadvantage' will differ and may well require different institutional strategies to address them. Some of the initiatives reported here are relevant to many or all of the forms of disadvantage identified, for example those dealing with staff development and training, or harassment, but they are described in one specific chapter for convenience, and with an emphasis on their relevance to that aspect of inequality. The final part of the book seeks to draw together the various threads, identifying the kinds of actions and initiatives available to managers at all levels within institutional hierarchies to identify their institution's values and priorities, and then to seek to bring about change.

As already noted, the subject of equality of opportunity in higher education is a vast one, which has in recent years generated a growing literature on analysis and advice. This book cannot cover everything; it is inevitably selective. There is little reference here, for example, to international students or to aspiring students from remote rural areas. Also, the somewhat arbitrary division of its content, with separate chapters addressing selected discrete dimensions of inequality, risks obscuring the message that each one of us is a unique individual and some of us may experience a multiplicity of disadvantages. However, we hope that readers will be persuaded by arguments on the importance of promoting equal opportunities and will find ideas and examples of good practice described here which can usefully be applied in their own institutions. In particular, managers may find helpful the models of how to identify and address inequalities of opportunity in their own universities and colleges. Like adherence to religion or feminism, one's best will never quite be good enough, but this book may provide a stimulus to progress in the right direction.

References

Committee of Vice-Chancellors and Principals (1997) *The Impact of Universities and Colleges on the UK Economy*. London: CVCP.

Committee on Higher Education (the Robbins Report) (1963) *Committee on Higher Education Report*, Cmnd 2145. London: HMSO.

Department for Education and Employment (1998) *Universities and Economic Development: Executive Summary*. Sheffield: DfEE.

Harris, R. I. D. (1997) The impact of the University of Portsmouth on the local economy, *Urban Studies*, 34: 605–26.

Higher Education Funding Council for England (1996) *Widening Access to Higher Education: A Report by the HEFCE's Advisory Group on Access and Participation*. Bristol: HEFCE.

Higher Education Funding Council for England (1997) *The Influence of Neighbourhood Type on Participation in Higher Education: Interim Report*. Bristol: HEFCE.

Higher Education Funding Council for England (1998a) *Widening Participation in Higher Education: Funding Proposals*: ref 98/39. Bristol: HEFCE.

Higher Education Funding Council for England (1998b) *Achieving the Learning Society: Annual Report, 1997–8*. Bristol: HEFCE.

Higher Education Funding Council for England (1998c) *Council Briefing*. Bristol: HEFCE.

Higher Education Funding Council for England (1999) *Higher Education in the United Kingdom*, 99/02. Bristol: HEFCE.

Higher Education Statistics Agency (1997a) *Students in Higher Education Institutions, 1996/7: HESA Data Report*. Cheltenham: HESA.

Higher Education Statistics Agency (1997b) *Students in Higher Education Institutions, 1995/6*, Reference Volume. Cheltenham: HESA.

Higher Education Statistics Agency (1997c) *Resources of Higher Education Institutions, 1995/6*, Reference Volume. Cheltenham: HESA.

HM Government (1998) *The Learning Age*, Green Paper. London: HMSO.

Hoggart, R. (1996) *The Way We Live Now*. London: Pimlico.

Hunt, P. (1998) Cloaks and daggers: the knives are out at Cambridge over calls to loosen gown rules, *THES*, 17 February.

National Committee of Inquiry into Higher Education (the Dearing Report) [NCIHE] (1997) *Higher Education in the Learning Society*. Norwich: HMSO.

Roberts, H. and Woodward, D. (1981) Changing patterns of women's employment in sociology, 1950–1980, *British Journal of Sociology*, 32(4): 531–46.

2

Why Should Universities Bother with Equal Opportunities? A Vice-Chancellor's View

Graham Upton

Introduction

My aim in this chapter is to identify issues of equal opportunities for, and among, students and staff in higher education using my own university as a case study. I start by setting the context, mainly using comments and data from the Dearing Report (National Committee of Inquiry into Higher Education, 1997), one of the central aspects of which is its focus on issues of widening access and equity for both students and staff. The merits of a strategic approach to equal opportunities are then discussed in relation to both the business case and agencies of change. Finally, equal opportunities initiatives at Oxford Brookes University are discussed and evaluated, and conclusions drawn.

The case for equal opportunities

At present the role of education in the UK is, perhaps, most often perceived from a functional perspective. First, it appears, education is seen as the engine for a competitive nation and its economy, and second as having utility for the consumers (students) in terms of jobs and careers, income and their material lives, and as a route to upward mobility. From primary school level through to higher education, learning and research, we now live in a public world of performance indicators, league tables and the 'bottom line'. There is some utility in this; in the ensuing debate about who are winners and who losers, it is clear that there has been some useful exposure of inequalities among and within disadvantaged groups. It can also be seen that in the last decade a more than doubling of the numbers in higher education has begun to open up opportunities – albeit limited – for members of these disadvantaged groups.

Minority ethnic groups and participation in higher education in the UK

Evidence collected for the Dearing Report (NCIHE, 1997) shows that minority ethnic communities overall are now better represented in higher education than white people. The Dearing Report's statistics show that in 1994, 12.2 per cent of the 18–20 year olds in higher education were non-white compared to the figure of 7.3 per cent of non-whites in this age group in the total population. But there are important differences here, including some related to social class. Modood (1993 cited in NCIHE, 1997) has commented that although most members of minority ethnic groups have a lower socio-economic class profile than white people, some appear to value education more highly than their white counterparts. In particular, women from minority ethnic backgrounds have been taking advantage of higher education: the 1991 census showed that 47 per cent of 16- to 24-year-olds in this category were in full-time education, compared with only 32 per cent of white women. The highest take-up rate was among Chinese women, with 66 per cent of women in this age group participating in full-time education, albeit that Chinese people make up only a very small proportion of the 5 per cent of individuals in the UK from minority ethnic groups (CRE, 1997). However, there was a low level of participation among Bangladeshi women and African Caribbean men and subject specialism also showed a strong ethnic bias, with African Caribbean students over-represented in arts and humanities courses, and under-represented on courses requiring high degrees of numeracy or on technical courses (3 per cent). In comparison, 92 per cent of Chinese and 48 per cent of white students took mathematical, science, engineering and technology courses.

In addition, detailed research shows that ethnic minority students remain concentrated in certain 'new' universities (the former polytechnics), predominantly those in London and the Midlands, where they are the local institutions for large minority ethnic populations (Modood, 1993). The Dearing Report commented that this concentration may also be partly explained by these universities being more diverse, more multiracial and more flexible in terms of their entry requirements and access programmes. However, exclusionary attitudes and behaviour by other universities may equally be responsible for this bias. The limited data on the actual experiences of ethnic minority students in higher education has indicated that many face overt discrimination and feelings of isolation, and that only limited attempts have been made by institutions to provide targeted and appropriate support (Singh, 1990; Bird *et al.*, 1992 cited in NCIHE, 1997).

Participation rates of women and men in higher education in the UK

The proportion of women undergraduates in the UK has doubled in the past 30 years to the point where there are now equal numbers of men and women studying for first degrees. However, like minority ethnic students, women tend to be concentrated in certain subject areas, such as education and the humanities. Indeed, a warning against 'too much optimism about overall progress towards equal participation by women' is given in the Dearing Report. The Report comments that mature students and those on access courses are more likely to be women. Problems of poor child-care facilities, transport problems, inflexible timetabling and insufficient academic and personal guidance have all been catalogued as additional obstacles for women students. These barriers also contribute to the higher drop-out rates of mature and part-time women students. The dominance of women in such student groups was highlighted in the Dearing Report as illustrating the persistent under-representation of working-class and unemployed men. Class remains an important issue for equal opportunities in higher education, and has been particularly relevant in the recent debate about the introduction of tuition fees.

The Dearing Report also indicated that women were still very much under-represented in postgraduate research degrees programmes, and at all levels in the academic staffing hierarchy. In this, the Report reinforced the comment made by the Hansard Society that, 'in bleak contrast with the position elsewhere, the number of women in senior academic posts is scarcely increasing' (Hansard Society, 1990: 10). Hansard exhorted universities to take action to improve the representation of women academics at all levels. However, subsequent research findings show there has been little activity: in old and new universities respectively only 20 per cent and 30 per cent of full-time academic staff are women, although there is probably a much higher proportion of 'non career' part-time and casual female lecturing staff in the less secure jobs (Bagilhole, 1993; NATFHE, 1998). Women were also poorly represented in senior positions: data from the 'new' universities showed that only 12 per cent of women staff members are in posts above that of senior lecturer – the most common grade for teaching staff – compared with 25 per cent of men (Bagilhole, 1993). As the Committee of Vice-Chancellors and Principals has acknowledged, such evidence suggests that universities 'cannot be held up as models of good practice' (Bagilhole, 1993: 262).

Approaches to equal opportunities

An increasingly diverse student population can make demands on institutions to provide different kinds of service and the promotion and delivery of greater equality should be seen as a strategic response to those new demands. In future this may also make better 'business' sense in a world where students, moving to become consumers, may be quick to assert their rights and demand what they consider value for their fees. In doing so, they are likely to look at their university's mission statement and goals – and although virtually all universities now apparently have equal opportunities policies, it is clear that by no means all put them into practice.

In 1997 a guide entitled *Higher Education and Equality* was developed jointly by the Committee of Vice-Chancellors and Principals, the Commission for Racial Equality and the Equal Opportunities Commission (Powney *et al.*, 1997). It encourages institutions to embed equal opportunities in their practices and operations, rather than treat it as an afterthought or 'add on'. Among the many points made in the guide, much is said about 'enhancing customer satisfaction', becoming 'an employer of choice' and avoiding the costs of discrimination. Clearly, equality is on the agenda as a business case.

A widely used model for implementing equal opportunities in the business world is that developed by Hammond and Halton (1990) which has been used as the basis of Opportunity 2000, the campaign for increasing the quantity and quality of women in business. In fact, few of the employers who signed up for Opportunity 2000 have got anywhere near achieving real equality of opportunity, which is worth noting by those promoting equal opportunities in universities (Opportunity 2000, *Annual Reports*). The Hammond and Halton model was derived from an analysis of effective strategies for changing organizational culture. Four main strands were identified: demonstrating commitment, changing behaviour, communicating ownership and making the investment. When applied to organizations claiming equal opportunities, it was found that these four were absent in all or part.

The cost of such omissions can be spectacular, in terms of both cash and bad publicity. This lesson has been learned the hard way by some universities faced with equal pay and harassment cases. In other public sector institutions, and in particular the National Health Service, the police and the armed forces, lack of attention to equal opportunities has led to large financial compensation payouts in relation to both discrimination and equal pay cases (*Equal Opportunities Review*, May/June 1997; *Equal Opportunities Review*, January/February 1998). Although this is clearly 'bad for business', such 'soft' or difficult-to-quantify policy areas, like equal opportunities, are often early victims of funding cuts, delivering short-term gains for possible long-term losses which can lead to the adoption of a minimalist approach (Blakemore and Drake, 1996).

Another problem which has beset the development of equal opportunities in the business sector is the tendency to use a top-down approach when promoting such policies, thereby reinforcing the hierarchical nature of most business organizations. In Kanter's study of successful change in corporations in the USA, she concluded that in the most innovative organizations 'there were large numbers of people at all levels who could grab and use power. And with this power to act came the chance to innovate' (Kanter, 1983: 24; see also Price and Priest, 1996). Increasingly, as minority groups establish a space and a voice, studies show that this type of active agency can get people working collectively and collaboratively for change; it can be a viable and inclusive equal opportunities strategy (Ledwith and Colgan, 1996).

There are important lessons here for universities, which are by nature different from most business organizations: they have flatter structures and pay much more regard to the importance of participative decision-making. In universities it is thus particularly important to maintain a balanced approach which emphasizes partnership and which recognizes that there is a dispersal of power and expertise around the organization. In this context, leadership is important but it is perhaps even more important to recognize the potential value of students and staff as active agents of change.

Equal opportunities at Oxford Brookes University

When Oxford Brookes (referred to as Brookes in the remainder of this chapter, for reasons of brevity) became a university in 1992, its mission statement included an aspiration to achieve 'Excellence through Diversity'. This has been an important 'driver' for our interest in, and approach to, equal opportunities. In this we had a good basis to work from as Brookes' equal opportunity policies had their roots, as a former polytechnic, in its local authority inheritance. This had provided a legacy of some well-developed policies in areas such as job sharing and career-break schemes. There were also significant support structures already in existence for students. For example, students with disabilities were provided with specially adapted accommodation, a disabled users' group met regularly and there was a specialist adviser in post. The institution had similar support systems for international and mature students, and there was a nursery for the children of staff and students (Price and Priest, 1996).

All the above structures were retained, following incorporation as a university, providing an important basis for subsequent development. Significantly, much of the thrust for this came 'from below'; from staff who in their academic and professional lives were committed to equality. It was just such a group which, in 1991, successfully bid for internal funding to commission an external study of equality at Brookes (University of Central Lancashire, 1993). When subsequently the governors and the (then) vice-chancellor set up the Equal Opportunities Action Group (EOAG), some of those original activists became members.

In their discussion of 'activists as change agents', Liz Price and Judy Priest (both previous heads of equal opportunities at Brookes) define activism as the 'roles we play when we take action to exert influence for, and on behalf of, ourselves and others who are disadvantaged or lacking power within our university' (1996: 37). They tell the story of the beginnings of the current equal opportunities approach, using Kanter's framework outlined above, of a three-stage model of political change: problem definition, coalition building and mobilization (Kanter, 1983).

Thus, the strategy at Brookes has always been one of systematically finding out what the issues are, investigating them and providing the evidence, then moving to consultation and, wherever possible, of actively working with key players in the wider university community to develop and agree policies and procedures. This is not to say that there has been no opposition, or inertia – itself a form of opposition – or ignorance in equal opportunities matters. These still exist but they do not deter. One of the great benefits of this approach to problem definition is that it fits well with 'normal' academic practices of research and inquiry. It is a familiar method in a university. It is also well known in any research community that the process of carrying out research raises awareness as well as providing evidence. At Brookes, efforts have consequently been made to carry out research and auditing wherever possible before any action has been taken. For example, a harassment survey was carried out in which 100 per cent of staff and 50 per cent of students received a questionnaire. In itself, this generated debate within the university but the evidence from the survey of extensive, endemic low-level bullying and harassment between and among staff and students provided indisputable legitimization for the development of the subsequent comprehensive policy, procedures, support systems and training. Harassment and bullying have not gone away, but members of the university community who experience it are now more aware that they have rights and systems of redress.

This is the sort of work which has begun to change the university's culture. In the University of Central Lancashire's report (carried out in 1991), Brookes was described as portraying a culture of middle-class complacency – a culture where 'exhibiting difference becomes increasingly difficult, be that difference one of gender, race, disability or sexual identity: gays and lesbians here would have to be bloody brave to come out' (University of Central Lancashire, 1993: 15). Now there is a Lesbian, Gay, Bisexual (LGB) self-organized group that was established partly with support from EOAG which helped in setting up open staff seminars on lesbian and gay employment rights and for staff who wanted to learn more about lesbian and gay issues. A group was also set up for those who wanted to raise awareness and campaign on LGB issues, irrespective of their own sexuality. This group made a start on evaluating the impact of employment policy and practices on such staff, and also opened up a debate with university counsellors about LGB issues (Equal Opportunities Action Group, 1996). Similarly an Ethnic Minority Staff Forum was initiated, largely by ethnic minority members of EOAG. This is a place where staff can meet in privacy and security to discuss issues, to gain mutual support and develop solidarity: the Forum has also organized events with guest speakers.

One of the major achievements of 1996–7 was the finalization of an equal opportunities policy for students. Surprisingly, although there were already commitments to equal opportunities for students expressed through a number of other documents such as the university's mission statement and the students' charter, there had been no overall equal opportunity policy for students. In the early stages this was developed with members of the students' union and advice was taken from other key members of the university. It was circulated to all schools and departments and taken through the major university committees. It generated much debate and monopolized almost all of the last meeting of the year's academic board. It covers recruitment and admissions, curriculum and teaching, support services, planning and monitoring, training and development and complaints processes (EOAG, 1997). Full implementation is yet to come.

As our approach to equal opportunities at Brookes has matured, we have increasingly come to realise the importance of locating equal opportunities in the curriculum. Over the past two years, EOAG has held a series of workshops with colleagues from across disciplines and Schools, where equal opportunities in the curriculum has been debated. This discussion has encompassed curriculum and syllabus content and materials, classroom practice and its associated social processes, the content and structure of our degrees and courses, recruitment of students and the staff profile which is largely white and middle-aged. For staff from entirely different disciplines, these discussions have offered the chance for important pedagogic debates which might not otherwise have happened, but the discussion has also spread into academic schools with the development of workshops on equality in the curriculum. Informing some of this has been a survey which we have undertaken of equality initiatives in the curriculum both at Brookes and in the wider field of higher education in the UK. This study detected a strongly felt need among committed academics, both in this university and elsewhere, to share, extend and develop good practice. As a result, a national conference on equal opportunities and the curriculum was held at Brookes in September 1997.

On employment issues, EOAG has actively supported the development of family-friendly policies. Early on it established and piloted a child-care network for those who could not, for whatever reason, use the university's nursery. It was at the forefront of discussions on job evaluation as a means of improving the position especially of lower paid non-academic women staff, and has had inputs to personnel policies and various other changes in order to ensure their equality implications have been identified. The EOAG is represented at meetings of the joint staff committee, which brings together staff from the personnel department and the university's recognized trade unions, and on the major university committees. It has also monitored promotion interviews since the process for promotion to principal lecturer was devolved to schools.

This leads to consideration of a critical area for equal opportunities, namely monitoring. How are we doing, and how do we know? In Brookes, student and workforce statistics are now regularly collected and published. The student statistics show small increases in the proportion of students from minority groups and a steady increase in the proportion of women students. However, so far there has only been limited movement in improving the proportion of senior women staff.

Organizing for change

A major strength of the approach at Brookes has been the way in which the Equal Opportunities Action Group has comprised staff seconded on a part-time basis from right across the university (including academic, administrative, and library staff). They work together with a half-time head of equal opportunities who reports directly to the vice-chancellor and is part of the university's Senior Management Forum. An additional important aspect has been the concept of 'outreach' into schools and departments. This works in two ways. First, there is a system of advisers who can be called on to run collaborative workshops on issues such as harassment training. Second, the EOAG has funded a number of small equal opportunity projects carried out by schools to support their strategic plans. Examples include harassment training for students and staff working in Students Union outlets such as bars and entertainment venues, and the development of equal opportunity approaches in open learning in the School of Education.

In the long term it is essential that all these activities should come to be seen as part of routine university development and activity. Meanwhile, however, it is this harnessing of commitment to equality within the university's community which it is hoped will ultimately lead to a culture where explicit equality values and behaviour become embedded across the whole university. For the time being, these initiatives are important investments for the university even though they cost little in financial terms – in 1996–7 eleven projects were undertaken in this way, at a total cost of just over £5,000.

At the same time, EOAG has funded a few larger projects which have been carried out by schools and departments within the university, supporting these with guidelines on research and ethics. An early piece of commissioned work was from the university's publishing department. This research, which examined issues of gender and ethnicity, led to a debate and action within that school, particularly in developing and widening the curriculum. This good practice has since stimulated other schools to take similar action. Being in the academic business, EOAG has also ensured that some of the research has been presented at academic conferences and published. Networking with and advising other institutions are also growing equal opportunity activities.

The future

At Brookes, much has been achieved in the five years since EOAG was established. There is a long way to go, however, and I suspect that it will be some time yet before we can claim that equal opportunities are embedded in all aspects of our practice and procedures. But that must be our aim. Special initiatives and financial support have an important part to play in stimulating change but in the long term they cannot and should not be maintained. Rather, there must be ownership of the principles of equality by all.

This, of course, does not obviate the need for continued monitoring or the provision of institutional leadership. It is also all too easy for equality to be seen as peripheral when there are budgets to be balanced and government policy changes challenge the way we do things. At a cost of £65,000 a year, out of an annual budget of £70 million, our support of equal opportunities is a small but essential part of ensuring that the environment which we provide at Brookes is one in which all staff and all students can work effectively, and make their maximal contribution to the pursuit of our ambitions as a university. This is not only important as a moral imperative but has significance in maintaining our existing activities and generating new business. At present, for example, we are, like many universities, endeavouring to increase our number of international students. Recently EOAG carried out a study of ways in which undergraduates do, and do not, work effectively together in multicultural groups when carrying out assessed work. It was clear that we will have to work to ensure that our international students are more widely recognized by staff and by our local students as having the right to be full participants in the educational process. For example, they should be helped to participate more fully in seminars and discussion groups. This work is to be followed up with an investigation of the experiences of international postgraduate students, and I have no doubt that the findings of both studies will have implications for re-examining our teaching and learning methods.

Similarly, our policy of regionalization, in which we hope to recruit students in increasingly large numbers from our immediate 'travel to learn' area, will also have important equality implications. In Oxford, for example, we have a large local minority ethnic population which is not yet proportionately reflected in our student body. Equal opportunity input in this area will clearly have an important contribution to make to the annual strategic planning cycle of the university.

Meanwhile, it is helpful to have external drivers, such as the Dearing Report and at the practical level, the equal opportunities criteria for HEFCE's Quality Assessment. This latter is the sort of mainstreaming which is needed if any institution of higher education is to move towards fully understanding and actually practising equal opportunities. HEFCE's requirements provide a useful way of focusing institutional minds on what equal opportunities actually are and how they contribute to the quality of education in a university. However, translating good intentions into practice is complex and there are certainly no quick fixes.

References

Bagilhole, B. (1993) How to keep a good woman down: an investigation of the role of institutional factors in the process of discrimination against women academics, *British Journal of Sociology of Education*, 14(3): 262–74.

Blakemore, K. and Drake, R. (1996) *Understanding Equal Opportunity Policies*. London: Prentice Hall/Harvester Wheatsheaf.

Bird, J., Ching Yee, W., Sheibani, A. and Myler, A. (1992) Rhetorics of access – realities of exclusion? Black students into higher education, *Journal of Access Studies* 17: 146–63.

Commission for Racial Equality (1997) *Ethnic Minority Women*. London: CRE.

Equal Opportunities Action Group (1996) *Report for 1995–6*. Oxford: Oxford Brookes University, EOAG.

Equal Opportunities Action Group (1997) *Report for 1996–7*. Oxford: Oxford Brookes University, EOAG.

Equal Opportunities Review. May/June 1997; January/February 1998.

Hammond, V. and Halton, V. (1990) *A Balanced Workforce?* Berkhamsted: Ashridge Management Research Group.

Hansard Society Commission (1990) *Women at the Top*. London: The Hansard Society for Parliamentary Government.

Higher Education Funding Council for England (1996) *Policy Statement on Equal Opportunities in Quality Assessment*. Bristol: HEFCE.

Kanter, R. M. (1983) *The Change Masters*. London: Unwin Hyman.

Ledwith, S. and Colgan, F. (1996) *Women in Organisations: Challenging Gender Politics*. Basingstoke: Macmillan.

Modood, T. (1993) The number of ethnic minority students in British higher education: some grounds for optimism, *Oxford Review of Education*, 19(2): 167–82.

NATFHE (1998) Casualisation grows, hits women hardest, *HE News*, March, p. 1.

National Committee of Inquiry into Higher Education (the Dearing Report) (1997) *Higher Education in the Learning Society*. Norwich: HMSO.

Opportunity 2000. *Annual Reports*. London: Business in the Community.

Pearl, M. and Singh, P. (1999) *Equal Opportunities in the Curriculum*. Oxford: Oxford Brookes University Equal Opportunities Action Group.

Powney, J., Hamilton, S. and Weiner, G. (1997) *Higher Education and Equality: A Guide*. London: CRE/EOC/CVCP.

Price, L. and Priest, J. (1996) Activists as change agents: achievements and limitations, in L. Morley and V. Walsh (eds). *Breaking Boundaries: Women In Higher Education*. London: Taylor & Francis.

Singh, R. (1990) Ethnic minority experiences in higher education, *Higher Education Quarterly*, 44(4): 344–59.

University of Central Lancashire (1993) *Excellence for All: Progressing Equal Opportunities at Oxford Brookes University*. Preston: University of Lancashire.

Acknowledgements

This chapter is based on work which has been carried out in Oxford Brookes University over a period of years. The documentation of that history for this chapter has been undertaken by Sue Ledwith, Senior Lecturer in the School of Business in Oxford Brookes University, and I am indebted to her for her help in collating that material and more generally in the preparation of this chapter.

Part 2

Some Specifics on *Un*equal Opportunitites

3

Gender: Students

Diana Woodward

Introduction

The proportion of women entering higher education today exceeds that of men. However, as recently as the 1960s women comprised less than 25 per cent of students (Brooks, 1997). The recency of this phenomenon means that women's place in the academy cannot yet be considered secure. This quantitative change has yet to be matched by a comprehensive qualitative change in the institutional culture of many universities and colleges. As Chapter 4 will show, the majority of these new entrants' lecturers are likely to be men, even in those subjects traditionally favoured by women, with few women in promoted posts in any disciplines who can serve as role models and provide female students with the informal sponsorship and guidance still useful in securing access to funded further study. This is important, as a research degree is the main route by which the next generation will be recruited to careers in university teaching. Until a substantial proportion of university teachers are women, including in promoted grades, they are at a disadvantage in seeking to challenge the status quo. Therefore the prevailing style of higher education on offer is likely to remain predominantly traditional and implicitly male in terms of its curriculum, its modes of teaching and assessment, and in the students' experiences of formal teaching, pastoral support and institutional support services. Greater gender parity of the staff base, in terms of both lecturers and support staff, is needed to provide the kind of empathetic support and services needed to enable women to flourish.

This is especially true for women who are not confident school-leavers entering university armed with good A-level examination passes. Mature women students, women from working-class homes and from minority ethnic groups, lesbians, mothers and (above all) women whose attributes encompass more than one of these groups may well need specific forms of support in order to succeed in higher education. The benefits can hardly be exaggerated of having an understanding tutor who appreciates the terror induced by a mature student's first class presentation, or the impact of a child's sudden illness on her mother's capacity to hand in a well-researched essay on time. Irrespective of which member of staff has been designated a student's tutor, students in trouble will approach someone whom they know and feel they can trust. Hence the importance of social diversity in the staff teaching team, especially in the early stages of undergraduate courses when student withdrawal rates are highest.

Of course, these are gross generalizations which do scant justice to those institutions where women's issues have been taken seriously. Furthermore, women themselves are a far from homogeneous group, with varying circumstances. Those with different socio-demographic attributes may need different types of support to enable them to succeed. However, before addressing these specific issues, a brief review of women's participation in higher education will provide a useful backcloth to the current position. It will show the massive extent and the speed of recent shifts in women's access to higher education. The struggle for women's full acceptance in the academy may be far from won, but much has been achieved within the past twenty years.

A short history of women's access to higher education in the UK

The early universities in the UK followed their European counterparts in providing an education for well-born young men seeking to enter holy orders. The Protestant Reformation liberated them from the Church's control, but as recently as the Great Exhibition of 1851, England (like Scotland) still had only four universities, at Oxford, Cambridge, London and Durham, producing a combined total of about 1000 graduates a year, most of whom were still destined for the Anglican priesthood. Following the political ferment of the 1840s in the United States and Western Europe, various movements began to demand civil rights in relation to citizenship, nationalism, suffrage, the abolition of slavery, and women's rights. English women suffered appalling discrimination in their attempts to secure access to higher education in the second half of the nineteenth century. This was justified by universities and colleges with recourse to paternalistic Victorian assertions about women's physical and intellectual capabilities, although in practice few women had access to the kind of academic schooling required for study at this level. The story of their struggle, notably to obtain medical training, is now well known. For many women, particularly in provincial cities, access to higher education was restricted to attendance at part-time university extension classes. In London there were two women's colleges by 1849, but neither really provided more than secondary-level education until London University permitted women to take its degrees in 1878 (Purvis, 1991).

The London Ladies Educational Association arranged separate women-only lectures, finishing on the half-hour and with the women admitted by a side door to minimize the risk of contact with male students. Women were finally awarded degrees at the Victoria University, Manchester, in 1880, at the Scottish universities in 1892 and at Durham University in 1895, but their participation was often hedged with restrictions. At Oxford University and, particularly, at Cambridge women's full access to lectures, examinations and graduate status was denied and frustrated for decades. Women were finally admitted as full members of the University of Oxford in 1920, but not at Cambridge until 1948 (McWilliams-Tullberg, 1975). There remained only two colleges for women at Cambridge until New Hall was founded in 1954, and it is only in the last decade that women have comprised more than a heavily outnumbered minority within the university.

Dissatisfaction with the narrow traditionalism of the ancient universities from the non-conformist churches and from industrialists in the major cities, among others, led to a series of initiatives designed to broaden access to higher education, culminating in the establishment of the 'civic' universities in Birmingham, Manchester, Liverpool, Sheffield, Leeds, Bristol and later, Reading, and of other institutes of learning which became universities many decades and mergers later. These institutions benefited from financial support from enlightened local philanthropists, whose values often included progressive attitudes towards education for women. All of these new civic universities admitted women (Dyhouse, 1995; David and Woodward, 1998). However, an evaluation of them made in 1913 now reads somewhat optimistically:

> The Archbishop of York recently stated that when the history of the last twenty years came to be written, it would seem that few social phenomena were of greater national importance than the rise of the new universities. As women enjoy in all these an equality with men as to degrees, scholarships and fellowships, appointments to staff, access to teaching, laboratories, libraries, etc., and almost universally participate in government through Court, Senate, Convocation and similar bodies, the new universities must, a fortiori, be of great importance and value in girls' education.
> (Sarah Burstall in the 1913 *Directory of Women Teachers*, cited in Dyhouse, 1995: 2)

For most of the previous century the principal strategies adopted by female protagonists to storm the bastions of male power (be they the universities, the medical profession or other social institutions) were strict conformity to prevailing norms about femininity and respectability, tireless lobbying, and gratitude for the support and sponsorship of influential men. Many young women faced implacable opposition from their families in seeking to enter higher education. In 1914 the mother of Vera Brittain (later to become a feminist writer, and mother of contemporary politician Shirley Williams) faced censure from the ladies of Buxton for permitting her daughter to prepare for entry to Oxford University, which must have been all the more galling as she did so reluctantly.

> 'How can you send your daughter to college, Mrs. Brittain !' moaned one lugubrious lady. 'Don't you want her ever to get married ?'
> (Brittain, 1933: 88)

Gradually the numbers of women obtaining university degrees grew and, as paid employment for middle-class women became a legitimate activity before marriage and a way to earn one's living if one did not marry, more of them entered professional employment. After the First World War, the Civil Service or teaching became acceptable forms of employment for unmarried women, the latter helping to increase the pool of well-qualified female applicants for university places. Women's range of occupational destinations remained narrow. As late as the 1970s, few women graduates went into careers in industry and commerce except in such traditionally female areas as personnel work, and many of them soon left or moved into teaching (Chisholm and Woodward, 1980). There was no conception, by the women themselves, nor by their educators or employers, that any discriminatory attitudes or practices underlay this situation; it was just how things were. From the end of the Second World War until the early 1970s, academic analyses of women's employment echoed popular sentiment with its liberal perception of teaching as an ideal career for women, and part-time work as the solution to women's 'conflict' between their domestic responsibilities and the benefits of employment (Myrdal and Klein, 1956). Some vivid first-hand accounts, by women who later achieved senior posts in higher education, of their struggles to sustain a career during this period are included in David and Woodward (1998).

Generations of young women were denied the opportunity of access to, or faced barriers in succeeding in, higher education. These barriers comprised the traditional attitudes of many parents, who felt that the investment and the deferral of entry into paid employment which it represented would be 'wasted' on their daughters, as they were unlikely to remain in a long-term career afterwards; the secondary education system, which (with the exceptions of the single-sex, selective, highly academic grammar and high schools, or independent schools) regarded its role as preparing most young women for entry into a narrow range of 'appropriate' occupations, and beyond that, for a life of domestic labour within marriage; and the universities themselves, which for years did nothing to challenge the sex-typing of subject choices which resulted from the guidance and curricula offered in girls' secondary schools, and even operated bars to restrict the proportion of women entering certain courses, such as medicine, or certain universities. The Asquith Commission of 1922 recommended that no more than 500 women students should be admitted to Cambridge University, fixing a ratio of 1 : 10 which had barely changed when I arrived in 1969. Oxford followed suit in 1927, fixing a ratio of 1 : 6 (Dyhouse, 1995).

The position of women students was beginning to change by the early 1970s, in the face of criticism based on equal rights and declining applications from well-qualified male applicants for certain courses. In the early 1970s, for example, the Civil Engineering Department at Leeds University (where I gathered some data for my PhD on gender differences in students' expectations) was investing considerable (male) staff time in visiting schools in an attempt to encourage women to apply to study there. Because fewer of these potential applicants than their male counterparts had the good passes in maths at A-level on which delivery of the curriculum was based, this gave rise to an internal debate about whether they should be set a lower maths requirement to broaden the numbers eligible to apply, or whether such applicants might then have difficulty in keeping up with the course.

Women and higher education in the UK in the 1990s

As noted at the outset, only in the very recent past have women overtaken men as entrants to degree courses. In 1994–5 they represented 49 per cent of all new students, a figure that has since risen to 53 per cent (HESA, 1997). The proportion of female undergraduates has doubled since the early 1960s, when the Robbins Report was published, and their former propensity to enrol at the post-1992 universities (the former polytechnics and colleges) and on part-time courses is no longer the case (NCIHE, 1997). However, differences persist between types and levels of study, and in the choice of discipline studied. In the 1996/7 academic year women comprised a bare majority of new students on first degree and taught postgraduate courses, and were almost three-fifths of entrants to 'other undergraduate courses' (such as diploma and certificate courses), yet were only two-fifths of the new students enrolled for research degrees (HESA, 1997).

This is largely a function of enduring gender differences in subject choice (examined below), in that the numbers of funded research studentships are very much greater in science and technology, and are scarcer in the social sciences and humanities. The provision of funded opportunities for advanced study reflects the gender profile of disciplines, to men's advantage. British students wishing to pursue full-time postgraduate research at British universities and who need funding to do so will typically apply first to the relevant research council for their chosen discipline. The largest of these, in terms of financial support for postgraduate study, is the Engineering and Physical Sciences Research Council (EPSRC), which in 1997/8 spent £77 million on 10,691 students following both research degrees and Masters level study (EPSRC, 1998). The next largest funder was the Economic and Social Research Council, which in 1995/6 spent £9.8 million on funding 382 research studentships and £6.7 million on 683 awards for Masters level programmes (ESRC, 1997). In 1998 the Arts and Humanities Research Board funded 556 awards for research degrees and 447 studentships for taught postgraduate courses. Barely one in four applications to it was successful, and fewer than half of the students holding a first-class degree won an award. So ten times as many student awards were given by the EPSRC than the ESRC or the AHRB. (The councils' websites provide useful up-to-date information.)

To provide some benchmarking data, in 1996/7 there were almost 1 million students on full-time undergraduate courses at British universities (HESA, 1997). (Almost all applications to the research councils for postgraduate funding are from full-time, not part-time, students.) The subjects covered by the

Arts and Humanities Research Board include about 18 per cent of these students, with the proportion of women varying between 71 and 53 per cent for different subjects. The ESRC's subjects cover 38 per cent of students, with the proportions of women ranging from 74 to 50 per cent, and the EPSRC's subjects cover 19 per cent of students, with the proportion of women ranging between 37 and 14 per cent (HESA, 1997). It is not possible to establish comparable data on the gender of applicants for research council studentships, and clearly there are other important sources of funding, such as universities' own scholarships, but their distribution almost certainly reflects the research councils' pattern of awards. It is therefore not perverse to infer, given the gender breakdown for students in these respective disciplines, that subjects which attract high proportions of men are vastly better endowed to support postgraduate study. The EPSRC funds ten times as many postgraduate students as the ESRC and AHRB, even though there are twice as many undergraduate students taking social science degrees and the same number taking arts and humanities degrees. In 1997/8 5854 PhDs were awarded by English universities to UK-based students in the sciences, engineering and technology, compared with only 1264 for all other disciplines (HESA data report).

This clear differentiation in terms of funding for different disciplines at postgraduate level is further compounded by women's under-representation in the workforce at senior levels within universities (see Chapter 4). As long as there are only a few prominent women researchers to provide encouragement or mentoring, or who are in a position to secure funded research studentships, or who can win research grants which generate employment for research assistants, young women nearing graduation will lack role models and may not have the sponsorship or access to networks required for their own successful transition to a research degree. As possession of a doctorate is now seen as a virtual prerequisite for entry into an academic career, the under-representation of women among research degree students bodes ill for any rapid transformation of the groves of academe.

The distribution of male and female students between disciplines has persisted over decades with surprisingly little change despite the entry of many more women students, except in those subjects where artificial barriers have been removed (such as medicine) or in those that have been added relatively recently such as business studies and computing. To illustrate the extremes of this distribution, the data for new entrants to higher education in the 1996/7 academic year reveal (HESA, 1997: 15) that women constitute only 14 per cent of full-time students and 7.5 per cent of part-time students on first degree courses in engineering and technology, but between 76 and 90 per cent of full-time and part-time students on first degree or sub-degree courses in the 'subjects allied to medicine' (nursing, physiotherapy and related subjects). The extent of this divergence is surprising, given the longevity of campaigns such as 'Women into Science and Engineering' and the recent 'Athena' project (from the CVCP's Commission on University Careers Opportunities) and the visible success of some men in reaching senior management posts in nursing who might be expected to serve as role models for other men. Even computing, which as a new subject might have been considered free from the gender-stereotyping long associated with engineering and nursing, is now firmly sex-typed as a male field of study, with women comprising only 19 per cent of new full-time undergraduates.

The Dearing Report (NCIHE, Report 5, 1997) noted that the majority of mature students and those on access courses are women. It reviewed the findings of various studies which showed that older women faced particular barriers in gaining entry to and succeeding in higher education. They are, almost by definition, less likely to have the standard educational qualifications for university entry, and frequently have poor child-care facilities and transport problems, and suffer from inflexible timetables, and insufficient academic and personal guidance. They often lack adequate time for their studies and may have poor time management skills. Although not mentioned in this section of the Dearing Report, their poverty exacerbates many of these problems and constrains choices. Taken together, it is no surprise that female mature and part-time students have above average drop-out rates.

Turning to gender differences in employment on graduation, we find that women graduates, like those from minority ethnic backgrounds, experience lower rates of unemployment than their male peers (DfE, 1993), but one reason put forward to explain this is that these groups may be willing to take a wider range of jobs, including those seen as not typical graduate-level posts (NCIHE, Report 5, 1997). Like their male peers, women graduates typically have higher earnings than their non-graduate counterparts, but still earn less than male graduates. Recent data from the Organization for Economic Co-operation and Development which examined the impact of terminal qualification on earnings for its 29 member countries show that graduates can expect to be earning between 20 and 100 per cent more than their non-graduate colleagues by the time they reach the 30 to 44 age group (OECD, 1998 reported in *THES*, November 27 1998). Women graduates in the United Kingdom and Ireland enjoy the biggest 'education premium', typically earning twice the salaries of their non-graduate female counterparts. However, in all countries women graduates earned less than their male counterparts. In the UK, gender differences in the choice of subject studies are translated into different choices of career, with more men entering higher-paid careers in commerce and industry and more women entering public sector employment and the caring professions (NCIHE, 1997).

What are the issues? Women students' experiences of higher education in the UK

There may now be parity in the numbers of men and women undergraduate students, with double the proportion of women students than at the time of the Robbins Report in 1963, but major differences persist in their experience of higher education. In addition to differences in the proportions of women students between subjects, women outnumber men as mature entrants and on access courses, but are under-represented on research degrees. However, a recurrent theme in this book is the need to distinguish between mere quantitative change and qualitative shifts in people's experiences within higher education. Success in meeting an institution's mission to broaden opportunity is not achieved simply by recruiting greater numbers of non-traditional students into the academy (with the criteria for determining what 'non-traditional' means varying between institutions and disciplines). It is much more important to ensure that these new types of students receive the kinds of support they require in order to thrive.

There is now an ample literature documenting the experiences of 'pioneer' women entering male occupational preserves such as engineering, construction, mining and manufacturing (see for example, Hearn *et al.*, 1989; Carter and Kirkup, 1990). A well-documented account of efforts to promote equal opportunities by breaking down the sex-stereotyping of certain occupations within the Toronto Transit Commission is provided by Colgan *et al.*(1996). However, their postscript notes the threat to the programme's continuation brought about by the election of a conservative administration. Women may experience ridicule and other forms of harassment, including even physical harassment, from men who resent and resist female encroachment into formerly male preserves. Even if their new male peers are not unwelcoming, there are the problems of confronting an androcentric organizational culture and challenging established custom and practice. The dominant experience for the first wave of women is a feeling of 'not belonging', of social discomfort, which eases when the point of a critical mass of incursors is reached, of say 10 per cent of the group. Until then, they feel that their performance is constantly being monitored and judged as women rather than as people.

Some of these issues which recur in 'pioneer' women's accounts will follow. They are culled from a range of documentary sources and my 25 years' experience in higher education as a lecturer, senior manager of both 'academic' and 'administrative' units, as an individual with institution-wide responsibility for dealing with sexual harassment cases, as a member of the UK's HM Inspectorate for Further and Higher Education, and as a leader of HEFCE subject review teams on visits to some 40 university departments.

Excessive visibility is a common complaint (Thomas, 1990; Carter and Kirkup, 1990). As one former engineering student recalled:

> 'I was in a class with 120 students. There were four women including myself... I still felt rather an oddity in my classes, and the [male] students I think treated us as rather an oddity ... As I recall, there was a certain kind of male momentum in the class which was not particularly receptive to incorporating women in the social groups. And I felt rather on the outside at that time.'
>
> (quoted in Carter and Kirkup, 1990: 65)

If male lecturers, technicians and fellow students are not used to working with women, they frequently lack a repertoire of appropriate behaviours for interacting with them. In conversation, this becomes apparent when male speakers make frequent allusions to their wives, sisters or girlfriends as female reference points. Another strategy is the exclusionary put-down:

'One of the very noticeable things about the girl scientists, and myself included, was that it took us about a year to establish ourselves. We didn't do very well in the first year, and that was partly sort of developing our confidence at just battering away at the system. For example, in electronics practicals there used to be a large number of boys who'd done electronics at school. We hadn't and you tend to get this terrible inferiority complex because you get all these blokes around muttering about these queer names for components. They say "Oh, you need a so-and-so and a so-and-so", and you think "I haven't got the foggiest idea what a so-and-so and a so-and-so is" (laughter). And especially in the first year you had to take your courage in both hands and keep on battering away at the demonstrators (all men) until you understood something.'

(anon. quoted in Carter and Kirkup, 1990: 59–60)

This woman went on to talk about the advantage of being in a women's college (at Oxbridge), where she did much of her study with a small group of other women, who supported each other strongly, in both academic and social terms. Women students in disciplines where they comprise a minority generally want to be treated exactly like the other students, rather than being singled out for special attention or assistance. However, in many departments in the pure and applied sciences, the dearth of recent new staff appointments has generated a profile which is predominantly white, male and nearing retirement. Their manners may be impeccable, referring to women students as 'ladies', for example, and their desire to assist them may be sincere, but their own social discomfort can lead to over-protectiveness which prevents women students from having the opportunity to learn from their own mistakes.

These attitudes are neatly illustrated in a doctoral study which compared students in physics and the humanities:

'We managed to get one lady on to our electronics course last year . . . I think the problems must be in schools. We just don't get the applicants . . . We must have about five or six [women students] altogether in a class of seventy.'

(Dr L, lecturer in physics, quoted in Thomas, 1990: 110)

Another physics lecturer quoted in the same study talked about his discussions with male applicants about their experience of Meccano (a construction toy popular in the 1950s) and motorbikes, which he equated with sewing for young women applicants:

'We quite often find people in the lab whose fingers are all thumbs and I'm sure that's because they're not used to doing delicate things with their hands. Now I always think the equivalent for the ladies who come in is in fact whether they do sewing or that sort of thing, which is just as delicate on the fingers, just as precise on the fingers as playing with little nuts and bolts. Now whether in that is the answer, that they're not used to mechanical things even though their dexterity is good, I don't know. It could be that we're going back years in their life to how they're conditioned when they're young . . . when they don't have the meccano and mechanical toys like that.'

(anon. quoted in Thomas, 1990: 110)

Women in male-dominated disciplines face the need to negotiate their identity as scientists and young women with their male fellow students and the (male) staff, whereas their male counterparts have no such equivalent dilemma.

'I find an awful lot of them [male students], if you speak to them. It's 'Aah, a girl spoke to me', you know . . . But in the lab, and computing, when you're sitting at the terminals and asking questions, that's a good way of making friends with the blokes ('cos the girls naturally are friends whether you're the same type of people or not, the girls all chat to each other), but I find you've got to make an effort with the blokes, to say 'Mmm, I can't do this, can you help me', sort of thing' ("Debbie", 1st year physics student).

Debbie is here developing a strategy to cope with a particular problem, in this case the problem of feeling excluded, of not having friends. There is not, as might be imagined, any deliberate deviousness in her strategy; she is simply aware that her male peers find a woman who is obviously a 'woman' (i.e. someone fairly helpless and not very good with computers) easier to cope with than someone who is both a 'woman' and a 'scientist'

(Thomas, 1990: 123).

Higher education is, we like to believe, a bastion of liberal or even progressive values. Thankfully, the kinds of overt, explicit harassment to which women pioneers have been subjected in certain manual trades has been rare in universities. However, a more sinister and long-standing feature of some corners of higher education has been the notion by some male academic staff that it is not unreasonable for them to form romantic liaisons with women students (a position – no pun intended – which was famously parodied in Malcolm Bradbury's novel, *The History Man,* where the central character was an unsympathetically portrayed 1960s-style philandering social science lecturer). This view has been vigorously challenged in recent years, with the critique mainly originating from groups of women staff or students, with the result that a number of institutions now have codes which require staff to disclose relationships with other members or students. In the case of students, the member of staff concerned will usually then be removed from direct involvement in assessment of the student's work, and may be subjected to disciplinary procedures.

This is a difficult area for senior management to address, as both students and members of staff are adults over the age of consent, and workplaces are prime sites for relationships to develop. To curtail adults' freedom to choose partners for sexual relationships could be regarded as an infringement of their civil liberties. However, the inherent inequality in any relationship between a senior person and a junior one, whether they are a student or a member of staff, has become acknowledged, for example by the National Association of Teachers in Further and Higher Education (the largest trade union for lecturers in the UK's post-1992 universities) in its guidelines. Likewise, the Association of University Teachers (the UK's principal lecturers' union in the pre-1992 university sector) asserts that 'a sexual/romantic relationship with a student will always involve serious risk and may involve serious difficulties rooted in the unequal power, and hence choice, of the parties concerned' (quoted in *THES*, August 7 1998). In 1995 at their annual conference, NATFHE passed a motion that 'consensual sexual relations between academic staff and students who they currently teach or assess . . . are ill-advised, unprofessional and to be discouraged'. This position is endorsed by the AUT and the National Union of Students. Drawing on research by Pam Carter and Tony Jeffs from Nottingham Trent University, NATFHE's report asserts that the huge majority of consensual relationships involved male staff and younger female students. Relationships of genuine mutuality were rare. Rather, the typical scenario was the 'predatory' male lecturer who 'engages in multiple concurrent or consecutive affairs'. Even in the cases of relationships between female staff and male students and homosexual relationships, equality was rare (cited in *THES*, 7 August 1998).

A typical institutional code of conduct on, or regulations governing, staff/student relationships might cover such features as the following: the incompatibility of such personal relationships with the professional responsibilities of staff; the need to declare such relationships to the head of department when they develop; and the need to remove the member of staff from teaching or assessment involving the student. Many institutions also require any relationship between members of staff to be registered, in order to promote transparency and to avoid allegations of nepotism.

However, the majority of women students thankfully do not have such experiences, although inequalities and prejudices based on gender persist. Women may have long formed the majority or a substantial minority of students in many disciplines in the social sciences and humanities, but even here they may suffer gender-based prejudices and lack the freedom they expect to pursue their intellectual interests.

References

Bradbury, M. (1975) *The History Man*. London: Secker and Warburg.

Brittain, V. (1993) *Testament of Youth: An Autobiographical Study of the Years, 1900–1925*. London: Gollancz.

Brooks, A. (1997) *Academic Women*. Buckingham: Society for Research into Higher Education and Open University Press.

Carter, R. and Kirkup, G. (1990) *Women in Engineering: A Good Place to Be?* Basingstoke: Macmillan.

Chisholm, L. and Woodward, D. (1980) The experiences of women graduates in the labour market, in R. Deem (ed.) *Schooling for Women's Work*. London: Routledge and Kegan Paul: 162–76.

Colgan, F., Johnstone, S. and Shaw, S. (1996) On the move: women in the Toronto public transport sector, in S. Ledwith and F. Colgan (eds) *Women in Organisations: Challenging Gender Politics*. Basingstoke: Macmillan.

David, M. and Woodward, D. (eds) (1998) *Negotiating the Glass Ceiling: Careers of Senior Women in the Academic World*. London: Falmer Press.

Department for Education (1993) *Statistical Bulletin on Women in Post-Compulsory Education, 29/93*. London: HMSO.

Dyhouse, C. (1995) *No Distinction of Sex? Women in British Universities 1870–1939*. London: UCL Press.

EPSRC (1998) *Annual Report*. London: EPSRC.

ESRC (1997) *Annual Report*. Swindon: ESRC.

Hearn, J., Sheppard, D. L., Tancred-Sheriff, P. and Burrell, G. (eds) (1989) *The Sexuality of Organisation*. London: Sage.

Higher Education Statistics Agency [HESA] (1997) *Students in Higher Education Institutions, 1996/7*. Cheltenham: HESA.

McWilliams-Tullberg, R. (1975) *Women at Cambridge: A Men's University, Though of a Mixed Type*. London: Gollancz.

Myrdal, A. and Klein, V. (1956) *Women's Two Roles: Home and Work*. London: Routledge and Kegan Paul.

OECD (1998) *Education at a Glance – OECD Indicators*. Paris: OECD.

Purvis, J. (1991) *A History of Women's Education in England*. Buckingham: Open University Press.

Thomas, K. (1990) *Gender and Subject in Higher Education*. Buckingham: Society for Research into Higher Education and Open University Press.

4

Gender: Academic Staff

Diana Woodward

A transatlantic case study

The *Boston Globe* ran a cover story in March 1999 about the experiences of women professors at the prestigious Massachusetts Institute of Technology (*Boston Daily Globe*, 21 March 1999). Some five years earlier, it reported, there had been 197 male staff in tenured (permanent) posts there, and 15 female. The women had assumed then that their numbers were low because, as 'everyone knew', girls did not like science. Three of them began to apply their skills of scientific analysis to their own situation, producing a report which presented evidence that women staff typically were allocated less than half the office space of men of equal status, were awarded lower salaries and less research funding; fewer women sat on the committees that made decisions about hiring staff and allocating funding; there had never been any women heads of department; and women staff who were offered jobs elsewhere were never offered inducements to stay, unlike their male colleagues. It proved untrue that girls disliked science: half of the six departments in the school of science had more women students than men, but the proportion of tenured women staff had not exceeded 8 per cent in two decades. There were only seven women, compared with 55 men, who were progressing towards achieving tenured posts. Not surprisingly, the women did not enjoy working at MIT. As one woman said, 'I was unhappy at MIT for more than a decade. I thought it was the price you paid if you wanted to be a scientist at an elite institution.' As their report said, 'The unequal treatment of women who come to MIT makes it more difficult for them to succeed, causes them to be accorded less recognition when they do, and contributes so substantially to a poor quality of life that these women can actually become negative role models for younger women.'

When these anomalies were initially pointed out, the senior managers at MIT (who were all white men) rejected these charges of inequality and even resisted producing the additional information requested by the complainants. However, instead of sitting back and waiting for a lawsuit, to their credit they then took another look at the data. This led them to admit that MIT had discriminated against women for years, in ways which were subtle and unintentional but, to the women concerned, were nevertheless all too real in their effects. The dean of the school of science became a convert to the cause. He set about redressing these inequalities, as well as establishing a broader enquiry into gender inequities, as requested by the women complainants, generating a report which was endorsed by the president of MIT. In the four years since these allegations were first made, MIT has raised women's salaries by an average of 20 per cent, to equal those of men; has increased the research money and space awarded to women; has appointed more women to key committees; and has increased the pensions of some retired women by $80,000 to $100,000 to equal that which they would have received had the salary inequities not existed. However, even the dean experienced difficulty in persuading his male department heads that any problem existed. They argued that women simply did not thrive in the competitive, masculine culture of MIT. However, the report, which has now been issued on the institute's Web page, acknowledges evidence of 'subtle differences in the treatment of men and women', 'exclusion' and even 'discrimination against women faculty'. Male cronyism, associated with the marginalization of women, created 'unequal access to the substantial resources of MIT'.

Since the first report was presented a year ago, MIT has made 'more progress in one year than was accomplished in the previous decade', according to one female member of staff. The dean of science expects to have a 40 per cent increase in the number of tenured women staff within a year, bringing the proportion of women on the staff to over 10 per cent for the first time. However, MIT is an elite, wealthy institution, capable of mobilizing significant resources to right proven wrongs, and the United States federal government is able to use the law to enforce equal opportunities in publicly-funded organizations. In the month preceding this announcement, the federal government filed a suit against Stanford University, an elite institution in California, for failing to do enough to aid the progress of women (*Boston Daily Globe*, 21 March 1999). Few higher education institutions outside the United States would be able to respond so swiftly or comprehensively, and women and other minority groups on the staff of universities in the UK, at least, have no similar legislation at their disposal. While they do have recourse to industrial tribunals, which may offer speedier and cheaper means of redress than do full court cases, they are designed to investigate individual alleged wrongs rather than to address systematic, structural inequalities.

The history of women in academic careers in the UK

The history of women's participation as students in higher education was outlined in the previous chapter. Their employment as teachers in higher education is largely a twentieth-century phenomenon (Dyhouse, 1995). The influx of women students into British universities in the late nineteenth century was not matched by commensurate changes in the gender of the staff, and women received little encouragement to continue their education to postgraduate level, which was necessary to gain entry to university teaching. Dyhouse has uncovered various statements from male professors and senior university administrators from the late nineteenth and early twentieth centuries about the undesirability (in their view) of appointing women staff to teach in mixed-sex universities and colleges. The situation changed somewhat after the First World War, when the likely shortage of suitable male applicants coincided with the passage of the Sex Disqualification (Removal) Act in 1919. However, women's appointments were dependent on the discretion and attitude of the male heads of department. Some women gained teaching appointments after becoming wardens of women's hostels or tutors to women students, or were coaches to female students rather than recognized lecturers. However, as late as 1939, Aberdeen University had only one woman appointed to a full lectureship. Not unexpectedly, women found it easier to gain appointments to train teachers than they did to secure lecturing posts in other subjects. However, these positions were somewhat anomalous and teacher training, as well as its students, was not regarded as fully equivalent in status to other fields of study, not least because the entry requirements were generally lower.

By 1931 the proportion of women teaching staff in British universities was about 13 per cent, a figure which remained fairly constant between the 1920s and 1970s (Rendel, 1980). Not surprisingly, women faced fewer obstacles to their professional development in single-sex institutions. Women were almost never appointed to senior positions in mixed universities and colleges, other than to designated women-only posts such as senior tutor for women students, even if their qualifications and credentials matched or exceeded those of their male counterparts. The burden of teaching and pastoral responsibilities associated with these positions left little time for personal research. Dyhouse (1995) documents other kinds of difficulty, apart from the ever-present institutionalized sexism of the time and personal antagonism from male colleagues, faced by women seeking academic careers before the Second World War. These included a sense that certain kinds of knowledge were 'inappropriate' for women, lack of sponsorship, and poor working conditions.

Most of the women who taught in British universities before the Second World War remained unmarried, partly because single-sex institutions offered an alternative lifestyle for unmarried women outside the parental home, but mainly because of the prevailing expectation in middle-class society, which lasted until well into the post-war era, that it was inappropriate for married women to pursue a career. Successive waves of post-war university expansion and the designation of colleges of advanced technology and later polytechnics tended to favour the growth of 'male' subjects such as science and engineering for reasons of national competitiveness, which expanded career opportunities for male academics. The incorporation of teacher training colleges into larger institutions of higher education in the 1960s and 1970s wiped out many senior posts formerly occupied by women. Even disciplines which have traditionally been popular with women students, such as the humanities, have failed to provide women academics with career opportunities comparable to those enjoyed by men in 'male' subjects, because of the cultural dominance of men and the way in which masculinity is perceived as advantageous (Thomas, 1990).

British women academics in the UK today

The position of women academic staff in higher education has been extensively researched, both in the UK and internationally. The reason for this is not hard to discern. The second wave of feminism in the late 1960s and 1970s was, not surprisingly, quickly embraced by women students and young staff in the social sciences, who soon applied their political analysis of oppression, injustice and inequality in the wider society in a bid to understand their own position in academe. Early studies exposed the invisibility of women in the canon of accepted scholarship, and charted the distribution of women staff in academic disciplines. Women were seriously under-represented as staff at all levels in the academic hierarchy, with their proportion declining steadily towards the apex. Denied positions of influence, they were unable in these early years of the new feminism to mount successful challenges to the curriculum, the distribution of resources or the ethos of masculinist higher education.

Although progress has been achieved since then, it has not been without the expenditure of a great deal of time and energy. Some women of the generation who comprised this 'first wave' of modern feminists attained positions of influence, becoming vice-chancellors, principals at both Oxbridge and higher education colleges, and the heads of quangos (quasi-autonomous non-governmental organizations). But the numbers of women are still small at the higher levels of university management and scholarship (see David and Woodward, 1998). At the time of writing there are five women vice-chancellors out of a total of 76 university-status institutions (including the constituent colleges of the University of London), and four women heads of the 17 general colleges of higher education. Data published by the Commission on University Careers Opportunities in 1998 showed that women made up 8 per cent of vice-chancellors, principals and rectors; 14 per cent of pro vice-chancellors or their equivalent; 15 per cent of deans; 24 per cent of registrars and administrative heads; and 12 per cent of directors of finance or estates, student services or personnel and human resources departments (reported in *THES*, 5 March 1999). In 1997–8 women still comprised only one-third of all academic staff and a mere 9.2 per cent of professors, an increase from 6.7 per cent in 1995 (*THES*, 15 May and 3 July 1998; *THES*, 28 May 1999). Data compiled by the Association of University Teachers in 1998 showed that 16 universities and colleges had no women professors and eight had no women senior researchers or senior lecturers (*THES*, 15 May 1998). There are no female professors in engineering, according to *THES*' analysis of information provided by HESA for institutions with over 500 staff in 1997–8, and they are a small minority even in disciplines where women constitute a sizeable majority of the students, such as education (where 70 per cent of the students are female but only 20 per cent of the professors are) and languages (where the comparable figures are 67 per cent and 16 per cent). The equivalent proportion of women professors in the United States is 20 per cent, where they earn on average 79 per cent of the salaries earned by their male counterparts (*THES*, 28 May 1999).

In the UK, there are major disparities between institutions and between subjects. For example, 37.5 per cent of the professorial posts at Robert Gordon University are held by women, the highest proportion in any university in the country. At eight institutions, less than 5 per cent of the professoriate are women, including the universities of Bradford, Heriot-Watt, Strathclyde, UMIST, and Salford. The universities of Westminster, Sunderland and Central Lancashire had no women professors at all at the time of the audit. All of the 'top ten' universities, ranked by the proportion of women professors, are 'new' post-1992 universities (mostly former polytechnics), but because the absolute numbers of women professors is so small, a university's position in this ranking can fluctuate wildly from year to year if just one or two women professors leave or are appointed. Of the 244 new women professors created between 1996 and 1998 (taking only those institutions with more than 40 professorships), 35 were in nursing and 52 in social studies, whereas by 1997–8 there were still only three female chemistry professors in the country, one in dentistry and three in agriculture.

Predictably, the highest proportion of women professors are to be found in traditionally 'female' disciplines, making up 33 per cent of all professors in health and community studies, 22 per cent in catering and hospitality management and 17 per cent in education, according to the AUT data. They comprise below 15 per cent of professors in all other subjects, falling to below 4 per cent in engineering and the sciences other than pharmacology (7.5 per cent), biosciences (5.9 per cent) and general sciences (14.3 per cent). However, even at South Bank University, which topped the 1996–7 rankings in terms of its proportion of women professors, only 2 per cent of its women academics were professors, compared with 4.4 per cent of the men academics. The liberal argument that gender equality in student numbers will over time be matched by the gender ratio in the professoriate does not hold true, based on these figures. As Professor Teresa Rees of the University of Bristol points out, both psychology and music have over 50 per cent women students, and have traditionally recruited a high proportion of women students, but there are only two women professors of music nationally and only one psychology professor in every seven is female (*THES*, 3 July 1998).

As argued elsewhere in this book, certain disciplinary subcultures can prove to be hostile environments for women. A senior academic working in construction and civil engineering at South Bank University contrasted her own working environment with that of colleagues working in disciplines with far higher proportions of women staff:

> 'Here, there is a very male culture, very few women, lots of swearing and thuggishness, whereas the other side of the university is very much a women's world.'
>
> (anon. quoted in *THES*, 3 July 1998)

In the same article, a woman in a science department in another university, who declined to give her name as she was seeking promotion, confirmed the perception of many women academics, that they must be demonstrably better than their male peers to get promoted:

'When I applied for promotion to senior lecturer, my head of department told me that I was producing more papers and bringing in more grant money than most of my male colleagues – but he still wasn't going to promote me. I was in that situation for five years. Then, when I finally did get promoted, life became a lot more difficult. The men would gang up on me in meetings. Everything I said and did was belittled. I set up several courses, and once it was obvious they were going to be successful, my responsibility for them was taken away and given to a man. I ended up keeping out of people's way, and getting on with my research.'

(quoted in *THES*, 3 July 1998)

There are similar echoes of exclusion, lack of recognition and outright discrimination in the accounts of their career development given by some British senior women academics in David and Woodward (1998). Even in subjects where women students predominate, the majority of academic posts have been and still are occupied by men, and in most departments the senior posts are still disproportionately taken by men. In academic life, as in certain other areas such as the legal profession, advancement can depend on patronage and sponsorship. Certain key experiences such as getting work published, receiving an invitation to become an external examiner or to make a plenary presentation at a conference, and being appointed to key committees often depend on receiving a recommendation from an 'insider'. Where men occupy most or all of the key positions in the networks through which recommendations are sought, it can be difficult or impossible for women to get started on the route to promotion by becoming visible and securing the necessary achievements. As Judi Marshall (professor of organizational behaviour at Bath University) has said in relation to her own career:

'I was very lucky. I wasn't very streetwise at the start of my career about things like refereed journals, but my supervisor was. Now I think the situation is very difficult for younger women. I didn't feel I had to push. But now you have to be in the right journals and have the right kind of publications.'

(quoted in *THES*, 3 July 1998)

Women accounted for a third of all academic staff by 1996/7 (HESA data cited in *The Guardian*, 13 April 1999). Even when women academics do manage to get promoted, their salaries are typically considerably lower than those of their male peers. Since their promotion chances are worse anyway, this constitutes a major source of inequality, both for universities as employers and for women academics during their working lives and in retirement. The average female academic will earn between four and five years' less salary than an equivalent man who works for the same number of years. In the 'old style' (pre-1992) universities, the average full-time male academic earns £4,300 more per year than his female colleagues, and considerable differentials have been found at all levels from professor to technical and administrative staff (*The Guardian*, 4 May 1999; Independent Review of Higher Education Pay and Conditions, 1999). Women are a third more likely than men to have fixed-term contracts and are 550 per cent less likely than their male counterparts to become professors (report of an analysis by the Association of University Teachers in *THES*, 5 March 1999).

Various explanations, ranging from the liberal to the radical, have been put forward to account for this picture of consistent disadvantage for women, with associated proposed remedies. Some arguments identify the historic under-representation of women in postgraduate study. These days few young academics will be appointed to permanent posts without a doctorate, yet men still outnumber women 6:4 as research students (HESA data for 1996/7). Women may have recently overtaken men as a proportion of all students, from 49 per cent in 1994/5 to 53 per cent in 1996/7, but their representation is highest in non-degree undergraduate and part-time study, and is lowest for research degrees. Many graduating students need explicit encouragement from their tutor to embark on a research degree, and will require advice about where to apply and how to secure funding. As Chapter 3 showed, the distribution of funded studentships is very unequally distributed across the disciplines, with the highest numbers concentrated in the sciences and engineering, exactly those subjects were women are most under-represented. The achievement of gender parity in entry to academic careers is therefore not yet in sight.

Apart from quantitative factors such as this, there is ample evidence (some of which is cited elsewhere in this book) that qualitative factors operate to the detriment of women academics. Women still have to achieve acceptance within the academy. The proponents of liberal arguments would point to the evidence about how recruitment and selection panels operate (and not just in higher education) to appoint people who share their own characteristics, as they implicitly or knowingly feel more comfortable about the prospect of working with them. Others would argue that institutional cultures in higher education (as in many other employment sectors) are manipulated by men to exclude or marginalize women, thereby making it harder to them to perform well and to gain the recognition required for advancement. Theoretical work about the position of women in the labour market, backed by data from a range of occupations and sectors, has been done by Hearn *et al.* (1989), Collinson *et al.* (1990), Witz (1992), Hearn and Parkin (1995), Ledwith and Colgan (1996) and Walby (1997), among others. These provide evidence of the ways in which women are confronted by additional barriers to career development in comparison with men. Many of the discriminatory practices which they face derive from traditional, patriarchal attitudes about the differences between men's and women's capabilities and what activities are appropriate for each sex. These attitudes serve to reinforce and perpetuate divisions between 'men's work' and 'women's work', and are even widely accepted as legitimate bases for discriminating against women. Where these verbal arguments fail to persuade, more overt forms of behaviour may be employed to exclude women from male work environments, such as verbal or physical harassment. While the use of such blunt instruments is rarely necessary in academic circles, there being ample scope for exercising discretion in appointments and promotions and for masking any misogynistic intent in the outcomes, their use is not uncommon between students and technical staff.

In the past couple of years concern has grown about the extent of masonic influence in higher education. At least 11 masonic lodges are affiliated to British universities (*THES*, 13 March and 20 November 1998), and at least two recent vice-chancellors are known to be freemasons. There have been unprovable assertions that women in certain institutions where the most senior posts have been held by alleged freemasons face a 'glass ceiling' beyond which promotion is impossible. Spokesmen for the masonic movement claim that it has no malign intent, and essentially operates like 'office five-a-side football teams, affiliated to a specific organization but with no powers over their management at all' (*THES*, 13 March 1998: 3). However, the Association of University Teachers argues that masons should disclose their membership, in the interests of transparency and the promotion of equal opportunities, in relation to their involvement in all procedures relating to recruitment, promotion, peer review, discipline and finance.

Marginalization and exclusion are not just matters concerning personnel procedures. The nature of the subjects studied or taught by women has also been a major concern for the post-1968 generations of feminist academics. Women began by scrutinizing the theories and literature in their own disciplines, finding them to be deficient and neglectful of women and their concerns, yet putting forward the male perspective as a universal truth. In the 1970s and 1980s, feminist critiques were published of the theories, assumptions and literature in many fields. Women's studies has become a recognized academic field in its own right (although its teaching is still often under-resourced and marginalized, despite its popularity with students). Scholarship in many disciplines has been forced into a radical reappraisal, as a result of feminist scholarship, leading to the generation of new theories, perspectives, methods and approaches. For a while, until the mid to late 1970s, it was possible to purchase virtually all new university-level publications which addressed women's issues. Gloriously, this has long since ceased to be possible. An explosion in the demand for feminist work has generated a sub-discipline of scholarship on women's issues within a very wide range of disciplines and fields, with their own journals and publishers' series. These have not only extended the breadth of the curriculum with their scholarship, but they have also challenged the accepted tenets and 'ways of seeing', adding new vigour to some moribund fields and making knowledge relevant to a wider cross-section of the academic community.

This politicization extended not only to the development of critiques of the methods, published scholarship and curricula where women were well represented. These women also created new forms of organization, influenced by feminist politics, within universities and colleges, the trade unions and professional associations. This was often done through forming women's sections within trade unions or more informally, through women's groups associated with the Women's Movement, with certain disciplines, or with political organizations based outside higher education. However, despite this slow but now probably irresistible tide of protest, even white women academics of middle-class origin are still far short of achieving parity with their male colleagues, and other groups of women staff within higher education such as administrators have fared even less well. Despite the significant achievements of the past quarter century, which are all the more remarkable when seen against the backcloth of centuries of male dominance of the university system, much remains to be achieved.

What can be done?

One priority must be to achieve greater parity in the staffing profile of academic departments between the gender of students and that of their lecturers. Many large organizations set gender equity targets, and monitor progress towards their attainment, using statistical reports issued regularly by personnel departments. Clearly a major shift cannot be achieved quickly where there is little staff turnover, and staff numbers are static or declining. However, this kind of target-setting can help to focus the collective consciousness of appointments panels on redressing past staffing imbalances, rather than having their members cite poorly understood principles about positive action or positive discrimination to justify appointing yet another male member of staff. Attention needs to be paid to rebalancing the hierarchy, as well as shifting the overall ratio of male to female staff. If the proportions of women in promoted posts fail to match the proportion of women students, then this too should be a priority. Similarly, women should not be over-represented in junior, hourly-paid and temporary posts. Equity by sex in salaries should also be monitored, with university-wide and sectoral comparisons provided if possible to provide comparitors for the department. Whenever opportunities arise to nominate a member of staff for a role or opportunity leading to staff development, care should be taken to ensure that all those eligible receive equal consideration, and again, this should be monitored.

In departments where there are few women students, the appointment of a 'critical mass' of several women staff may help to address the skewed student profile, if these women are encouraged to take part in recruitment fairs and to teach on first-year courses, before students choose to specialize, where they provide role models and known 'friendly faces' for students. However, they should not become 'token women', who are asked to take part in committees or to undertake administrative or pastoral duties to a greater extent than their male peers, as this will consume time which could otherwise be spent on their own research and career development. They should be assigned women mentors, if necessary from outside their own department, and could be encouraged to establish an informal peer support network, either within the department or with colleagues from elsewhere in the institution. They may wish to have a senior woman colleague join a male head of department for their annual performance review meeting.

The culture of a department is likely to require attention if it has not hitherto had a critical mass of women academic staff. Do the prevailing styles of communication reflect best practice in avoiding sexist language and inappropriate humour or banter? Do staff invariably treat each other with genuine respect? What messages are conveyed by members' body language in meetings? It might be worth gathering anonymous returns from members of staff about these matters and, if necessary, commissioning some equal opportunities training to improve current practice. Of course, steps must be taken to ensure that the form of it is appropriate for the identified issues and that this staff development is actually experienced by those who most need to review their attitudes and practices.

Is there any evidence, whether explicit or implicit, that women's preferred sub-disciplinary specialisms are regarded as commensurate with men's/mainstream ones (these two are, of course, synonymous) in relation to the curriculum and its delivery and research activities?

Evidence abounds of the disadvantage and discrimination experienced by women academics within certain disciplines. Women in science and engineering seem to fare particularly badly, as we have seen already. Only 3 per cent of British science professors and fellows of the Royal Society are women. A delegate to a recent European conference on women in science described the career path of women like herself:

> 'At the beginning there is an iron gate, then a sticky floor. At the top there is a glass ceiling, and in between a hurdle race.'
>
> (anon. quoted in *THES*, 8 May 1998.)

Recently the 'Science Alliance' was formed, based on a coalition between four trade unions with members in higher education, to press for greater equity for women scientists in universities. Its charter has an action plan calling for equal pay, an equal and transparent promotion system and flexible working patterns (*THES*, 20 March 1998). This could form a useful part of an equal opportunities strategy for a faculty or department.

References

Collinson, D. L., Knights, D. and Collinson, M. (eds) (1990) *Managing to Discriminate*. London: Routledge.

Commission on University Career Opportunity (CUCO) (1994) *A Report on Universities' Policies and Practices on Equal Opportunities in Employment*. London: CUCO.

David, M. and Woodward, D. (eds) (1998) *Negotiating the Glass Ceiling: Careers of Senior Women in the Academic World*. London: Falmer Press.

Dyhouse, C. (1995) *No Distinction of Sex? Women in British Universities 1870–1939*. London: UCL Press.

Hearn, J. and Parkin, W. (1995) *'Sex' at 'Work'*. Hemel Hempstead: Prentice Hall/Harvester Wheatsheaf.

Hearn, J., Sheppard, D. L., Tancred-Sheriff, P. and Burrell, G. (eds) (1989) *The Sexuality of Organisation*. London: Sage.

Independent Review of Higher Education Pay and Conditions (the Bett Report) (1999) London: The Stationery Office.

Ledwith, S. and Colgan, F. (eds) (1996) *Women in Organisations: Challenging Gender Politics*. Basingstoke: Macmillan.

Rendel, M. (1980) How many women academics: 1912–1976? in R. Deem (ed.) *Schooling for Women's Work*. London: Routledge and Kegan Paul.

Thomas, K. (1990) *Gender and Subject in Higher Education*. Buckingham: Society for Research into Higher Education and Open University Press.

Walby. S. (1997) *Gender Transformations*. London: Routledge.

Witz, A. (1992) *Professions and Patriarchy*. London: Routledge.

Additional reading

Acker, S. (1994) *Gendered Education*. Buckingham: Open University Press.

Bagilhole, B. (1993) How to keep a good woman down: An investigation of the institutional factors in the process of discrimination against women academics, *British Journal of the Sociology of Education*, 14(3): 262–74.

Brooks, A. (1997) *Academic Women*. Buckingham: Society for Research into Higher Education and Open University Press.

Davies, S., Lubelska, C. and Quinn, J. (eds) (1994) *Changing the Subject: Women in Higher Education*. London: Taylor & Francis.

Eggins, H. (ed.) (1997) *Women as Leaders and Managers in Higher Education*. Buckingham: Society for Research into Higher Education and Open University Press.

Lie, S. and O'Leary, V. (1990) *Storming the Tower: Women in the Academic World*. London: Kogan Page.

Malina, D. and Maslin-Prothero, S. (eds) (1998) *Surviving the Academy: Feminist Perspectives*. London: Falmer.

McCauley, J. (1987) Women academics: a case study in inequality, in A. Spencer and D. Podmore (eds) *In a Man's World: Essays on Women in Male-Dominated Professions*. London: Tavistock.

McWilliams-Tullberg, R. (1975) *Women at Cambridge. A Men's University, Though of a Mixed Type*. London: Gollancz.

Morley, L. and Walsh, V. (eds) (1995) *Feminist Academics: Creative Agents for Change*. London: Taylor & Francis.

Purvis, J. (1991) *A History of Women's Education in England*. Buckingham: Open University Press.

Rassool, N. (1995) Black women as the 'other' in the Academy, in L. Morley and V. Walsh (eds) *Feminist Academics: Creative Agents for Change*. London: Taylor & Francis.

Safia Mirza, H. (1995) 'Black women in higher education: defining a space/finding a place, in L. Morley and V. Walsh (eds) *Feminist Academics: Creative Agents for Change*. London: Taylor & Francis.

Stiver Lie, S., Malik, L. and Harris, D. (eds) (1994) *World Yearbook of Education 1994: The Gender Gap in Higher Education*. London: Kogan Page.

Walsh, V. and Morley, L. (eds) (1996) *Breaking Boundaries: Women in Higher Education*. London: Taylor & Francis.

5

'Race' and Ethnicity

Karen Ross

Multicultural Britain – tolerance and disavowal

It has become a fashionable commonplace in the late 1990s to think of the UK as a country which has sloughed off, lizard-like, its dark, distasteful colonial past and parades a public face which beams 'tolerance' and a happy-clappy multiculturalism. No matter that, in the 1997 General Election in the UK, the British National Party put up a total of 56 candidates who received 35,393 votes, averaging 632 per constituency, or 1.35 per cent of the total vote. No matter that 12,000 racially motivated attacks were reported to the police in 1994–5, compared with 4,300 in 1988 – an increase of 175 per cent in six years (Modood *et al.*, 1997). Racism isn't a problem any more, allegedly, so any criticisms of continuing unequal opportunities are now deemed to be an example of special pleading. But more than 20 years after the Race Relations Act (1976) was made law in the UK, the testimonies of the UK's various minority ethnic communities suggest a society which is some way off the public rhetoric of diversity in equality, as in the Commission for Racial Equality's seductive mantra of 'all different, all equal'. Even the very public debate surrounding the Stephen Lawrence inquiry, subsequent trial, independent inquiry and the publication of the inquiry report (the Macpherson Report) on the whole hateful case in 1999 is seen, in many influential quarters, as being a bit over the top, as in 'if the teenager had been white, would there have been this fuss?' Of course, if Stephen Lawrence *had* been a white boy, then the crime would not have been committed in the first place but if, as a white teenager, he had been stabbed and killed in a 'routine' teenage altercation, would the police enquiry have been so flawed and amateur?

A few facts of British life

In April 1991, at the time of the last Census, 55 million people were counted as resident in the UK and of these, just over 3 million (about 5.5 per cent) were classified as 'ethnic minority' which, for British purposes, means visibly ethnic by skin colour, that is, *not* white. The largest minority ethnic group[1] according to census statistics are South Asian communities (49 per cent), followed by African Caribbean (22 per cent), African (7 per cent), Other Asian (6.6 per cent), Chinese (5.2 per cent) and Others (9.6 per cent). Although concerted discussions about the multicultural nature of British society – most often displayed through a rhetoric of problematization – is a relatively recent phenomenon, what is rather less understood is the UK's history as a country both of settlement for migrants and a country which has benefited enormously from the labour (not to mention creativity and talent) of 'non-white' people, in times of war and times of peace.

The earliest recorded presence of people of African descent in Britain was in the third century when an African garrison was stationed at Hadrian's Wall (Fryer, 1984). This means that people from minority ethnic backgrounds lived in Britain before the 'English' came here, a fact that, by itself, begs the question, who put the 'multi' in multicultural? It also asks, rather cogently, what does 'Englishness' or 'Britishness' actually mean? In particular, what are the prerequisites for joining the British National Party – ancestry, settlement, blood, skin colour? When I was a doctoral student, I worked in a further education college in the Midlands and I remember discussing the media's portrayal of minority ethnic groups with a class of 16-year old white students. We got to talking about the BBC and one of them said that the British Broadcasting Corporation was obviously for white people because it had 'British' in its title, the inference being that to put 'British' and 'Black' together would obviously be oxymoronic. But the vast majority (96 per cent) of 'Caribbean' children under the age of 16 have been born in Britain, together with 94 per cent of 'Indian' children and 94 per cent of 'African Asian' children (Salt, 1996). At what point do they cease being described as second-generation immigrants in favour of the simpler (and more accurate) descriptor of 'British'? When they score for England or throw the javelin for Britain?

'Race', ethnicity and higher education in the UK

Most higher education institutions (HEIs) in the UK pride themselves on their equal opportunities policies (EOPs): their recruitment advertisements are embellished by the now ubiquitous slogan of 'we are an equal opportunities employer'. Their various mission statements speak of a respect for diversity, a 'tolerance' of cultural traditions, a commitment to creating a 'level playing field'. But these same HEIs are often hard-pressed to provide demonstrable evidence of how they actually implement their EOPs and/or what they do with their monitoring data. How far do they/will they really go in celebrating diversity? Will they build a Temple, Gurdwara, Mosque or Synagogue on campus; provide a prayer room in the learning centre; include halal meat or kosher food in the refectory; take swift action against racist remarks, by students or lecturers; train staff in diversity issues? In short, are HEIs welcoming places for minority ethnic students and staff and how do they demonstrate putting their money where their rhetoric is?

During the 1997 general election campaign in the UK, the Labour Party's primary message, the one with which the Party hoped to woo the electorate, was the politically correct promise – Education! Education! Education! With a rising tide of racist violence sweeping across Europe and a significant 'anti-foreigner' discourse pervading the political agenda, education, in all its myriad forms, is an appropriate vehicle through which to challenge racism and discrimination and bring about social change. But the promotion of an anti-racist strategy in educational arenas, of anti-oppressive practices in recruitment, of multicultural curriculum development, is currently under threat and no longer regarded as self-evidently 'good'. In the late 1980s, an enquiry into the circumstances surrounding a racially motivated murder at Burnage High School, Manchester, made headline news for several weeks with an almost hysterical response or, as Grosvenor (1997) puts it, the hype of a new 'moral panic', a panic fuelled by the national media which culminated in an indictment that the school's 'Anti-racist policy led to killing' (*Daily Telegraph*, 26 April 1988 cited in Gillborn, 1995: 36). While the enquiry team were supportive of the aims of anti-racism *per se*, they criticized the way in which it was carried out at Burnage on the grounds that it was a form of 'symbolic, moral and doctrinaire anti-racism' (Gillborn, 1995: 43). What the enquiry seemed to be saying was that anti-racist education is acceptable provided that it is not too discomfiting for white people. As Neal points out, rather sadly, the attacks on anti-racist strategies in education as evidenced by the controversy surrounding Burnage and its aftermath, find a resonance with the more contemporary backlash against political correctness (Neal, 1998). What these two 'anti-' positions share is a reluctance to accept that change is required if multicultural Britain or any other multicultural society, is to have any kind of stable future: we cannot afford any more racist murders or nailbomb attacks in the centre of multicultural, multi-ethnic neighbourhoods.

But even the legality of positive action strategies are now being questioned, for example, training places 'reserved' for minority ethnic candidates to redress under-representation have been challenged, successfully, under allegedly anti-racist legislation itself.[2] Trow, writing a polemic against what he describes as 'benign racism', condemns affirmative action programmes designed to enhance the opportunities of minority ethnic students to achieve university places in the United States by saying, 'We in America are discovering that all "positive discrimination" accomplishes is to shift a handful of the most talented (and usually the most economically advantaged minority) students from the most highly selective universities into other excellent, if slightly less selective, universities' (Trow, 1999: 18). The patent lie contained within that damning statement, that affirmative action strategies only benefit affluent non-whites, does not seem to trouble Professor Trow who, as a securely tenured staffer at the prestigious UCLA Berkeley campus, does not deem it necessary to provide any evidence or statistical support for his malevolent rhetoric.

In some organizations, policies to promote equality of opportunity have been

downgraded and reclassified as 'all different, all equal', implying a static celebration of diversity rather than an active pursuit of an anti-racist practice. I was
recently involved in providing equal opportunities training to a group of staff
in an HEI in south-west England. I began by asking for participants' definitions
of 'equal opportunities' and, not surprisingly, there were different views but
most seemed to converge on the idea of everyone starting off at the same point,
the 'level playing field' analogy. When pushed to think about positive action
strategies, most participants thought such actions were illegal, demonstrating a
typical lack of understanding between 'positive action' (legal) and 'positive discrimination' (illegal). The latter is illegal because it means that a 'special' case is
made for, say, a minority ethnic candidate to be given a post simply on grounds
of ethnicity rather than suitability for and/or ability to do the job, level of qualification and so on. The former is legal because it means that, all other things
being equal – suitability, qualifications, experience, standards – a minority
ethnic candidate will be offered the job in preference to a white candidate as a
way of redressing existing imbalances in, say, the ethnic composition of a
department. But before we have equality of opportunity, we have to have equality of access: minority ethnic lecturers and students first have to be selected
before they can compete on the magical/mythical level playing field.

Unfortunately, most of the participants in the training workshop failed to
accept what they considered to be an extremely subtle distinction between the
two strategies and believed that *any* attempt to redress what (they admit) are
undoubtedly 'real' racial imbalances in a given staff or student group is inher-
ently 'unfair' and 'prejudiced'. 'Two wrongs don't make a right' was a typical
response to the question of promoting positive action strategies, and a desire to
recruit on grounds of merit only was the strategy of choice, not understanding
that 'merit' is rarely the 'real' reason for making appointments but rather the
right 'fit' – 'I'd be glad to appoint a non-white lecturer but the rest of the
department wouldn't like it.' An example of this occurred in 1989 when the
Commission for Racial Equality received allegations from Leicester Racial
Equality Council that an Asian applicant for the post of Principal at Hinckley
College of Further Education had been discriminated against on racial
grounds. The CRE decided to take on the case and its final report stated that:

> The discouraging findings of this formal investigation into lecturer
> appointments in further education in Leicestershire County Council is
> that discrimination can still occur in the most unexpected places – in this
> case, an FE college of a local authority with a long-standing equal oppor-
> tunities policy . . . The investigation found that an Asian applicant for the
> post of Principal at Hinckley College had been rejected on racial grounds
> – although six of the nine people present at the interview thought that
> he was the better candidate. The job was offered to an internal, white
> candidate.
>
> (CRE, 1991: 5)

While the proven case of racial discrimination occurred in the further education sector, higher education institutions are, arguably, some of the other

'unexpected' places in which such discriminatory practices could also take place – we are not immune and cannot afford to be complacent.

Minority ethnic students and higher education in the UK

The Race Relations Act (1976) includes a section on discrimination 'by bodies in charge of educational establishments' (including university and other HEI governing bodies), whereby it is unlawful for the body responsible for an educational establishment to discriminate:

(a) with regard to the terms of admission to the establishment;
(b) by refusing or deliberately omitting to accept an application for admission;
(c) in the way it affords a pupil whom it has admitted to the establishment access to any benefits, facilities or services, or by refusing or deliberately omitting to afford such access; or
(d) by excluding such a pupil from the establishment or by treating him [sic] unfavourably in any other way.

(Home Office, 1977: 16)

Twenty years on and in the specific context of HE, to what extent are we sure that some of us/them are not acting unlawfully?

Rates of participation in post-16 education among British students

The staying-on rates for minority ethnic pupils in post-compulsory education provide an interesting corrective to the common-sense perception that minority ethnic pupils do badly at school and are therefore not eligible to apply for entrance into the higher education sector, although the global statistics on race and education obscure very real differences between minority ethnic groups. Jones (1993) reports that 56 per cent of 16- to 19-year-olds from minority ethnic backgrounds were in full-time further education compared with 37 per cent of young white people. In the Policy Studies Institute's 1994 survey of ethnic minorities [sic], which included an 'added-in' white sample, they found that the staying-on rates for 16- to 19-year-old whites (56 per cent women; 43 per cent men), Caribbeans (57 per cent men; 46 per cent women) and Pakistani/Bangladeshi women (54 per cent) are more or less the same, but higher for Indian/African Asian women (66 per cent) and significantly higher for Pakistani/Bangladeshi men (71 per cent) and Indian/African Asian men (81 per cent) (Modood *et al.*, 1997).

Interestingly, most studies of participation in post-compulsory education show that social class operates as a significant factor in the propensity to leave school at 16, but such patterns are not evident in the staying-on rates for minority ethnic students, with some commentators suggesting that high educational aspirations are a non-class-based feature of South Asian groups (see for example, Vellins, 1982; Brennan and McGeevor, 1987; Modood, 1993). Modood goes so far as to say that part of the rationale among South Asian communities to encourage high academic achievement in their children is a consequence of a certain 'mentality' among those groups which manifests as an 'over-riding ambition to better oneself and one's family, matched by appropriately high levels of deferred gratification . . . This by itself does not eliminate racial bias, but does considerably lessen its impact' (Modood cited in Fuller, 1997: 179). Of course, staying on in post-compulsory education does not necessarily lead to students applying for a place in university or college – or getting accepted.

Rates of participation in higher education programmes in the UK

Although hard to pin down statistically, as ethnic monitoring at the application stage is a relatively new phenomenon, there has been a strong view that, traditionally, students from minority ethnic backgrounds have not comprised a significant section of the student body in higher education. And within the small percentage of minority ethnic students, differential rates of participation have been identified between students from different minority ethnic backgrounds (see for example, Vellins, 1982; Ballard and Vellins, 1985).

However, from 1990 the national organizations responsible for the centralized processing of undergraduate applications to universities, polytechnics and colleges of higher education – UCCA (the Universities Central Council for Admissions, superseded by UCAS – Universities and Colleges Admissions Service – in 1992) and PCAS (the Polytechnics Central Admissions System) – began to ask applicants to state their ethnic origin, so it is now possible to map the progress of non-white applicants in their search to secure a place in higher education. In the first two years of ethnic monitoring (1990 and 1991), only Bangladeshis and 'Black Others' were proportionately less represented than whites in admissions to polytechnics, although both these former groups, together with 'Black Caribbeans' and Pakistanis were under-represented in acceptances to universities (Modood and Shiner, 1994: 1).

In other words, universities were less likely to accept a minority ethnic applicant than polytechnics and colleges and within those acceptances, Bangladeshis and 'Black Others', so termed, were the least likely to secure a place. Looking at the statistics on minority applications during 1990 and 1991, Modood argues that four general points emerge: (a) there were wide variations in higher education applications between different minority ethnic groups, where some, such as Chinese or Black Africans were strongly over-represented while others, such as Bangladeshis, were consistently under-represented;

(b) that the over- and under-representation of different minority ethnic groups changes over time; (c) successful applicants were often skewed towards the polytechnic rather than university sector; and (d) there were differential success rates (between admission and acceptance) among minority ethnic candidates. So, what are the causes for these differences – serendipity or discrimination?

Since UCCA and PCAS first started publishing data broken down by ethnic origin, a debate has ensued over why the rates of admission success are so markedly different between whites and minority ethnic applicants (the latter having a greater failure rate). By way of explaining the differences, UCCA (1991) pointed to:

1. The low number of applications from ethnic minorities for courses with low entrance requirements, notably teacher training courses, which at 12.6 have the lowest mean A-level points score of accepted applicants.
2. The high number of applicants from ethnic minorities, for competitive courses. More than 20 per cent of applications from ethnic minorities were for courses in medicine and law, three times that of whites. With mean A-level points scores of 26.7 and 25.5 respectively, these were the hardest subjects in which to gain a place.
3. The tendency for ethnic minorities to apply to a limited set of universities. While only a third of whites applied to a university in their home region, 44 per cent of Asian applicants and 52 per cent of African and African Caribbean applicants did so in 1991. When considering the geographical location of ethnic minorities this means that, in 1992, 41 per cent of Asian and 50 per cent of African and African Caribbean applicants applied to the 35 institutions in London and the south-east, compared with 20 per cent of white applicants.
4. The greater tendency for ethnic minority applicants to have achieved their A-level grades through resits. In 1992, 12 per cent of applicants with two or more A-levels had re-sat some or all of their examinations to get their final grades.
5. Ethnic minorities have lower average A-level scores than whites.

(Modood and Shiner, 1994: 5–6)

What seems to be suggested by a consideration of these five factors is that they disallow racial discrimination as a possible factor in the selection of applicants: UCCA reported that once these factors were taken into account, 'any apparent racial bias largely disappears' (1991: 8). These five factors suggest, therefore, that minority ethnic applicants have aspirations which far exceed their qualifications and their over-reaching is further exacerbated by the limited geographical scope of their applications, sounding suspiciously like a variation on the 'blaming the victim' syndrome.

Not entirely satisfied with UCCA's explanation, the Committee of Vice-Chancellors and Principals of the Universities of the UK (CVCP) commissioned the Centre for Research in Ethnic Relations at Warwick University to investigate the importance of these five factors, since clearly something was at play in the admissions process. The subsequent study did indeed confirm that all five factors were important in the process (Taylor, 1992) but linked them to class-related structural inequalities in accessing higher education rather than discrimination, and emphasized the importance of equal opportunities policies. Not satisfied with this rather lame conclusion, the PSI used the complete datasets from UCCA and PCAS for 1992 applicants and subjected them to a variety of statistical tests to explore more precisely the weight of each of UCCA's identified factors. In conclusion, the authors of that study argue that:

> The key conclusion of this report is . . . that even after significant academic and social factors are taken into account in the form of a rigorous multi-variate analysis, some ethnic differences in the rates of admission to university and polytechnic remain unexplained.
>
> (Modood and Shiner, 1994: 46)

However, the authors were unwilling to name 'racial discrimination' as the explanation which dared not speak its name.

Several years on, what has changed? Between 1994 and 1998, the proportion of minority ethnic applicants to university rose from 11.3 per cent to 12.8 per cent, although most of the increase was from Asian applicants, since the proportion of African and African Caribbean applicants actually fell from 3.7 per cent in 1996 to 3.04 per cent in 1998. Nonetheless, on the face of it, this looks reasonably healthy, given that only 5 per cent of the British population are from minority ethnic backgrounds, albeit with a generally younger age profile than white Britons. But what is harder to explain is the differential success rate of applicants: for 1988 the figures were 77 per cent for white, 74 per cent for Asian and 65 per cent for African and African Caribbean applicants.[3] Although, as Table 5.1 indicates, the success rate of minority ethnic applicants has gradually improved over the past few years, the fact that such a large gap remains between success rates gives continuing cause for concern.

Table 5.1 clearly shows that African and African Caribbean applicants tend to have an older age profile (only 38 per cent of applicants in 1996 were under 21 compared with 78 per cent of white and 80.7 per cent of Asian applicants) and applicants from all minority ethnic communities tend to have the less traditional qualifications such as General National Vocational Qualifications (GNVQs), Higher National Certificates (HNCs) and Higher National Diplomas (HNDs) rather than the more traditional A-levels. Do these features make them less attractive to higher education institutions? Modood (1994) certainly claims that they do.

What is also worthy of note is the variability of acceptance rates onto different level programmes, e.g. there is a much greater proportion of acceptances for minority ethnic candidates onto HND courses than degree programmes than for white applicants. For African and African Caribbean applicants, 9.8 per cent of women and 14.4 per cent of men successfully gained an HND place, compared with 10 per cent of women and 14 per cent of men from Asian backgrounds and 5 per cent of white women and 9 per cent of white men. It is not

Table 5.1 Applications, acceptances and ethnicity of applicants

Ethnicity	Applications	Degree acceptance	HND acceptance	% success
Black African, Black Caribbean and Black 'other' women				
1996	7,424	4,004	438	60
1995	7,592	3,836	544	58
1994	6,940	3,205	438	52
Black African, Black Caribbean and Black 'other' men				
1996	6,177	3,270	552	62
1995	6,305	3,134	517	58
1994	6,037	2,767	438	53
Asian women				
1996	14,949	9,521	1,124	71
1995	14,103	8,467	1,232	69
1994	12,886	7,460	1,105	66
Asian men				
1996	17,241	10,524	1,675	71
1995	16,473	9,742	1,846	70
1994	15,589	8,964	1,597	68

Source: derived from UCAS annual report (1996)

possible to discern whether these differences reflect the first choices of applicants but it is clear that nearly twice as many African, African Caribbean and
Asian students graduate with qualifications which are viewed as of lesser value
(i.e. HND) than those awarded to white students.

As well as differential acceptance onto programmes of different level, minority ethnic students are granted places at universities or other HEIs in different
proportions to white students. For example, African Caribbean and Indian students are more likely to get accepted at HEIs in the 'new' university sector than
other minority ethnic students, whereas Chinese and Bangladeshi students are
more successful in gaining places in 'old' universities (Modood and Shiner,
1994). In addition, as indicated by the UCCA data, minority ethnic students
are more likely to apply to universities and HEIs close to home than white
counterparts, which means that the majority of minority ethnic students apply
to relatively few HEIs.

There is also considerable variation in the subjects studied by African and
African Caribbean, Asian and white students and especially the choices made
by women and men across all ethnic categories. The most popular subject categories for white women students were social studies and business/administ-
ration, followed closely by education. For white men, the most popular

choices were business/administration, engineering and technology, and mathematical sciences and informatics. African and African Caribbean women showed the same primary preferences as white women (social studies followed by business/administration) but the third most popular subject choice was mathematical sciences and informatics, followed by subjects allied to medicine. Education was the fifth most popular subject for this group. For African and African Caribbean men, mathematical sciences and informatics was the most popular category, followed by engineering and technology and business/ administration, that is, their subject choices, although ranked differently, were the same as for white male students.

For Asian women, business/administration and social studies were again the most popular choices, followed by subjects allied to medicine and mathematical sciences and informatics. For Asian men, mathematical sciences and informatics was the most popular category, followed by business/administration, engineering and technology and social studies. It is clear to see, from these subject choices, why so many teachers are white women: education appears as a significant subject category for only one group of students, white women. This fact goes some way to explaining why potential students argue that the further and higher education sectors are unwelcoming to them, since they do not see non-white role models to encourage them in.

Minority ethnic students' experiences of higher education in the UK

So, having leapt all the hurdles which face every prospective university entrant, but having probably also faced other issues earlier in their academic career, such as low teacher expectations, lack of support, overt or covert discrimination (see for example, Modood, 1997), a minority ethnic student finally achieves a place to study at university. What are her/his experiences? When seeking to find examples of empirically-based research on the topic, I came across very little. Bird suggests that there has been a

> noisy silence about black students and no codification of their experiences. Part of the silence may be based upon the idea that the liberal academy is not a site of discrimination. Another part may follow from the idea that existing structures, such as codes of practice on racial abuse and harassment are working. A final part may follow from the belief that where there are complaints of discrimination they are ill-founded or exaggerated.
>
> (Bird, 1996: 5)

Similarly, Dorn (1991) argues that higher education has been the victim of its own ideology, where discrimination has been rendered invisible as a consequence of the espousal of a liberal rhetoric which makes it almost impossible to talk about even the possibility of unequal treatment. My own experiences of attempting to deliver equal opportunities training, as I suggested above, bears this out absolutely – lecturers do not believe that their own colleagues are capable of behaving in a racist way, let alone think about the impact or import of their own behaviour .

In response to this woeful lack of material, Bird (1996) set out to examine the experiences of minority ethnic students in south-west England (Bath and Bristol). Set out below are a selection of quotes from minority ethnic students about the attitudes of fellow students and staff members:

'You are getting white people talking and lecturing about racism and yet they won't confront their own racism.'

'He [a black student] was looked down upon . . . one of his lecturers said something like, "I don't think I'm going to see you next year, you won't be here" . . . he was waiting to kick him off the course basically.'

'When I have done placements I am very conscious that I am an Asian and [that] is not very common . . . I am aware of racism.'

'I don't see any black or Asian lecturers . . . if there was a black or Asian lecturer, how would they be received by all the white students . . . I think the way things are they would not be received well.'

'Where is this equal opportunity thing?'

'There was no black tutor to relate to [even though] there is a high percentage of us [black students] here.'

(Bird, 1996: 22)

Bird goes on to argue that, when comparing student and staff views of ethnic diversity in higher education (Bird *et al.*, 1992), there seemed to be more awareness of the issues and more reflexivity on the part of minority ethnic students than was evident from the discussions with white staff and students. Trotman Reid (1990) also argues that the scarcity of minority ethnic staff in higher education is partly to blame for some of the difficulties which many minority ethnic students experience when trying to find someone they can relate to.

Training to teach in the higher education sector in the UK

As students in Bird *et al.*'s study have stated, one of the key issues facing minority ethnic students in higher education is the lack of role models, as lecturers, researchers or other staff. As we saw earlier, the lack of interest of minority ethnic students choosing to embark on teacher training programmes, at both undergraduate and postgraduate level, has a clear knock-on effect in terms of role-modelling for subsequent cohorts of students. Why teaching and lecturing are seen as such unattractive options for minority ethnic students is unclear but it is a worrying trend. One reason could be that as there are demonstrably few non-white lecturers, minority ethnic students may feel that they are not pre-pared to study for a profession where they will continue to be in a highly visible minority. It is in fact very difficult to get an accurate picture of the number of minority ethnic lecturing staff in the UK, since not even the DfEE collects data on ethnicity: however the National Association of Teachers in Further and Higher Education (NATFHE) does collect 'ethnic' data on their membership form and their 1994 print-out showed that 2.27 per cent of their 75,000 members were from minority ethnic backgrounds (Mirza, 1995). The most recent attempt to quantify the number of minority ethnic staff and explore their experiences can be found in the findings of a study commissioned by a consortium of agencies including the CRE and the CVCP (Modood and Fenton, 1999). Among other things, the authors found continuing evidence of institutional racism, unequal treatment, blocked promotion prospects and less advantageous terms and conditions: 20 per cent of the minority ethnic partici-pants in their study stated that they had experienced racial discrimination from staff and/or students. These findings give us little cause to believe that more than twenty years of legislation, enacted to protect the rights of the UK's minority ethnic communities, have made any significant impact on their lives and life chances. The findings also suggest that the legislation is no longer working – if indeed it ever did.

Singh suggests that minority ethnic students who are qualified to enter higher education tend not to train for teaching because they expect to encounter pupil and teacher racism (Singh, 1988). In a study by Siraj-Blatchford, minority ethnic student teachers reported experiencing discrim-ination, stereotyping and overt racism from co-students and lecturers at uni-versity and from staff and pupils in school while on teaching practice (Siraj-Blatchford, 1991). Later work by Blair and Maylor (1993) again con-firmed the largely negative experiences of minority ethnic student teachers, where the latter stated that they were often treated as 'professional ethnics', as people who could (and should) provide lecturers and teachers with 'specialist' information about aspects of 'race' and 'culture', to the exclusion of other aspects of teaching and pedagogy (cited in Fuller, 1997: 28). Racism was a factor in the ability of these student teachers to form relationships with their co-students and lecturers, leaving them anxious about their progress and wor-ried that by drawing attention to their experience of racism, they would then jeopardize their chances of successfully completing their degree (see also Crozier and Menter, 1993). The small amount of work which has been carried out with minority ethnic student teachers suggests that the time spent on teach-ing practice often provides the worst experience of open racial hostility but that reporting back such experiences to lecturing staff is too often met with scant regard and minimal support, leaving students isolated and alienated (Siraj-Blatchford, 1993; Showunmi and Constantine-Simms, 1995).

Improving access

Although the number of students from minority ethnic backgrounds applying for places at higher education institutions has increased steadily during this decade, the majority of these students are concentrated in relatively few higher education institutions, leaving a great many institutions largely bereft of non-white students. These are therefore seen as possibly unwelcoming places for local minority ethnic students to seek admission. Jewson *et al.*'s study of university undergraduate prospectuses for 1990 argues that most prospectuses represent non-white students as overseas students rather than as evidence of their own 'home-grown' multi-ethnic student population, actively recruited from their local catchment communities (Jewson *et al.*, 1991). This can be a rather off-putting strategy for minority ethnic students who already have a folkloric understanding of what HEIs do and who they are for. Even in areas which have significant minority ethnic populations, knowledge and information about opportunities in higher education are often poor among school pupils.

Work with five inner-city schools with proportions of black students ranging from 5 to 30 per cent in the Bath and Bristol areas, where there are four HEIs, produced a depressing picture common to many urban areas nationally. Few of the black students had ever visited the HEIs; few had been told about the HEIs and about what they had to offer; few aspired to HE; many saw HEIs as not for them, but for bright, middle-class white students (Bird, 1996: 35).

Better links could be forged between schools and their local HEIs, with staff and students visiting each other, generating a two-way flow of information sharing and open communication. This is already happening, to some extent, via the COMPACT system which provides precisely this kind of link between schools, HEIs and local businesses, but evaluation work has yet to be carried out on the extent to which this initiative delivers more minority ethnic students into higher education.

School-HEI link: case study 1

As part of an initiative to improve the links between schools and HEIs, a secondary school in the Bath/Bristol area with a significant number of minority ethnic students (20 per cent or so) was approached by Bird *et al.* (1992) with a view to trialling and developing a link which would go beyond the conventional liaison system and instead build on some of the initiatives developed through student mentoring schemes (Bird, 1996).[4] School staff were initially suspicious about the motives of the local HEIs and worried that there would be an unacceptable burden of new tasks generated by the link. After lengthy discussions, a set of principles were devised to guide the development of the relationship.

(a) the link work should relate to other things the school was doing, e.g. careers guidance;
(b) the links should be useful to the school and provide some kind of pay-off in

both the short and the longer term – altruism doesn't deliver the national curriculum;

(c) work with HEIs should raise the profile of HE in general and not operate simply as a recruiting tool;

(d) minority ethnic students in HE should be involved in the work with the school and should have that work formally recognized, preferably through accreditation;

(e) both minority ethnic and white school pupils should be involved in the project.

As well as these principles which were laid down at the beginning of the process, a number of guidelines emerged as the project developed:

- give students a central role in the link
- work across the age range in schools
- try to develop flexible entry to HE
- work with ethnically mixed groups of students
- involve parents.

Community outreach

In addition to formal and informal links with schools, Bird argues that higher education institutions should make more effort to disseminate information to minority ethnic communities more generally and to work directly with minority ethnic community and liaison workers to (among other things) allay fears and rumours about what higher education is actually like and to provide communication bridges between community and higher education providers (Bird, 1996). In the Inner London Education Authority's innovative study of equal opportunities and further education (Sammons *et al.*, 1989), the project team found the use of local community networks for the marketing and publicity of courses to be a positive feature of a number of the courses which were seen as examples of good practice:

> . . . using the ethnic press; local community groups or centres; AEIs [adult education institutes] and local education shops were mentioned as important for publicizing some courses. In certain colleges, particular attention was paid to providing publicity materials in local community languages.
>
> (Sammons *et al.*, 1989: 7)

Of course, marketing strategies employed in the further education sector can make the easy journey across to higher education without too much difficulty. Crucially, 'there are, therefore, two steps for HEIs: knowing communities and getting trust' (Bird, 1996: 55). The easiest way to 'know' local communities is to use a strategy of 'community profiling' (see Further Education Unit, 1995), which essentially means using available Census data to map the local minority ethnic community, analysing age profiles and assessing the potential for taking up existing and local higher education opportunities. The 'getting trust' bit is rather more difficult and involves the development of sensitive relationships over periods of time: a first step is to discover what community organizations actually exist within the locale of an HEI (for example, whether there is a local Race Equality Council) and which ones would like to start a dialogue.

Community liaison – case study 2

An interesting initiative taken by Goldsmiths College, University of London, is its Caribbean Centre. Set up in 1979 as a local community project, it is still run by local people, most of whom are volunteers (Breinburg, 1994). The idea originated from discussions between a group of local Caribbean people and senior staff at Goldsmiths. The rationale for the Centre, in those early years called 'The Centre for Caribbean Students', was first to develop Caribbean Studies at all levels, college-wide and accessible to all, with the expressed aim of encouraging non-Caribbean people to come and learn together with Caribbean participants; and second, to encourage more minority ethnic people, but particularly those of Caribbean origin, to access higher education across all academic programmes.

   Accordingly, the Centre developed a number of short courses, including both 'recreational' and award-bearing programmes in Caribbean Studies, Legal Studies and Criminal Justice Studies. The Centre has also forged links abroad, including the Netherlands, the Caribbean itself, Canada and the United States and has a visiting/exchange programme with the Caribbean Centre at the University of Amsterdam. The Centre has also been highly successful in increasing the number of African Caribbean students entering higher education, although Breinburg argues that the Centre has been much less successful in enabling (potential) lecturers and researchers to gain employment within higher education (Breinburg, 1994).

Ethnic monitoring[5]

The most that the majority of higher education institutions are likely to do within the limits of their expressed equal opportunity policies is to monitor the ethnicity (along with all the other variables present on the admissions form) of their applicants and then file the results. Without a clear idea about the point of ethnic monitoring – even at its most basic level, let alone a more elaborate system which attempts to monitor the learning experience – it is easy to sideline ethnic monitoring as just another crazy politically correct stunt, designed to embarrass HEIs about their lack of minority ethnic students. Even the most well-intentioned HEI, though, needs to have a system of monitoring (including ethnic monitoring) which has specific aims and objectives, which can be tested, is adequately resourced and has trigger points for action. The Commission for Racial Equality's definition of 'ethnic monitoring' is:

. . . the use of ethnic records to analyse and evaluate how a school or college operates. It is a continuous process, and can:

- reveal patterns of racial inequality;
- identify any barriers or obstacles that might account for the differences between ethnic groups;
- help identify remedies to such problems.

An effective ethnic monitoring system should be able to show whether differences between ethnic groups are due to racial discrimination or to other reasons.

(CRE, 1992: 9)

In the course of writing this chapter, one quality assurance manager I spoke to articulated a common problem. While there was a tacit recognition among some staff that the members of minority ethnic communities were under-represented amongst the student population, precisely who had responsibility for tackling the problem seemed much more ambiguous. Key staff are provided with lists of students on their courses, disaggregated by variables such as ethnic background, but there are no formal procedures where anomalies could be discussed and remedies sought. The routine response seems to be that minority ethnic students are simply not applying and that this is hardly the fault of the institution. That factors other than academic ability are at play in the selection process is simply denied, or possibly not understood, by most staff working in higher education.

The procedure for setting up an effective ethnic monitoring system is usefully summarized by Bird (1996 especially pp. 95–106), but crucially requires a number of ingredients: liaison and working with the student union; ownership by staff and students; provision of an overt rationale for introducing the system; sensitive classifications; clear use of data; integration with general equality policies and equality audit procedures (adapted from Bird, 1996).

Supporting minority ethnic students

Unless minority ethnic students are studying at a higher education institution which has a significant local minority ethnic population, they are likely to feel highly visible and possibly isolated in what is probably a white-dominated environment. There are, in any case, significant issues about ownership when institutions think about setting up group-specific support initiatives: at the very least, concern and interest in such a support activity needs to come from members of the relevant group themselves, with the institution perhaps providing the supporting framework to enable such groups to function. As Bird points out, when support structures for one group, in this case minority ethnic students, are initiated, they are often criticized as 'special treatment' by those who feel that they are losing out or by those who feel that their power is being challenged and control subverted.

Some white students felt that black students were getting extra recognition and representation within the departmental structures. In essence, they were failing to recognize the extent to which existing structures within faculties and departments were heavily dominated by white people . . . some staff were [also] uneasy about the black students' role and influence, particularly on curriculum issues.

(Bird, 1996: 83)

Unsurprisingly, the evaluation of the support group from its members was overwhelmingly positive and such an initiative can perform a number of useful roles for its members: support if things go wrong; a safe space to discuss 'race' issues; and a pressure group.

National Mentoring Consortium – case study 3

In 1992, a mentor scheme was set up at the University of East London (UEL) by a careers advisor who, when he was appointed in 1991, was the only minority ethnic careers advisor working in the higher education sector.[6] His job was primarily to address the specific needs of African, Caribbean and Asian students at UEL and to increase the success rates for minority ethnic graduates seeking employment (Stewart, 1996). UEL then set up a pilot mentoring scheme to address some of the disadvantages experienced by minority ethnic students. The main disadvantages were identified as follows:

- African, Caribbean and Asian people are more likely to be graduates than other groups, but are twice as likely to be unemployed. Minority graduates are only half as likely as white graduates to be offered employment in their final year.
- Minority ethnic students have to make more applications than white students before obtaining interviews.
- As a result of the pattern of past exclusion of minority ethnic groups from areas of the labour market, many students lack basic information about employers' requirements and recruitment practice and the preparation they need to maximize their employment opportunities.
- This lack of information and preparation often results in a poorer performance in applications, interviews and at assessment centres.
- With the under-representation of ethnic minority groups in many areas, students often knew no one who could offer guidance and they frequently needed encouragement to apply for prestigious employers' graduate recruitment schemes.
- There is evidence of direct and indirect racial discrimination in the procedures by which organizations recruit graduates from universities in the 'milk-round'.
- Within the universities and in earlier educational institutions many ethnic minority students feel misunderstood and unsupported by the

staff, may lack confidence in their own abilities and in some instances, have higher drop-out rates.

(Stewart, 1996: 6)

The National Mentoring Consortium (NMC) grew out of the UEL pilot project and, in 1996, the NMC had 12 participating universities (providing mentees) and 46 participating employers (providing mentors). The NMC links minority ethnic undergraduates in a one-to-one relationship with an employed mentor in order to provide professional expertise, personal development, support and encouragement. In particular, it aims to support students through their studies and to:

- prepare students for the world of work;
- encourage and prepare them to apply for graduate management training schemes;
- increase their awareness of different types of career and the preparation needed to apply;
- provide role models to whom students can relate, who will encourage them to maximize their potential; and
- provide customized personal development training for students.

(Stewart, 1996: 7)

The 'mission' of the NMC is, broadly, to prepare and develop high calibre minority ethnic undergraduates for successful recruitment into graduate management training schemes. It is clear how the mentees benefit, but what do participating employers get out of involvement in the scheme? The scheme suggests that the benefits to companies include access to the largest ethnic minority network in the country, a 'head start' in graduate recruitment, management training for mentors and development opportunities for mentors. The individual mentors are offered the opportunity to benefit from personal and professional development opportunities, improved training, enhanced management skills, networking, and a sense of fulfilment and camaraderie. The participating universities can take advantage of: improved access to and links with the wider community, progression of equal opportunities provision, and highly focused careers advice and personal development training for their African, Caribbean and Asian students.

When Stewart evaluated the scheme, she interviewed 19 mentors and 18 mentees representing four separate cohorts of mentor–mentee relationships since 1992 (Stewart, 1996). Findings from the study included the following:

Mentors' views: 92 per cent found the scheme challenging, 95 per cent found it rewarding, 91 per cent found it valuable, 63 per cent had developed at a personal level and 85 per cent had recommended the scheme to others.

Mentees' views: 95 per cent found it challenging, 97 per cent found it rewarding, 95 per cent found it valuable, 80 per cent had developed personally, 97 per cent felt their awareness of the career world had been extended, 82 per cent had recommended the scheme to others and 45 per cent felt that their academic work had improved.

Overall, the success of the mentoring relationship depended on a number of factors including the selection and preparation of the student; the matching of mentor to mentee; and the induction and training provided to the mentor (CRE, 1996). Interestingly mentees identified advantages in having a mentor from the same ethnic group as well as from a different ethnic group, as the three quotes below indicate:

'It enabled me to question my prejudices about Asians . . . if I had an African/Caribbean mentor I would have had preconceived ideas of what to expect.' (African male mentee/ Asian male mentor)

'[There were] advantages in the way that he was able to identify problems faced by ethnic minorities, but it was difficult for him to answer questions on discrimination' (African female mentee/ white male mentor)

'We were able to be more open with us both being black.' (Caribbean female mentee/Caribbean female mentor)

(Stewart, 1996: 19)

Participating universities were very positive about the actual and potential benefits which they had derived from the scheme, at both the institutional and the student level. These benefits included the creation of a model for student support, guidance in equipping students for work placements and graduate recruitment, and the implementation of equal opportunities and the creation of a welcoming and supportive environment for minority ethnic students. This latter is something that all of us working in higher education would be pleased to see as a reality in our own institutions.

Targeted programmes to encourage more students from minority ethnic backgrounds to consider higher education, and to support existing black and Asian students are becoming much more commonplace, especially in HEIs which serve and/or are situated in a multicultural neighbourhood. Innovative projects, such as the development of the Junior University at Bradford which aims to attack the ongoing intergenerational pattern of educational disadvantage among Bradford's minority ethnic community by accessing the University's facilities to school pupils, or London Guildhall's establishment of the Bengali Education and Advice Centre[7] are forward-looking responses to the problem of under-recruitment of minority ethnic students and show what is possible with well-researched, properly supported strategies which genuinely widen participation to higher education.

Notes

1. I use the term 'minority ethnic' throughout this chapter to signal the unequal relationship between majority ethnic groups (in the British context, this means 'white' people) and minority ethnic groups but without wishing to downplay the myriad ethnicities and differences which are necessarily subsumed under this one crude descriptor. However, for the sake of brevity and in an attempt to distinguish easily between majority and minority communities, I beg indulgence to use this term here.

2. For example, for a number of years, the BBC allocated a small number of places on its main training scheme to minority ethnic candidates but was challenged, successfully, by the Freedom Association (a right-wing campaigning group) under the Race Relations Act (1976) on the grounds that such allocation disadvantaged white applicants.
3. Data provided by UCAS to the author, 12 May 1999.
4. For a more detailed discussion of ways to forge relationships between schools and HEIs and what they should include, see Bird, 1996, especially pp. 36–51.
5. See the CRE's *Ethnic Monitoring in Education* (1992) booklet for a detailed discussion of how to 'do' ethnic monitoring in such a way as to be helpful in strategizing for equality.
6. For an in-depth discussion of the National Mentoring Scheme and its evaluation, see Stewart, 1996.
7. Both these initiatives are described in summary in Woodrow *et al.*, 1998.

References

Ballard, R. and Vellins, S. (1985) South Asian Entrants to British Universities: a comparative note, *New Community*, 12(2): 260–5.

Bird, J. (1996) *Black Students in Higher Education: Rhetorics and Realities*. Buckingham: Society for Research into Higher Education and the Open University Press.

Bird, J., Myler, A. and Yee, W. (1992) *Widening Access to Higher Education for Black People*. Bristol: University of The West of England/Employment Department.

Blair, M. and Maylor, U. (1993) Issues and concerns for Black women teachers in training, in L. Siraj-Blatchford (ed.) *'Race', Gender and the Education of Teachers*. Buckingham: Open University Press.

Breinburg, P. (1994) Aspects of the Caribbean Experience. Published paper given presented to the conference 'Future of Multi-Ethnic Britain: Challenges, Changes and Opportunities' (organized by the Runnymede Trust/Commission for Racial Equality/EC/All-Party Parliamentary Group on race and community). University of Reading, September.

Brennan, J. and McGeevor, P. (1987) *Employment of Graduates from Ethnic Minorities: A Research Report*. London: Commission for Racial Equality.

Commission for Racial Equality (1991) *A Question of Merit: Report of a Formal Investigation into Lecturer Appointments in Leicestershire*. London: CRE.

Commission for Racial Equality (1992) *Ethnic Monitoring in Education*. London: CRE.

Commission for Racial Equality (1996) *A Positive Mentor Attitude: Evaluating the Success of the National Mentoring Consortium – Executive Summary*. London: CRE.

Crozier, G. and Menter, I. (1993) The heart of the matter? Student teachers' experience of school, in L. Siraj-Blatchford (ed.) *'Race', Gender and the Education of Teachers*. Buckingham: Open University Press.

Dorn, A. (1991) Notes on ethnic minority participation in HE. Unpublished paper presented to the Widening Participation in HE conference (organized by the Polytechnics and Colleges Funding Council). London.

Fuller, M. (1997) *Education and Race*. Unit 4, Block 5, *Equality and Education: Exploring Educational Issues*. Buckingham: Open University Press.

Further Education Unit (1995) *Community Profiling*. London: Further Education Development Agency.

Gillborn, D. (1995) Renewing and refocusing anti-racism: the view from education. Published paper in the Conference Report 'Challenge, Change and Opportunity: The Future of Multi-Ethnic Britain'. London: The Runnymede Trust.

Grosvenor, I. (1997) *Assimilating Identities: Racism and Educational Policy in Post-1945 Britain.* London: Lawrence and Wishart.

Home Office (1977) *Racial Discrimination – A Guide to the Race Relations Act, 1976.* London: HMSO.

Jewson, N., Mason, D., Bowen, R., Mulvaney, K. and Parmar, S. (1991) Universities and ethnic minorities: the public face, *New Community*, 17(2): 183–99.

Jones, T. (1993) *Britain's Ethnic Minorities.* London: Policy Studies Institute.

Mirza, S. H. (1995) Black women in higher education: defining a space/finding a place, in L. Morley and V. Walsh (eds) *Feminist Academics: Creative Agents for Change.* London: Taylor & Francis.

Modood, T. (1993) The number of ethnic minority students in British higher education: some grounds for optimism, *Oxford Review of Education*, 19(2): 167–82.

Modood, T. and Fenton, S. (1999) *Ethnic Minority Staff in Higher Education.* London: Policy Studies Institute.

Modood, T. and Shiner, M. (1994) *Ethnic Minorities and Higher Education.* London: Policy Studies Institute in collaboration with UCAS.

Modood, T. and Shiner, M. (1997) *Ethnic Minorities in Britain: Diversity and Disadvantage.* London: Policy Studies Institute.

Neal, S. (1998) *The Making of Equal Opportunities Policies in Universities.* Buckingham: Society for Research into Higher Education and Open University Press.

Salt, J. (1996) Immigration and ethnic group, in D. Coleman and J. Salt (eds) *Ethnicity in the 1991 Census.* Volume 1: *Demographic Characteristics of Ethnic Minority Populations.* London: HMSO.

Sammons, P., Arora, K. C., Banerjee, K. and Kapoor, S. (1989) *Equal Opportunities for Ethnic Minorities in Work-Related NAFE: Identifying and Developing Good Practices in Colleges.* London: ILEA.

Showunmi, V. and Constantine-Simms, D. (1995) *Teachers for the Future.* Stoke-on-Trent: Trentham Books.

Singh, R. (1988) *Asian and White Perceptions of the Teaching Profession.* Bradford: Bradford and Ilkley Community College.

Siraj-Blatchford, L. (1991) A study of black students' perceptions of racism in initial teacher training, *British Educational Research Journal*, 17(1): 35–50.

Siraj-Blatchford, L. (1993) Racial equality and effective teacher education, in L. Siraj-Blatchford (ed.) *Race, Gender and the Education of Teachers.* Buckingham: Open University Press.

Stewart, M. (1996) *A Positive Mentor Attitude: Evaluating the Success of the National Mentoring Consortium.* London: Commission for Racial Equality.

Taylor, P. (1992) *Ethnic Group Data for University Entry.* Report to the CVCP Working Group on Ethnic Data. Warwick: University of Warwick (CRER).

Trotman Reid, P. (1990) African-American women in academia: paradoxes and barriers, in S. Stiver Lie and V. E. O'Leary (eds) *Storming the Tower: Women in the Academic World.* London: Kogan Page.

Trow, M. (1999) Beware this benign racism. *THES*, 18 June.

Universities Central Council for Admissions (1991) *Statistical Supplement to the Twenty-eighth Report (1989–1990).* Cheltenham: UCCA.

Universities and Colleges Admissions Service (1994, 1995, 1996) *Annual Reports.* Cheltenham: UCAS.

Vellins, S. (1982) South Asian students in British universities: a statistical note, *New Community*, 10(2): 206–12.

Woodrow, M. (1998) *From Elitism to Inclusion: Good Practice in Widening Access to Higher Education.* London: CVCP.

Useful addresses and contacts

Commission for Racial Equality
Elliot House
10–12 Allington Street
London SW1E 5EH
Tel: 020 7828 7022

National Mentoring Consortium
Cumbrian House
217 Marsh Wall
London E14 9FG
Tel: 020 8590 7000

Policy Studies Institute
100 Park Village East
London NW1 3SR
Tel: 020 8468 0468

6

Disability

Karen Ross

Introduction

Equality campaigns tend to run in cycles (and often circles). The rather hedonistic tenor of 1960s Britain gave way to a decade in which demands for gender equality became particularly intense, culminating in the Sex Discrimination Act (1975). The Race Relations Act (1976) followed the next year, and race and gender were often conflated as symbolic of a more general institutionalized malaise of oppressive practice perpetrated by white, middle-class men upon everyone else. During the 1990s, after 20 or more years of anti-sexist, anti-racist legislation (albeit with precious little to show for their respective 'successes' in terms of real progress), campaigns which fought for the rights of other marginalized and oppressed groups became much more visible, in particular gay/lesbian and disability rights campaigns.

This is not to say that campaigns for the rights of these oppressed groups have not been ongoing with a significant history – for example, 1981 was deemed to be the International Year of Disabled People and began the United Nations' Decade of Disabled People – but the campaigns (and disabled campaigners in particular) became significantly more public and significantly more vocal during the 1990s. Marches and demonstrations signalled an escalation in demands for equal rights since social policy on disability rights seemed to have been peculiarly resistant to change. The key issue was/is still not about charity or special pleading but about the right to full citizenship. Campbell and Oliver (1996) argue that, although the Decade of Disabled People was comprehensively ignored by governments, statutory and voluntary bodies alike, disabled people themselves made it the most important decade in their own history with the setting up of numerous pressure groups and disability-led organizations which formed the base of a real disability rights movement that got active in the 1990s: 'The emerging disability movement has now emerged' (Campbell and Oliver, 1996: 167).

Definitions and terms

So what do we mean by disability? The UK's Disability Discrimination Act (1995) (hereafter called the DDA) was, in many ways, a landmark Act, long-awaited by the disability rights movement but regarded, retrospectively (and even before its enactment by many) as a pathetic and powerless piece of legislation that compromises many of its original aims (those which had not already been abandoned or argued out of existence during the Bill's protracted passage through Parliament). However, it does stand as the most recent effort to 'protect' the rights of disabled people. For the purposes of definition, then, the DDA states that a disabled person is a person who has a disability and who can therefore seek protection under the law as a person having a disability if he or she has a physical or mental impairment which has a substantial and long-term adverse effect on his or her ability to carry out normal day-to-day activities (Doyle, 1996). The Act is, in fact, very vague on defining precisely what 'impairment' and therefore 'disability' actually means, although as it is informed by a medical model of disability, it is likely that a medical diagnosis will provide the final judgement. As Hahn puts it, somewhat cynically, 'disability is defined by public policy. In other words, disability is whatever policy says it is' (1985: 294).

But it *is* important to be clear about what we actually mean when we use a term such as 'disability' because there is considerable controversy over who should and should not be included under that definition. During 1996, I carried out a research project for the BBC which focused on the views held by disabled people towards the portrayal of disability on television. As someone who is committed to using a social rather than medical model of disability, I was keen to include individuals who experience mental ill-health and learning difficulties as well as people who have more 'obvious' sensory and physical disabilities. The sponsors and I had several lively debates before it was agreed to include mental ill-health and learning difficulty in our definition of disability but then, when I came to conduct the research, I found just as many differences in opinion among the participants over who could be 'legitimately' described as disabled. A later study, again for the BBC but this time focusing on disabled listeners and radio, yielded the same variation on who could legitimately be described as disabled. For the purposes of this chapter, my working definition of 'disability' encompasses any individual who feels they are socially, culturally and/or economically disadvantaged (either actually or potentially) because of a physical, sensory or psychological impairment. As Oliver puts it, much more elegantly:

> All disabled people experience disability as social restriction, whether those restrictions occur as a consequence of inaccessible built environments, questionable notions of intelligence and social competence, the inability of the general public to use sign language, the lack of reading material in Braille or hostile public attitudes to people with non-visible disabilities.
>
> (Oliver, 1990: xiv)

Disability politics – from medical to social perspectives

Estimates of the extent of disability in the UK vary enormously, from 'official' statistics – which are derived only from numbers of people claiming some form of disability benefit – to more populist estimates of 1 in 8 of the population; this is seen as a 'reasonable' estimate if we accept that many older people are disabled in some way but may not be claiming benefit and therefore are not 'recorded'. The great majority of disability activists argue that 'disability' is a socially constructed concept which has medical/biological underpinnings which serve to pathologize individuals, making them both victim of and responsible for their own 'impairment' (see for example, Finkelstein, 1980; Barton, 1988; Oliver, 1990, 1996; Morris, 1991). The medical model of disability has a number of features which force dependency that are most easily described by way of couplet descriptors – tragic but brave, bitter and twisted, helpless and hopeless.[1] This view of disability is one which is clearly individualized and absolves 'society' or 'culture' from any responsibility either for the construction of disability as a problem/disease category or to generate solutions (although legislation can be construed at least as a 'political' solution).

Reading disabled people's own testimonies of their lived experiences demonstrates graphically how the medicalized view of disability has shaped and determined their lives in highly 'social' ways and the way in which such a common sense approach to disability becomes internalized and individualized very easily. In fact, one of the most prolific writers on disability politics, Michael Oliver, argues that the medical model of disability is a misnomer and that rather there is an individual model which includes psychological and medical aspects, underpinned by a theme of personal tragedy which he then counterpoises with the 'social' model (Oliver, 1983, 1996). In both the quotes which follow, this medical/individual nexus is clearly visible:

> 'I think disability was very much illness-based for me. I was ill. I was perceived to be ill by everybody including the professional people and other people that visited me. I think I perceived myself as being ill, though in retrospect I certainly wasn't most of the time. I was ill at times but I wouldn't have said that was the predominant feature. The predominant feature throughout my institutional life was the fact that I was left in bed a lot of the time when I could have been up. Because I couldn't dress and wash myself, the staff did for me what they felt was adequate and sometimes it was totally inadequate. I was very much kept where they wanted me to be kept.'
>
> (Ann MacFarlane cited in Campbell and Oliver, 1996: 36–7)

The social model of disability is, obviously, antithetical to the medical model it seeks to challenge, and locates 'society', that is, us, as the generator of an ideological discourse and construction of disability which demeans, oppresses, marginalizes and devalues people with disabilities. As Lisicki argues, the challenge to the medical model through experiential learning was initially mounted at an individual level, since proactive disability campaign groups are a relatively recent phenomenon, and even then, resistance was instinctive rather than initiated as a predetermined political act of defiance.

> 'I had begun to realize the oppressive nature of the medical model but on a very individual level. At that time I did not know any better but they [the doctors] would want to do experimental operations and I let them. I just believed them and didn't know to resist. I didn't know to say no. It didn't take very long to learn – within four years I was saying to consultants, 'Stuff your operations up your arse'. I didn't know it as a medical model. All I knew was that all these doctors were really screwing people. And they are still doing it. They are chopping bits off people because they don't know how to deal with them.'
>
> (Barbara Lisicki cited in Campbell and Oliver, 1996: 37–8)

Disability in British higher education contexts[2]

In common with other attempts to locate empirically based work on 'minority' groups and their relation to and experience of higher education, there is very little work to be found which addresses issues of disability within higher education. Hurst (1996) argues that even sociological studies of disability and education have tended to ignore higher education, instead focusing on primary and secondary education and more specifically on the tension between integration as opposed to 'special' education. The experiences of disabled staff in any education sector has been routinely ignored.

But monitoring the numbers of applicants with different disabilities and special needs did at last became possible for the first time in the application year 1992–3. Before then, the application forms used by UCCA (Universities Central Council for Admissions) and PCAS (Polytechnic Central Admissions System) asked the applicant to indicate any problems, primarily to open the dialogue between the applicant and the relevant higher education institution (HEI). By the application year 1992–3, UCCA and PCAS were using a joint application form in preparation for being merged as the Universities and Colleges Admissions Service (UCAS), with notes for applicants. Current notes (1998/9) relating to disabilities and special needs (paragraphs 20–22) are reproduced below.

> [20] Disability/special needs – institutions within UCAS are very willing to help students with disabilities. In order to allow institutions to provide the best available support for you they need to know about the nature of your disability and how it might affect your studies. The information you provide does not affect judgements concerning your academic suitability for a course and is treated confidentially by institutions. However, it enables data to be collected from which the progress of equal opportunities for disabled students in higher education can be monitored.

[21] If you have a disability or special need and may require extra support in your study, fieldwork or accommodation, please enter in the left-
hand box the code from the list below that is most appropriate to you. If
more than one applies to you, please use code 8. If you have no needs arising from your disability or special need e.g. you are short-sighted but your
vision is corrected by spectacles, use code 0 . . . If you are a registered disabled person, please enter R in the right-hand box . . . applications from
registered and non-registered disabled persons will be treated in exactly
the same way. If you have used any code other than 0, use section 8 on
page 3 of the form to describe your disability and indicate clearly what
needs you have.

Disabilities or special needs/support required
0 You do not have a disability or special need or are not aware of any
   additional support requirements in study or accommodation.
1 You have dyslexia
2 You are blind/partially sighted
3 You are deaf/hard of hearing
4 You are a wheelchair user/have mobility difficulties
5 You need personal care support
6 You have mental health difficulties
7 You have an unseen disability e.g. diabetes, epilepsy, asthma
8 You have two or more of the above disabilities/special needs
9 You have a disability or special need not listed above.

[22] If you have a disability or special need, you are also strongly advised
to read the introduction to the UCAS Handbook 1998 entry. It is very
helpful to all concerned if you contact institutions at an early stage to discuss your special needs.
                (UCAS notes accompanying application form 1998/9)

    The proportion of students with disabilities applying (and being accepted)
for a university place has remained more or less constant over the past six years
for which statistics are available, as Table 6.1 demonstrates.[3] Notifying UCAS
of a disability does not appear to result in an increased chance of rejection and
the most frequently mentioned type of disability and/or special needs have also
remained stable over the six-year period. The largest category of self-identified
disability is 'special learning difficulty', most usually dyslexia.
    Stowell's research, undertaken more than a decade ago, sought to quantify,
among other things, the extent of provision for disabled students in higher education and he found that of the 80 HEIs who took part in the study, just over 40
per cent had no students with special needs, 5 per cent ran special courses only,
49 per cent provided access to mainstream programmes only and the remain-
ing 5 per cent offered access to mainstream programmes and ran special
courses (Stowell, 1987: 92).
    The report *Widening Participation in Higher Education* (1992), published by the
Polytechnics and Colleges Funding Council (PCFC), usefully summarizes

Table 6.1 Percentage of students with disabilities applying/being accepted for a place in a higher education institution through UCAS (n.b. based on different applied/accepted totals)

Disability/special need	1994		1996		1998	
	Applied	Accepted	Applied	Accepted	Applied	Accepted
Dyslexia	0.74	0.74	1	1	1.29	1.31
Blind/partially sighted	0.13	0.11	0.16	0.15	0.09	0.09
Deaf/hard of hearing	0.24	0.24	0.17	0.16	0.17	0.17
Wheelchair user/mobility problem	0.10	0.10	0.12	0.11	0.11	0.12
Personal care support	0.02	0.01	0.01	0.01	0.01	0.00
Mental health difficulties	0.05	0.04	0.05	0.05	0.06	0.05
Unseen disability	2.84	2.85	2.27	2.29	1.98	2.04
Two or more disabilities	0.10	0.10	0.17	0.17	0.18	0.17
Other disabilities/special needs	0.33	0.32	0.31	0.31	0.36	0.38
Total with disabilities or special needs	4.55	4.51	4.27	4.24	4.28	4.33

Source: see note 3

some of the barriers which function to exclude or at least make very difficult the increased participation of students with disabilities (cited in Johnstone, 1995: 176):

1. Market and policy limitations: the mission, shape and geographical location of the HEI influenced both the extent to which it was proactive in widening participation and the groups it could target positively.
2. Physical environment: the nature of the HEI's site could restrict its ability to expand the number of students with physical disabilities.
3. Student support: as a result of changes in the system of student support, many potential students from under-represented groups were said to be put off by the perceived costs of embarking on higher education.
4. Funding: providing for students from under-represented groups was seen to be expensive by many institutions. To enable an HEI to provide appropriate programmes with sufficient support and the necessary academic infrastructure, additional resources were required.

Within an equal opportunities context, many higher education institutions have committed themselves to widening access to more 'non-traditional' students or under-represented groups, for example, students from minority ethnic communities or older learners, but improving the participation rates of people with disabilities has often not been part of a proactive strategy. For example, in the Royal Society of Arts' report on widening access, they refer to encouraging greater participation among 'the disabled' (Ball, 1990: 35) as very much a passing comment. One, perhaps quite cynical, reason for not being that interested in attracting disabled students is that widening access to higher education on other grounds, say, racial equality or encouraging older students, does not cost the higher education institution very much in financial terms, since all it is really doing is making itself more friendly to a wider pool of potential students.

In other words, in the same way that employers have woken up to the financial implications of ignoring the creative talent and potential of half the work force, i.e. women, so higher education institutions are recognizing that any under-recruitment could be remedied by making better efforts to encourage 'non-traditional' aspirants to study with them. But to encourage more disabled students to apply often has significant financial implications in terms of physical access to the facilities, additional learning support, special adaptations and a variety of other kinds of one-off modifications which might have to be made to enable individual disabled students to enjoy a quality educational experience. Higher education institutions may therefore think quite hard about how far they want to transform the rhetoric of equality of opportunity into a reality for disabled students when there are (sometimes significant) financial considerations. As Hurst points out, although the 1990s have seen some HEIs developing good practice in this area, the majority have done very little:

> If challenged about this the most frequent responses cited costs to explain their lack of action. Certainly there was no incentive to spend money on adapting facilities or employing appropriate staff since the institutions were not given additional allowances for this work.
>
> (Hurst, 1996: 127)

But as Moreton points out so cogently,

> It is unlikely that anyone would suggest reducing the number of people being trained in medicine, engineering and the like simply because their resource cost per person is up to four times higher than those being educated in the arts. Science graduates are not turned down because they need all manner of expensive equipment to facilitate their experiential learning in the laboratories. Potential students with disabilities ought not, therefore, to be turned away because they need a special toilet, or a wider doorway, a phonic ear or some Braille output to facilitate theirs.
>
> (Dr Terry Moreton, Adviser for Disabled Students, University of Leeds, quoted in Corlett and Cooper, 1992: 31)

However, as the concluding chapter of this book points out, the Higher Education Funding Council for England (HEFCE) is currently making concerted efforts to strongly encourage HEIs to provide a more supportive environment for students with disabilities, largely through the provision of a special funding programme into which HEIs bid to progress particular strategies that will not only encourage more individuals with disabilities through the doors but also better provide for those students with disabilities whom they already have. But given the negative associations of disability in terms of additional financial and other support structures, many prospective students do not indicate that they have a disability on their application form. As we have seen, prior to 1992 applicants were asked simply to tick a box if they had a disability, but since 1992, when UCAS replaced UCCA and PCAS, higher education applicants have been asked to complete a section in which a range of disabilities can be indicated. In theory (and the practice has not yet been tested), this should encourage students with disabilities to be more candid in their disclosures, and the guidance notes to the application form stress that the information will be used to enable accepting institutions to make appropriate provision in advance of enrolment. However, as with so many things, the theory is a little different from the practice, not just institutionally but also attitudinally from non-disabled student peers. Camilla Reed had a leg amputated just before starting her degree course and her experiences of prejudice from her peers make humbling reading for those of us who are also non-disabled.

> During the first weeks of university, I went to sign up with the sailing club and was told that I would be allowed to go sailing if I wore the false leg. The thing is worth thousands of pounds – it's not something I can get wet – and there is no good reason why I can't sail without it: people with one leg have sailed the Atlantic.
>
> (Camilla Reed cited in Bower, 1999: vi)

When Reed was asked why she didn't fight for her rights, she has a very pragmatic response: 'Even if I did pursue it and win, what would be the point of fighting my way into a society that didn't want me there?' (Reed quoted in Bower, 1999: vi).

Financial support for students with disabilities: the British example

The unit costs of a student in higher education has, for some time, been acknowledged as proportionately more expensive for disabled than non-disabled students, since the former may require personal care, specialist equipment, note-takers, special exam arrangements and so on. Students who are studying full-time for a first degree or similar level programme (such as a Higher National Diploma) are likely to be eligible for a mandatory grant from their Local Education Authority which includes three extra allowances for people with disabilities. The Disabled Students' Allowances (DSAs) are intended to pay for any extra costs which higher education students incur as a direct result of their disability. For 1999–2000, the three allowances are:

- a general allowance of up to £1,350 per annum;
- an allowance for non-medical personal helpers (e.g. sign language interpreters) of up to £10,250 per annum;
- an allowance for major items of specialist equipment (e.g. a computer) of up to £4,055 over the academic programme as a whole.[4]

However, disabled students who study part-time are not entitled to any of these additional awards (although in some circumstances students studying part-time on an initial teacher training course may be eligible) and it is ironic that it is often a consequence of their specific disability that makes part-time study the only viable option. For students attempting to finance postgraduate study, there are very few sources of funding, and this applies equally to disabled students, unless the course is for a Post-Graduate Certificate in Education, in which case grants are mandatory and disabled students are also entitled to the Disabled Students' Allowances.

Being a disabled student in British higher education

As with other aspects of disability and higher education, the experiences of disabled students within higher education settings have not received much in the way of serious research attention. Where work has been undertaken (see for example Hurst, 1992, 1993), it has often emerged that disabled students are more concerned about coping as a student, e.g. living on a grant and costs of books, than how they experience student life as a *disabled* person: they identify primarily with the concept 'student' rather than the term 'disabled'. The rejection of 'disability' as the determining characteristic of individual personhood among students in Hurst's study was echoed in work I undertook, with a focus on television (see comments earlier), where many participants argued that they were not interested in joining their local cerebral palsy or arthritis care or mental health survivors' group because, although they might share a disability or impairment with other group members, they would not necessarily have anything else in common. In other words, while they 'accepted' their disability, it was only a *part* of their lives, and disabled people often expressed a much greater preference for joining a mainstream social activity group such as skittles or bowls than being 'ghettoized with another load of cripples', as one participant put it rather forcefully (Ross, 1997).

Legislative responses in the UK

It was arguably the Further and Higher Education Act (1992) which began to address the needs of disabled students. It introduced a unified system of finance and control across the education sector as a whole and expressed an explicit concern (articulated by the then Secretary of State for Education) that the new funding councils should pay particular attention to meeting the educational needs of disabled people. The Higher Education Funding Council for England (HEFCE) responded by setting up an Advisory Group on Widening Participation and in 1993–4 set aside £3 million for special initiatives, some of which higher education institutions could bid for to support their own projects in the area. Two projects funded by the initiative are described further in this chapter (see also the discussion in the concluding chapter). In 1999, HEFCE pledged £6 million to be spent over three years, beginning in January 2000, to improve provision in higher education for disabled students. The three-year special initiative has three related strands which means that most HEIs will be eligible to bid for some funding for particular projects (Townend, 1999: 1):

- Strand 1 targets institutions with little or no current provision for disabled students and aims to increase the number of HEIs making appropriate provision, to maximize students' choice;
- Strand 2 focuses on the promotion and transfer of knowledge, by HEIs who are already taking positive actions with disabled students, to a wider constituency, including staff with specific responsibilities for 'disability' but also other academic and resources staff;
- Strand 3 is to fund activities which bring together and build upon complementary provision and expertise between HEIs.

Controversially, the new Disability Discrimination Act 1995 (DDA) excludes access to education from its prohibition on discrimination in the provision of goods, facilities and services, in direct contrast to the position under sex or race discrimination law: however, employment in educational establishments *is* covered by the terms of the Act. It is ironic that education is recognized as crucial in beginning to meet the aspirations of disabled people to enjoy full and equal opportunities and 'the new right to freedom from discrimination in employment . . . will be undermined if educational opportunities are not equally available to disabled persons to enable them to compete with a well-qualified labour force as they seek to enter the competitive labour market' (Doyle, 1996: 155).

However, although the Act specifically exempts discrimination within educational contexts from its ambit, it does address the issue of access to education by way of modifications to existing education legislation, mainly the Further and Higher Education Act 1992. For example, the DDA charges higher education funding councils to have regard to the requirements of disabled people, whereas in the previous legislation the Department for Education and Employment only provided guidance to the higher education funding councils that they should have regard to the needs of disabled students in HEIs. The higher education funding councils are then empowered to make grants, loans or other payments to the governing body of a higher education institution conditional on a requirement that the governing body should publish Disability Statements outlining current policy, current provision and future activity/policy development for disabled students. It is currently envisaged that such Disability Statements will be made public and reviewed every three years. Explicitly, the Disability Statement should contain general information on policies and procedures relating to disabled students on:

- equal opportunities;
- access and admissions;
- examinations and assessments;
- quality assessment, monitoring and evaluation of support services;
- staff development and training programmes;
- provision of financial assistance to disabled students;
- charging students for certain facilities.

(HEFCE Circular 8/96, paras 12–13)

If a higher education institution does not have policies for all the above areas, it should nonetheless provide an overview of its policies affecting disabled students. With regard to current provision, the Statement should describe the nature and range of provision for disabled students including:

- names and titles (and contact details) of the coordinator and member of senior management responsible for disabled students;
- examples of the types of information, advice, services and materials available, and a broad picture of how the institution provides support;
- academic services and support arrangements (for example, special provision for examinations and marking);
- informational technology provision;
- a general description of the physical environment;
- specific information on medical facilities, transport, religious and spiritual worship, external services and award ceremonies.

(HEFCE Circular 8/96, para 14)

The higher education sector in the UK as an employer of disabled staff

As with statistics on minority ethnic staff working in higher education, figures on disabled staff are almost impossible to track any down. Intuitively, based on my own experience of working in four higher education institutions in both the 'old' and the 'new' university sector, disabled staff were even less in evidence than disabled students, if numbers are estimated purely on the crude strategy of identifying staff with 'visible' disabilities. One reason for the relative paucity of disabled lecturers could be the requirement for students wishing to train as teachers to be 'medically' fit. The sometimes arbitrary (and therefore discriminatory) nature of the outcome of a medical examination which potential teacher training students must undertake if they have indicated that they have a disability on their application form, is something that the Royal Association for Disability and Rehabilitation is actively pursuing (RADAR, 1993). A second reason could be that as disabled people are significantly underrepresented in the higher education student population generally, there are obvious knock-on effects in terms of the size of the pool of potential recruits for jobs in higher education.

Strategies for inclusivity in higher education

Of course, with the enactment of the Disability Discrimination Act 1995 in the UK, notwithstanding the inexcusable exclusion of the education sector from large parts of the Act, it becomes almost irresistible for higher education institutions to produce measurable or at least memorable results in short periods of time (Johnstone, 1995), leading to a quick-fix mentality. Here, a one-day workshop on disability awareness, there a new piece of software for dyslexic students (but without the technical support to enable students to actually use it). The alternative to such strategies, which merely allow HEIs to tick off 'disabilities' from its equal opportunities list, is to embrace the principles of a learning support environment, a primary aim of which is to ensure that an appropriate management structure and organizational infrastructure is securely in place and accessible to *all* learners (Johnstone, 1995). As Dyson *et al.* (1994) point out, the effectiveness (or otherwise) of a learning support strategy rests on the idea that learning is a fully participatory process and challenges the notion that learning is simply the incremental acquisition of a hierarchy of knowledge.

Crucially, the needs of individual students must be taken into account if they are to receive an educational experience which is as good as that of their non-disabled peers: slotting in to a pre-existing institutional framework for learning support *can* be helpful to disabled students but what is, arguably, of even greater value, is encouraging the HEI itself (i.e. the staff) to change, adapt and become aware of valuing difference and respecting student choices which might make life more complicated for their lecturers but must be worth the additional organization to maximize inclusivity. Examples might include providing handouts in larger print, always speaking directly to a class (instead of talking with their backs to students), accepting work which is cassette- rather than paper-based, and so on.

Skill (the National Bureau for Students with Disabilities) has evaluated HEFCE's special initiative for widening participation for students with special needs and reports that although most of the projects which were supported were successful in meeting their immediate objectives, some found it difficult to establish these new ways of working as permanent features of their institution's provision (Skill, 1996). New services would often outlive the short period for which funding from HEFCE was available and once this support evaporated, institutional enthusiasm and commitment sometimes fell away as well. From the evaluation, however, Skill was able to identify two factors which were more likely to bring about lasting institutional change: first, a clearly articulated commitment to long-term change from senior management, combined with the high level of strategic support required; and second, creative forward-planning by project workers who had anticipated the need to embed new practice before funding ran out. The Skill evaluation (1996: 2–3) placed significant importance on the role of senior managers in the successful (and lasting) implementation of quality services to disabled students in higher education (see also chapters 9 and 10 in this volume) which are summarized below:

Mission statements, strategic plans and publicity material
- the inclusion of a clearly articulated commitment to support for disabled students within the institution's mission statement and strategic development plan;
- the inclusion in strategic plans of clearly articulated and well-communicated policies on the division of responsibility for the provision of learning support across the institution to all students, including disabled students;

- specific references to disabled students in statements on other institutional goals, for example, goals in relation to employment practices;
- the inclusion of a clearly articulated commitment to support for disabled students in departmental and faculty mission statements and in development plans. Such commitments could be differentiated to suit the culture and discipline of different departments;
- clear references in all publicly available documents (prospectus, handbook, charter, annual report, forward plans, etc) to institutional policy and practice on support for disabled students;
- a willingness to use, and advertise the use of, a range of communication modes such as minicom, Braille, large print and audio tape for everyday internal information exchange on all issues, not just disability matters.

Staffing, staff development and staff support
- a clearly understood and visible two-way line of accountability between senior management and all members of staff on matters relating to support for disabled students, with one named senior manager responsible for ensuring implementation and coherence of policy;
- support for informal networks of staff and students which are concerned with provision for disabled students;
- encouragement of, and support for, collaboration with key external agencies/organizations;
- inclusion in staff induction and development programmes of disability awareness training and material concerning support for disabled students;
- inclusion in staff appraisal schemes of questions relating to staff's experience of, and need for, training in issues relating to support for disabled students;
- awareness among central support and administrative staff of the particular needs of disabled students.

Quality assurance and management information
- a system for monitoring the quality and extent of support to disabled students as part of the institution's overall quality assurance procedures;
- a commitment to encourage student feedback and a willingness to consult students on issues relating to the continuing development of policy and provision;
- a centralized management information system which can collect data relating to progress of disabled students from application to post-degree placement.

The National Bureau for Students with Disabilities (Skill) also recommends a list of questions that HEIs need to ask themselves when considering equality of access to students with disabilities (Corlett and Cooper, 1992: 8):

- Do you make careers visits to special schools?
- Do you have subtitled or signed versions of publicity videos for deaf and hard of hearing people?
- Do your recruitment and admissions staff have a good knowledge of the

facilities, funding and adaptations available to students with disabilities? Do they address these points when invited to speak, or when dealing with enquiries?

- Is the prospectus welcoming to, and informative for, applicants with disabilities?
- Are your open days accessible to people with disabilities?

Improving physical access

The built environment of an higher education campus may present no problems to some disabled students. To others, however, it can become a source of constant frustration and, in extreme cases, can restrict student choices and, therefore, equality of learning opportunity. Higher education institutions with older buildings on their campus or split sites face problems in making all their facilities accessible, but even newer campuses may find the costs of total accessibility prohibitive (Corlett and Cooper, 1992). But many institutions have adopted a policy of making adaptations as they go along and as individual needs arise, for example:

> We tended to think that these problems were isolated events which might never occur again. For instance, if we put a ramp down to a library we had a particular individual in mind. We sometimes wondered if we were justified in spending all that money on just one person . . . we needn't have worried. Such ramps are now practically worn out – not just by students in wheelchairs but by the throngs of other wheeled traffic such as porters' trolleys, shopping trolleys and baby buggies and people who prefer slopes to steps.
> (John Mitchell, Chair of the Principal's Advisory Committee on Disability, Sheffield Hallam University, cited in Corlett and Cooper, 1992: 28)

Students should be given access to as much of the campus as possible, which may necessitate any or all of the following (Corlett and Cooper, 1992: 28):

- developing wheelchair routes or installing ramps indoors and outdoors
- widening doors
- installing or adapting lifts
- providing accessible toilets
- providing clear and raised signs and maps around the site
- installing extra lighting and contrasting pipework

Supporting disabled students – case study 1

Middlesex University, in its Disability Statement, organizes its support for disabled students through its specialist information, advice and support facility known as The Able Centre. The Centre has a full-time coordinator and administrative assistant who work in close collaboration with a range of other colleagues in student welfare, the counselling service, careers, admissions, academic departments, students' union, and so on. The range of services available include:

Visual impairment and blindness
- closed circuit TV scanners in libraries, plus a number of text scanner readers;
- VDU enhancement of all server-led computer terminals for enlargement and colour variation;
- support via the RNIB Express Reading Service.

Hearing impairment and deafness
- most major lecture theatres have induction loops and local area systems have been installed at library issue and student office counters
- the setting up of the Sign Language Bureau, offering interpreters
- the provision of note-takers.

Specific Learning Difficulties (Dyslexia)
The Able Centre provides primary assessment, refers to educational psychologists and gives ongoing support.

The Able Centre also gives advice to students who are purchasing equipment by means of a Disabled Students Allowance from their Local Education Authority. A small bank of equipment is held for lending out on a short-term basis (e.g. lap top computers, cassette recorders, radio transmitters/receivers, specialist keyboards and induction loops). Training is also provided so that students become confident in equipment use and care.

Supporting disabled students – case study 2

The University of Sussex has a special needs coordinator who deals with most disability-related issues and there are also several part-time members of staff who provide learning support advice for those who think or know they have dyslexia. The staff provide equipment assessments, referrals to specialist units within the Sussex area and continued support throughout a student's higher education career. The University sends out a Special Needs Questionnaire to students who have declared a disability, to ensure that appropriate preparations are made prior to their arrival. The Students Union publishes an 'access around campus' guide giving information on how to access the various parts of the campus: it is written in a lively style and is informative rather than patronizing. It also makes explicit that not all the facilities/teaching rooms at the University are fully accessible and that prospective students would be advised to check out potential access problems before enrolment.

Supporting disabled students – case study 3[5]

The Open University's Disability Statement (1997: 3) makes an explicit commitment that the University will:

- provide information, advice and guidance to enquirers, applicants and current students which includes clear statements for each course/qualification route of any specific barriers to study about which disabled students will need to be aware;
- provide personal advice and counselling for individual disabled enquirers, applicants and students;
- give explicit consideration to the accessibility of new courses to disabled students, both in relation to course design and to the approval of patterns of teaching and assessment;
- provide a range of direct support for disabled students;
- aim to negotiate barrier-free physical access to face-to-face teaching and student support opportunities at study centres and residential school sites.

The Open University provides an extensive range of specialized services and facilities to disabled students, which can be categorized as follows: alternative media course materials; equipment loan schemes; information technology provision; communication support staff; tutorial support; curriculum development; resident school facilities; examination and assessment facilities; financial awards; physical environment; Open University Students Association. In addition to services provided directly, the OU's Statement also makes clear that the environment, both human and physical, needs to be flexible, so an extensive programme of disability staff development, including disability awareness for all staff, and resource materials, workshops and seminars for Associate Lecturers and staff in Regional Centres is also ongoing.

Making the commitment – establishing a disability coordinator[6]

Before setting up a service for disabled students, there are a number of questions which a higher education institution needs to answer (Skill, 1997: 11):

- Does it see provision for disabled students as primarily a welfare or an equal opportunities issue?
- Is the coordinator's role seen as primarily supporting students, or does it also encompass influencing policies, attitudes and structures across the institution?
- Do institution staff see a coordinator as someone who might support them in their work with disabled students, or someone on whom they can 'dump' students?
- Is the institution prepared to set up a range of specialist services, or is the coordinator role seen as a lone post?

From the outset, higher education institutions will need to decide whether the intended service is to be run for students or with students. While it is of course possible to set up an adequate scheme for students without their involvement, it seems common sense, particularly when starting from scratch, to involve precisely those students whose needs the service intends to meet. For Skill, appointing a disability coordinator is possibly the single most important step a higher education institution can take towards developing good provision for disabled students: a good coordinator provides a focus and a force for change and a first point of contact for both students and staff (Skill, 1997).

The transformative potential of information technology

The exponential growth of IT in terms of both hardware and software has had significant benefits in transforming the learning environment for students with disabilities. As well as microelectronic technology, which allows remote control of door movements and thus increases independence, new communications technologies enable more students with sensory disabilities to learn in 'mainstream' environments (Vincent, 1993). Visual display units attached to voice-sensitive switches have begun to revolutionize communication for physically disabled and hearing-impaired students, and voice-activated software allows students to use their voices rather than a keyboard to 'type' their essays and do other computer-based tasks. Optical scanning devices linked to Braille printers and voice synthesizers can also support visually-impaired students in their learning.

Moreover, as Hegarty (1993) and Wolff (1986) have pointed out, the existence of such technological innovations has encouraged more disabled people to think seriously about studying in higher education institutions. However, as indicated earlier, new information technologies are only as good as the person using them and the mere provision of a sophisticated computer workstation with expensive software will not, of itself, necessarily guarantee independent learning. The support structures are especially important as is the careful matching of student with available and appropriate IT. In Hawkridge and Vincent's study of IT in the further education sector (Hawkridge and Vincent, 1992: 219–20), they report on the strengths and limitations of computers, for students and staff, all of which have equal relevance to higher education:

1. The new technology can give students with disabilities and special educational needs a wider choice of courses and enhanced educational and employment opportunities. This is broadly true for all aspects of disability and special educational needs, but the new technology can provide enablement, access or opportunities with proper assessment and re-assessment of individuals' needs, training for students and their teachers and carers, information, advice and technical services.

2. Because providing the technology, assessing and training students and

others, and using the technology are complex activities, further education colleges need 'facilitators' with access to advice, experience and good practice. Students will then have opportunities that, in turn, can increase their independence.

3. The new technology can enable students to acquire skills that match current and future requirements in employment. Many employers are still unaware of this.
4. Staff training must be continued, particularly in how the technology can meet individual needs. Students' expertise and experience should be recognized because they have made significant contributions to staff development.

Disability awareness training

The (often sadly negative) experiences of organizations which have supported race awareness training suggest that extreme sensitivity and careful planning needs to be employed in the design, delivery and evaluation phases of any training programmes which are about raising awareness of equal opportunity issues, and disability training is no exception. Hurst (1996) suggests that there are several issues which need to be considered when developing disability awareness training. Who delivers the training and who receives it are two crucial elements to decide upon early in the process.

One view is that the whole of a staff group should participate in such training but in large organizations such as higher education institutions, this ideal solution is very costly, both in financial and human resource terms. It is also the case that even if such training is, notionally, 'compulsory', there will be all sorts of reasons given why some staff can't attend, usually by precisely the staff who would benefit most: much equal opportunities training is, for all practical purposes, delivered to participants who are already largely 'converted'. An alternative is to target specific groups of staff, such as academic counsellors or personal tutors. The 'who' question is also contentious but even at a base level, it would seem appropriate to use trainers who have personal experience of the issues about which they are being tasked to train, and this usually means that the trainers themselves are disabled. A related set of issues concerns the timing of the training, whether to offer it systematically at the beginning of each academic year, say, or whether it should be provided to individuals who have already begun working with disabled students and/or staff, in order to answer queries or discuss aspects of working relations which have occurred.

Tecknowledge.able – disability awareness case study

In 1994–5, the University of Wolverhampton applied to HEFCE's special initiative fund to create and publish the 'tecknowledge.able' pack (text and video materials). This aimed to provide accessible training materials geared to informing and updating tutors in higher education about new and developing technology that could assist students with disabilities to access learning materials and perform on an equal footing with other students. It also aimed to inform the design and delivery of changing teaching and learning strategies. At a general level, it was developed to provide information and reference materials for staff who either discover that their class includes a student with a disability or who are interested in further developing their understanding of disability issues and enabling technology. By mid-1997, the University had distributed more than 350 packs and they continue to receive regular requests for the material. One of the University's own staff, a special needs tutor, made the following comments when asked to respond to an evaluative questionnaire on the pack: 'Best 100-page booklet to provide information on equipment, support and funding in the country. List of organizations and suppliers (in appendix) very useful. Typeface and layout of booklet excellent. Text written at appropriate level – not patronizing, not too technical.'

How disability friendly are you? A case study and agenda for action

To conclude this chapter, there follows a description of a disability audit, undertaken in 1993 by Sheffield Hallam University (hereafter described as 'Sheffield Hallam' for brevity) which was also awarded a grant under the HEFCE special initiative fund, to undertake a systematic audit of the facilities and services which the University made available to support disabled students. The 'principles' generated in the process serve as a useful blueprint for higher education institutions to consider when thinking about disability issues in the context of equal opportunities in an higher education setting.

Two fundamental concepts guided the Sheffield Hallam team's explicit approach: first, a recognition of the social model of disability and the forms of oppression associated with social attitudes towards and responses to disability; and second (following from the first), a commitment to acknowledge disability 'cultures' and self-determination (Sheffield Hallam University, 1994). Using a set of principles relating to independent living, the team then applied them to the specific context of higher education (Hurst, 1996). The first principle is about information and access to that information. For blind students, for example, materials should be available in an accessible format such as Braille or audio cassette; for students with visual impairments, materials should be available in large print, and so on. Access to information must also be applied to recruitment initiatives, so that, for example, there are sub-titles on promotional videos, and prospectuses are available in different formats.

The second principle relates to peer support. The project team were keen to involve as many disabled students (and staff) in the project as possible, not least in terms of gaining active participants to their existing Disabled Students' Forum. The third principle concerns housing. Although many universities provide specially adapted accommodation, this can be both expensive and segregationist, and so the team suggests that universities should put pressure on local housing providers to ensure that a range of suitable accommodation is made available in areas close to universities. Technical aids was a fourth area that the project team looked at, affirming that disabled students had a right to have whatever equipment was necessary to enable them to learn effectively and independently. A fifth principle encompasses access to the physical environment of the institution. While many higher education institutions, through a programme of conversion and modification, have made most of their facilities accessible, there are still significant problems, especially with institutions which are multi-site. The final principle considered by the team is accessible and affordable transport, bearing in mind that even 'free' transport such as inter-site buses is often not adapted for students/staff with mobility problems.

The examples given above have been selected for the purposes of illustration and the omission of other, similarly important and innovative initiatives, is not meant to imply a value judgment on their various merits.

Notes

1. For a discussion of 'learned helplessness', see Swain (1989, 1994).
2. For an excellent guide on the realities of managing for equality the experiences of disabled students in higher education, see Corlett and Cooper (1992). This guide takes higher education institutions through a series of issues to be considered, including how to promote themselves to potential students, processing applications, hosting open days, enrolment, staff development, flexible teaching aids as well as associated issues such as recreation, accommodation and student welfare services.
3. This data was despatched to the author from the Universities and Colleges Admissions Service and represents the findings of monitoring exercises undertaken by UCAS in 1996 and 1998.
4. *Bridging the Gap: A Guide to the Disabled Students' Allowances (DSAs) in Higher Education in 1999–2000*. London: DfEE.
5. For further details of the Open University's full range of services and facilities offered to disabled students, please see the OU's Disability Statement and/or contact the OU direct.
6. For a highly detailed description of establishing a disability coordinator and developing services, see Skill (1997) *The Coordinator's Handbook*.

References

Ball, C. (1990) *More Means Different: Widening Access to Higher Education*. London: Royal Society of Arts.

Barton, L. (ed.) (1988) *The Politics of Special Needs*. Brighton: Falmer Press.

Bower, I. (1999) A tough climb, *The Guardian*, 27 April.

Campbell, J. and Oliver, M. (1996) *Disability Politics: Understanding our Past, Changing our Future*. London and New York: Routledge.

Cooper, D. (1996) Legislation: a practical example – young people and education, in G. Hales (ed.) *Beyond Disability: Towards an Enabling Society*. London: Sage in association with the Open University, 134–87.

Corlett, S. and Cooper, D. (1992) *Students with Disabilities in Higher Education: A Guide for all Staff*. London: Skill.

Doyle, B. J. (1996) *Disability Discrimination: Law and Practice*. Bristol: Jordan Publishing.

Dyson, A., Millward, A. and Skidmore, D. (1994) Beyond the whole school approach: an emerging model of special needs practice and provision in mainstream secondary schools, *British Educational Research Journal*, 20(3): 301–17.

Finkelstein, V. (1980) *Attitudes and Disabled People: Issues for Discussion*. New York: World Rehabilitation Fund.

Hahn, H. (1996) Disability policy and the problem of discrimination, *American Behavioral Scientist*, 28(3): 290–8.

Hawkridge, D. and Vincent T. (1992) *Learning Difficulties and Computers: Access to the Curriculum*. London: Jessica Kingsley.

Hegarty, I. (1990) Can further education for students with disabilities be justified? Unpublished MEd thesis; Manchester University.

Hurst, A. (1992) Widening participation in higher education and people with disabilities, *Personnel Review*, 21(6): 19–36.

Hurst, A. (1993) *Steps Towards Graduation: Access to Higher Education for People with Disabilities*. Aldershot: Avebury.

Hurst, A. (1996) Reflecting on researching disability and higher education, in L. Barton (ed.) *Disability and Society: Emerging Issues and Insights*. Harlow: Longman, 123–46.

Johnstone, D. (1995) *Further Opportunities: Learning Difficulties and Disabilities in Further Education*. London: Cassell.

Morris, J. (1991) *Pride Against Prejudice*. London: The Women's Press.

Oliver, M. (1983) *Social Work with Disabled People*. Basingstoke: Macmillan.

Oliver, M. (1990) *The Politics of Disablement*. Basingstoke: Macmillan.

Oliver, M. (1996) *Understanding Disability: From Theory to Practice*. Basingstoke: Macmillan.

Open University (1997) *Disability Statement*. Buckingham: Open University.

PCFC (Polytechnics and Colleges Funding Council) (1992) *Widening Participation in Higher Education*. Bristol: PCFC.

Ross, K. (1997) But where's me in it? Disability, broadcasting and the audience, *Media Culture and Society*, 19 (4): 669–77.

Ross, K. (1999) An audience with the listeners: researching disability and radio. *Report to the BBC*. Cheltenham: Cheltenham and Gloucester College of Higher Education.

Royal Association for Disability and Rehabilitation (1993) *So You Want to be a Teacher?* London: RADAR.

Sheffield Hallam University (1994) *Follow the Yellow Brick Road*. Sheffield: SHU.

Skill (National Bureau for Students with Disabilities) (1996) *Making Change Last*. London: Skill.

Skill (1997) *The Coordinator's Handbook*. London: Skill.

Stowell, R. (1987) *Catching Up? Provision for Students with Special Educational Needs in Further and Higher Education*. London: National Bureau for Handicapped Students/SCPR.

Swain, J. (1989) Learned helplessness theory and people with learning difficulties: the psychological price of powerlessness, in A. Brechin and J. Walmsley (eds) *Making Connections*. London: Hodder and Stoughton.

Swain, J. (1994) Taught helplessness? Or a say for disabled students in schools, in J. Swain, V. Finkelstein, S. French and M. Oliver (eds) *Disabling Barriers – Enabling Environments*. London: Sage in association with the Open University, 155–62.

Townend, R. (1999) New special initiative on disability, *eQuip Bulletin*, 3, February: 4.

Vincent, T. (1993) Foreword, in S. Broadbent and S. Curran (eds) *The Assessment, Disability and Technology Handbook*. Oldham: North West Access Centre.

Wolff, H. (1986) The disabled student in 2001 – deserted or liberated by new technology?, *Educare*, 24: 3–9.

Useful addresses/contacts

British Council of Organisations of Disabled People (BCODP)
Litchurch Plaza
Litchurch Lane
Derby DE24 8AA
Tel: 01332 295551
Minicom: 01332 295581

British Dyslexia Association (BDA)
98 London Road
Reading
RG1 5AU
Tel: 01189 662677
Fax: 01189 351927

CANDO Information Service (services to students with disabilities)
http://cando.lancs.ac.uk

eQuip Team (HEFCE Special Initiatives)
Coventry University
Alma Building
Alma Street
Coventry CV1 5FB
Tel/fax/voice/minicom: 01203 536369
Website: http://www.hefce.ac.uk/initiat/sldd/equip.html

European Access Network (European NGO promoting equal opportunities in HE)
Tel: 020 7911 5769
Fax: 020 7911 5132
Website: http://ulb.ac.be.EAN/ean.html

Skill: National Bureau for Students with Disabilities
Chapter House
18–20 Crucifix Lane
London SE1 3JW
Tel: 0800 328 5050
Text: 0800 068 2422

Teaching and Learning Technology Support Network
University of Wales, Bangor
Information Services
Sackville Road
Bangor
Gwynedd LL57 1LD
Tel: 01248 382425

Useful resources

- Directory of resources available from HEFCE-funded disability projects (HEFCE 98/60)
- Directory of resources available from disability projects funded by HEFCE (Skill)
- Disability statements: a guide to good practice (HEFCE 98/66)
- Guidance on base-level provision for disabled students in higher education institutions (HEFCE 99/04)

7

Sexual Orientation

Diana Woodward

Introduction

Sexual orientation may be regarded as a 'hidden inequality' in higher education as in most other kinds of organization. (As an example of what it feels like not to be out of step with the predominantly heterosexual world, take the experience of a friend who was asked politely in a Provincetown bookshop on Cape Cod in Massachusetts – a well-known summer resort for lesbians and gay men – whether she qualified for the lesbian discount on her purchases! She did.) In universities, those who profess to support equal opportunities may feel that they can identify and empathize with the members of other disadvantaged groups, such as women, those from minority ethnic groups, mature students, and disabled students and staff. This is not so in relation to lesbians and gay men, unless they choose to reveal their sexual orientation. Even the customary badges of gay and lesbian identity such as having very short hair, or particular configurations of ear-rings and body piercing, or wearing 'butch' clothes such as combat trousers, leather jackets and Doc Marten boots, have now been appropriated as heterosexual fashion items, thereby losing their status as reliable signifiers of a person's sexual orientation. Thus many people believe that they have never met any gay men or lesbians, because they have encountered no one resembling these stereotypes or who has 'come out' to them (that is, disclosed that they are gay or lesbian). Furthermore, some individuals have unsympathetic attitudes to gay, lesbian and bisexual people, because of their own political or religious beliefs or merely from long-held prejudices which have never been successfully challenged. Under these circumstances it is perhaps not surprising that many senior staff, lecturers and members of support departments in higher education feel ignorant and ill-equipped to identify what kinds of support gay and lesbian students and staff may need, and to provide it.

This chapter will seek to articulate some of the issues which need to be addressed before gay, lesbian and bisexual students and staff can feel fully accepted members of the academic community, with the same rights and opportunities as everyone else. Then we will turn to the kinds of actions which institutions need to take, to help bring about this situation.

What are the issues ? The experiences of gay men and lesbians within society

It has been estimated (often with spurious precision, using questionable definitions and methods of data collection) that about one in ten women and probably a rather higher proportion of men identify themselves as homosexual. Kinsey and his colleagues found, for example, in their pioneering study of 4,000 white American males published in 1948, that one in ten men had been exclusively homosexual for the past three years, and 37 per cent had had 'some homosexual experience to the point of orgasm'; in their companion study of 6,000 women published in 1953, they found that 13 per cent of women had had physical homosexual experience by the age of 45. Wellings *et al.* (1994), in their survey of 18,876 British adults, found rather lower figures: 6.1 per cent of men and 3.4 per cent of women reported ever having had homosexual experiences, of whom 1.4 per cent of the men and 0.6 per cent of the women respondents had had a same-sex sexual partner within the last two years. According to the researchers, these figures are broadly consistent with the results of other European studies, apart from a Norwegian study which found no difference between the men's and women's figures for homosexual experiences. As Norway arguably has the most progressive and egalitarian gender relationships in Europe, and Wellings' research team found the gap between men's and women's ratios to decline from the older (45–59 years) to the younger age-groups (16–24 years), it may be that the social pressures which have formerly inhibited women from engaging in homosexual activities are weakening.

Many people who regard themselves as gay or lesbian are celibate, by choice, fear or circumstance. Since the resurgence of the women's movement in the early 1970s, numbers of women have come to identify themselves as lesbian as a result of their feminist convictions, which may or may not have a physical expression. They are likely to be part of a lesbian subculture or community. But many people who come to realize, at some point in their lives and not necessarily just around puberty, that their preferred sexual orientation is towards their own sex, do so in isolation and keep this knowledge to themselves, especially if they live in rural communities, far from the anonymity and established gay scene of the big cities. Under these circumstances, moving away to enter higher education or to join the armed forces represent choices which do not need too much explanation to family and friends, but which will allow the individual to explore their emergent sexual identity away from the social controls of their home environment. For those who do not already have gay and lesbian friends, or who are not involved in political activism concerning sexual politics, there are few places to meet other gay men and lesbians apart from bars, and even here nobody is safe from being identified, with the risk of being 'outed' later (that is, of having one's sexual orientation made public against one's wishes). The recent popularity of gay and lesbian venues with 'straight' people compounds this danger, as they cannot be trusted to understand or to observe the code against outing people, or to appreciate the likely adverse consequences. Some men use public places such as toilets or open spaces to meet other men for sex, but many of these are men who would define themselves as predominantly heterosexual. This behaviour is illegal; homosexual acts are only legal between consenting adults, in private (and there has never been legislation proscribing lesbian sexual acts).

Let us debunk a few myths. Contrary to the stereotype, not all gay men and lesbians are promiscuous, preferring to live in stable relationships or alone, and we enjoy social contact with and support from our friends, just like other groups within the population. The *Sexual Behaviour in Britain* study (Wellings *et al.*, 1994) found that half of the men and two-thirds of the women who reported ever having had a same-sex partner had only had this one. Many paedophiles are heterosexual; the notion that most gay men are social isolates who prey on young boys is a damaging stereotype which may be a very long way from the truth, but which is still used as a basis for discrimination against gay men and lesbians seeking to work with children. Lesbians and gay men are often parents, whose children may have been born within heterosexual unions before they identified themselves as gay or lesbian, or are conceived as the result of either clinical intervention or the actions of a willing male friend assisted by a turkey baster. The numbers of women and men who are bisexual appears to be greater than previously thought: the *Sexual Behaviour in Britain* study found that between 2.5 per cent and 5 per cent of men not currently living with a same-sex partner (that is who are or have been in heterosexual long-term relationships: married, cohabiting, divorced, widowed, and separated; or who were single) and between 1.2 per cent and 3 per cent of women had had a same-sex partner at some point, and various studies have found that around four out of five adults who report having had same-sex sexual contacts have also had heterosexual intercourse. Many conceal this aspect of their identity, either because they are in stable relationships, including marriage, and fear the opprobrium of being 'discovered to be homosexual', or they fear being 'discovered to be heterosexual' where this involves betrayal of their gay and lesbian partners and their same-sex community.

Despite the pervasive belief that the UK is a tolerant society, most of whose citizens are favourably disposed towards equal rights for gay men and lesbians, the reality for many homosexuals is that they dare not disclose their sexual orientation at work or to members of their close family, for fear of homophobic or discriminatory reactions. However, it is the fortunate few who have no need to fear opprobrium or discrimination at work, rejection by family and friends, or homophobic attacks in the street. A survey commissioned by MIND, the British mental health charity, found that nearly three-quarters of the gay men and lesbians who responded had experienced prejudice and discrimination and more than one in five had suffered physical and sexual violence (MIND, 1997). Similarly, a national survey conducted for Stonewall (Palmer and Mason, 1996) found that one in three of the gay men who responded and one in four lesbians had experienced violence within the past five years because of their sexuality. These problems were compounded by lesbian and gay people's encounters with mental health professionals working in the National Health Service, more than half of whom attributed their mental health problems to their homosexuality. Similar findings come from a recent qualitative study of the experiences of gay men, lesbians and bisexuals of mental health services conducted by the Project for Advice, Counselling and Education (PACE, 1998). As Judi Clements, chief executive of MIND, said when launching the MIND (1997) report: 'Despite the fact that homosexuality has not appeared in the list of mental health problems for more than 20 years, it is clear that many mental health professionals still consider homosexuality to be a mental illness.'

It is salutary to acknowledge the recency of the shift away from regarding homosexuality as criminal or sick behaviour. Until 1967 male homosexuality was a criminal offence in the UK (and it has still been only partially decriminalized, with a higher age of consent and more stringent controls on the location and circumstances of legal gay sex than heterosexual activity). It was only removed from the list of psychiatric disorders by the American Psychiatric Association in 1974 to be replaced by the equally ominous diagnosis of 'sexual orientation disturbance' (Wellings *et al.*, 1994). Since the late 1960s, the politicization of homosexuality has had an impact in academe just as feminism has, leading to its repudiation as a manifestation of clinical or social deviance and paving the way for a number of excellent theoretical and empirical studies of gay and lesbian issues (Faderman, 1985, 1992; Lesbian History Group, 1989; Weeks, 1989).

Even this recent limited acceptance of homosexuality in the academic and scientific communities has outpaced change in public attitudes: modern Britain is a predominantly homophobic society. The *Sexual Behaviour in Britain* study (Wellings *et al.*, 1994) found that 70 per cent of its male informants and 58 per cent of its female ones regarded sex between two men as 'mostly' or 'always' wrong, as did 64.5 per cent and 59 per cent respectively in relation to sex between two women. Younger respondents were barely more tolerant than older ones, although in other studies young people, women and people with high educational achievements have been found to be less disapproving of homosexuality. Twenty per cent of respondents in the *Sexual Behaviour in Britain* study believed these behaviours to be 'not at all wrong'. Fully 11 per cent of women who had had same-sex sexual experiences and 19 per cent of men believed such behaviour to be wrong. One can only imagine the impact for their mental health of this dissonance between their beliefs and their behaviour.

Homosexuality may no longer be regarded as 'sick', although it may still under certain circumstances be 'criminal', but negative public attitudes and internalized low self-esteem can foster mental health problems. The indices of personal distress are generally far higher for gay men and lesbians than for other members of society (although there are clear difficulties in identifying people as homosexual for the purpose of collecting statistics such as these). Much of the literature on this issue originates in the United States, where gay and lesbian groups have been more vocal and effective than in the UK in undertaking research and securing services and facilities geared to meeting their needs. One study estimates that one-third of lesbians are alcoholics because of the significance of 'the bar' in lesbians' social lives and because drinking is used to cope with the stress, alienation and despair of rejection by society and one's family. Another national American study of almost 2,000 lesbians found that one-third were worried about their alcohol consumption or had sought treatment for substance abuse in the past (Bradford and Ryan, 1988). Suicide rates for American lesbians have been estimated to be between two to seven times higher than for the 'straight' female population for the same reasons (Deevey and Wall, 1993), and it seems plausible that figures of this order may well also apply in the UK. There are indications from British lesbian health conferences and other sources within the lesbian community of high rates of self-harm through mutilation and eating disorders, but as yet, there is no reliable evidence about their incidence (see for example *Dykenosis*, 1998).

The experiences of gay men and lesbians in higher education

Let me tell you about some people whom I have encountered in the course of my career in higher education. One of my first tasks when I became a Dean in the late 1980s was to handle a student appeal. The student was a lesbian who had been thrown off the course having failed her exams. The case looked fairly clear-cut. However, on further investigation it emerged that she had suffered two years of mounting ridicule and hostility from several of her lecturers, particularly one who made a play of his 'traditional attitudes'. She had sought to counter his rampant and unrepentant misogyny by writing 'hers' instead of 'his' throughout an essay, which he then refused to mark. The continued harassment by these lecturers, after her complaints about them in Course Committee meetings were ignored, led her to feel more and more isolated and uncomfortable about coming to classes, and so her work suffered. We won the case, she repeated her year and graduated, and when I met her several years later she was by then established in her chosen career.

At about the same time, a male colleague died of AIDS. Apart from being a lecturer, he was a member of one of the caring professions, as was his long-term partner, who had looked after him through his decline. Because of this, neither had felt able to disclose their relationship, nor the nature of Don's illness (not his real name), other than to a very few close friends. You can imagine the distress and problems of nursing a dying partner, trying to manage with minimum time off work, and grieving for that person after their death, all without the informed support of colleagues and line manager.

Three students whom I know well, aged in their late twenties or early thirties, are each bright, able people capable of going far in their careers. One felt from an early age that she was a lesbian. Growing up in a working-class family, in a mining district, she was making very good progress at secondary school, enjoying particular encouragement from her class teacher and her English teacher (who were a married couple) until they saw her kissing another teenage girl in a bus shelter. Their support was instantly withdrawn, to be replaced by distance and hostility. Her family provided no empathy or support. This student left school early and experienced a series of major personal problems (including homelessness and an addiction problem) until she was fortunate enough, in her twenties, to get a place at an adult residential college, from which she entered higher education. She is now confident and outgoing, and is preparing to become a social worker, putting her own experiences to good use in championing the needs of older people and individuals with disabilities.

Another student is a young man who has recently come to regard himself as gay. He was attacked by a man with a heavy piece of wood as he left a gay pub, in a 'respectable' suburban community. Although he reported the incident to the police, he declined to give them his name, for fear of what might be done with this information. The previous year he became very distressed at his treatment in the laddish culture of a men's hall of residence, but felt powerless to challenge it effectively. As far as he knew, there were no institutional policies or procedures which he could cite to demonstrate the unacceptability of the other students' behaviour. Another student, a lesbian, abandoned her place in the halls of residence at her university, following a period of harassment which the university had apparently failed to tackle effectively.

The third person already held a responsible post as a university lecturer when she began a postgraduate course on a part-time basis at another institution. She was suspended from work for alleged gross professional misconduct, following complaints from two colleagues when her same-sex long-term partner, who was already lecturing part-time at that institution, applied for a permanent post. She had already voluntarily declared this relationship, in accordance with institutional procedures about consensual relationships and was careful to avoid taking any part in the appointment process. At the time of writing she is awaiting an Industrial Tribunal hearing, after losing an appeal against the decision to demote her, and she believes that she can show that male colleagues found guilty of serious breaches of contract within the institution's internal procedures have been much less harshly treated. During this process she has received a great deal of support from her colleagues, both locally within her own institution and nationally within her professional association.

All of these people have experienced terrible isolation, and their behaviour has been judged to their detriment in a way that heterosexuals can barely imagine, both at work and at leisure, in private and in public places, because of their sexual orientation. This is particularly pernicious when it happens within higher education, given our professed values and claims to offer insight and enlightenment, opportunity and support, to members of the academic community.

The experiences of gay men and lesbians in higher education are, sadly, often no more positive than the discrimination and homophobia which are all too often encountered in the wider community. The students' unions in many universities and colleges have LGB (lesbian, gay and bisexual) societies which tend to provide a social network rather than actively engaging in political campaigning, apart from organizing a coach to take members to Pride in London (the annual summer celebration of gay and lesbian sexuality). However, very few prospectuses are gay-friendly, even those published by universities who are rightly proud of their otherwise sound record on equal opportunities issues. To quote from one typical prospectus, under a section headed 'Opportunities For All':

> The diversity of the student community at [. . .] reflects the University's active commitment to equal opportunities for men and women of all ages, from all social, educational and ethnic backgrounds, and for people with disabilities.

Note the absence of any mention of sexual orientation. Sports teams, the chaplaincy and student support services generally receive wide coverage, but the only hint to a prospective student who wants to apply to a university where gay men and lesbians are positively welcomed, or who is uncertain about their sexual orientation, was the single prospectus (from a selection chosen as likely to demonstrate the most commitment to equal opportunities), issued by South Bank University, which mentioned its Lesbian and Gay Society in a list of students' union societies. This is important because, as indicated earlier, many prospective students who know that they are lesbian or gay, or think that they may be, will want to find a place to study where there are social networks of like-minded people. The prospectus and the student-produced guides to universities and colleges provide this information to guide their selection of a place to study.

Staff trade unions in higher education have long been active in promoting equal opportunities, including sexual orientation issues. A recent study by the National Association of Teachers in Further and Higher Education (NATFHE) of its lesbian, gay and bisexual members found that half felt able to be open about their sexuality at work but the majority of them were only 'out' with close associates and colleagues whom they trusted. The rest, who hid their sexuality at work to avoid discrimination, reported feelings of oppression and invisibility, especially when homophobic comments and 'jokes' were made (Colgan, 1998). Several believed their careers had suffered because of their sexuality and some had experienced harassment at work. Three-quarters of the respondents reported that their institution's equal opportunities policies covered sexuality but most felt that they were ineffective.

A pamphlet issued by the 'AUT and Proud group' of the Association of University Teachers (1998) includes a 'witness account' of an ideal university working environment for gay, lesbian and bisexual staff:

> 'My university has an excellent EO policy. Two members of staff development and two members of personnel are gay/lesbian, so issues get considered constantly. I'm out to my boss. My partner is invited to informal and formal social events at work and I am invited to hers. I am given

compassionate leave to support her both in her parenting and in her caring of parents. It is understood that I have to arrange my holidays around her child's school timetable.'

The invisibility of sexual orientation as an issue in the equal opportunities agenda

In relation to the other topics covered in this part of book, the paucity of relevant material and information on sexual orientation in higher education is striking. Other equal opportunities issues – notably gender, 'race', maturity and educational disadvantage – have become topics for discussion, policy development, implementation and monitoring, to the extent that some battles have now been won, and if not, then at least the rhetoric of 'political correctness' is now evident in many universities and colleges. Progress lags behind in the area of disability, it can be argued, with still far too much evidence of a 'charitable' approach based on individual cases, and not enough politicized discussion about equality of access and esteem and entitlements. But in relation to issues about sexual orientation, few institutions appear to have developed policies or procedures for students or staff about freedom from discrimination or harassment. This may arise from the lack of pressure to do so from social institutions in the wider society and the law, such as exists in relation to discrimination on grounds of sex and race and to a lesser extent disability: in this country, it is not illegal to discriminate on the basis of sexual orientation. But also, lesbian and gay students and staff are often unidentifiable and invisible, making it difficult to identify and respond to their specific concerns. And these concerns can be life-threatening: research by the London Lesbian and Gay Teenage Group found that one in five young gay men and lesbians had attempted suicide (Sanders and Burke, 1994). A four-year study of 190 lesbian, gay and bisexual school pupils across the UK conducted by Ian Rivers, a psychology lecturer at the University of Luton, found that half have contemplated suicide, 40 per cent have attempted it and nearly a third have tried to do so more than once; the majority (82 per cent) reported having been called names, 71 per cent had been ridiculed, 60 per cent had been hit or kicked and 59 per cent had had rumours spread about them (Rivers cited in *The Pink Paper*, 13 February 1998). Rivers found that although bullied lesbian and gay schoolchildren were more likely to experience depression in later life than a control group of gay men who had not been bullied, they had less internalized homophobia. As one young man from Northern Ireland told him, 'When you've been through hell at school, coming out isn't so bad'.

A television programme broadcast in September 1997 about 'gay-bashing' included some interviews undertaken in a Belfast Working Men's Club. All of the people interviewed said that they had never met a gay man or lesbian. Since it is estimated that perhaps 10 per cent of the population are lesbian or gay, it is a pretty safe bet to say that they *have* encountered gay men and lesbians who were too frightened to be 'out'. The same applies in higher education. 'Out' students and staff are a small, brave, politicized minority. The rest keep their heads down, denying to others and often to themselves that they are different, because of a rampant homophobia which they have often internalized. Pressures to seek acceptance by conforming to the norms of the lesbian and gay subcultures lead to uniform dress codes and appearance, but this means that lesbians who do not fit this stereotype may not be identifiable by straight society unless they choose to advertise their sexual orientation in a different way, for example in academe by writing and publishing on lesbian topics. Other equal opportunities issues concern groups who are fairly readily identifiable, either visually or through data held on them, or by self-identification – although there are clearly issues about whether students and staff choose to identify themselves as belonging to a minority ethnic group or having a disability, lest there be unforeseen negative consequences of this revelation. But lesbian and gay students and staff may be anywhere on a spectrum from being fully 'out' and hence readily identifiable, being out only in certain settings and contexts, 'closet' but acknowledging this identity to themselves, or they may well be struggling to establish a stable sexual orientation. Institutional policies, practices and systems need to be very sensitively developed to reflect the diversity of this situation.

In some disciplinary and professional fields it can be acceptable or even seen as a mark of exotic individuality for members of staff to be publicly identified as lesbian or gay – for example, in the creative arts and humanities. These people provide role models for students, but often within a narrow range of stereotypes. It is far harder to find 'out' staff in traditionally male disciplines, where there is more emphasis on the results of work than on the creative process and its subjective aspects and relationships. To be an 'out' engineer may pose problems for relationships with professional peers, but of itself is unlikely to result in formal exclusion or dismissal. In contrast, it can be dangerous and threatening to be 'out' in other fields, especially those associated with professions such as school teaching, health care and social work, where working with children or vulnerable people may be regarded as incompatible with overt homosexuality by the kind of ignorant people who think that all gay men want to have sex with boys.

This is not to say that it is impossible to be an 'out' teacher or nurse, as that is clearly not so, merely that to do so carries potentially far greater risks which many people understandably feel unable to countenance. In other fields same-sex friendships may be tacitly condoned, but only so long as people are discreet about them: they are never openly discussed. This is a more liberal, tolerant position than naked prejudice (akin to 'don't ask, don't tell', to cite President Clinton's policy on homosexuality in the US military), but it still forces people into self-censorship of what they tell colleagues and of their behaviour (no overt physical expressions of affection are permitted) and leaves people isolated in times of trouble from understanding colleagues. For people whose participation in the informal culture of the workplace is a source of pleasure which enhances their satisfaction with their job, it may be hard to imagine never discussing what you did at the weekend, or talking about your holiday, for fear of dropping incriminating clues about a stigmatized lifestyle. Examples of this kind of close-knit organizational culture where homosexual relationships are a taboo subject include the police force, the military, schools, many hospitals and, in higher education, women's colleges before most went co-educational in recent years.

But being closet in itself entails first, acknowledging the force of homophobia, and second, deciding not to mount a personal challenge to it. The best protection against criticism is to be 'out', which deprives your opponents of their best weapon. This is easy to assert for confident, politicized academics in secure employment but the world looks very different for young and older students, and for junior or socially isolated members of staff who are struggling with their sexual orientation and hence their whole sense of self. Here are two accounts of how women coped with their lesbianism when they were students:

> 'I came out at college by having a large poster of two women locked in an embrace on my wall. It worked a treat. To start with I had come out to individuals but no one was too freaked out, especially as I had a girlfriend, so they weren't worried I was going to pounce. Because I've never had a severely negative reaction to my face, I've not held back on coming out since I've started college. It's not so much 'coming out' as just being me, and part of being me is that I'm a dyke, take it or leave it. I've always been out at work. I've never said clearly, 'By the way, I'm a lesbian', but I just let it be known. I talk about my partner or girlfriend and if people are too horrified they'll steer clear of me next time. But then I work in a nice intellectual atmosphere where most of my colleagues read *The Guardian* and it would be most improper of them to react otherwise. I think some of them actually think it gives them credibility to have a lesbian couple as friends. But I am fully aware that a large section of the population would happily beat me up and/or rape me if the situation permitted it.'
>
> (National Gay and Lesbian Survey, 1992: 83)

> 'I had my first lesbian relationship at university. It was a very agonizing period in my life as the relationship was conducted secretly and sporadically, with a lot of hurting on both sides as a result. We both felt totally isolated as lesbians, although a lot of our contemporaries must have known what was going on. Because of the secrecy and self-doubt, the relationship was doomed from the start . . . I take no pleasure in living a secret life and keeping my lesbianism a secret has always been a burden to me. I have never come out to my 38-year old brother since he is very family orientated and ridicules gays, nor to my father because I was too frightened; he is now dead. . . . at that stage I began to work up to telling my mother. It was very difficult as I feared being rejected, but in the end it wasn't as bad as I had imagined. She said that, although she was surprised, she was not shocked. It took her a long time to accept, but now she is fond of my girlfriend, and gets a lot of support from us emotionally . . . I have come out at work when my workmates have started ridiculing gays. I tend to keep

quiet unless someone is being anti-gay . . . I think I have chosen a line of work which is independent of others, in the world of entertainment where attitudes are a bit more "liberal" than in the establishment. I believe that being out at work would lead to problems for most people and I would never blame them for keeping quiet about it. I feel a little resentful that some avenues seem to be closed to me precisely because I have stopped myself from pursuing a career in the mainstream.'

(National Gay and Lesbian Survey, 1992: 87–8)

What can be done?

For those readers who have persevered up to this point in the chapter, we are almost certainly now addressing the converted: that is, people who are committed to the cause of promoting equality of opportunity but who are currently likely to have varying levels of familiarity with what are the main issues facing lesbians and gay men in higher education and what steps can be taken to address their concerns. The preceding section has sought to identify the wide diversity of circumstances and outlooks of people who are lesbian and gay, or who are struggling to determine whether they are or not. Here are some measures which universities and colleges can take to address these issues.

Raising the issue: establishing what is the existing situation

Often committees or groups of activists in universities and colleges will decide to launch a survey of the experiences of gay, lesbian, bisexual and transsexual students and staff. This has the objective of establishing from those most directly concerned what they see as the main issues which need to be tackled through concerted action, but also it serves to alert the wider community to the institution's commitment to this issue. Depending on the nature of the group initiating the survey (formal university committee, students' union, loose-knit group of activists or whatever) and the resources at its disposal, this may be a large or small enterprise, which will yield results varying in scope and reliability.

Experience from several universities and colleges indicates that surveys which request information on homophobia and discrimination are likely, whatever their provenance and arrangements for data collection, to bring in only a few responses as it will be difficult to persuade anyone other than already 'out' staff and students to complete and return the survey forms. However, lack of quantity does not signify lack of quality. A survey undertaken recently at the University of Southampton elicited 25 usable completed questionnaires from students and members of staff (Clarke *et al.*, 1997) and some of their finding are summarized below.

Two-thirds of the respondents in the study, who included academic and 'support' staff and students were 'out' to all their peers. Those who had only disclosed their sexual orientation to certain peers or to none explained why they were not fully 'out:

'not being taken seriously as an academic'

'I would be concerned if I thought colleagues might not trust me completely with students'

'discrimination with respect to promotion and research funding'

'ostracization by students who do not understand that gay people are human'

'rejection from friends, verbal abuse in halls [residential student accommodation on site]'

'be looked at differently'.

The coping strategies used to conceal their sexual orientation included 'lying' about having a boyfriend and feigning an interest in the opposite sex. None of the questionnaire respondents had experienced physical abuse within the university but several reported instances of verbal abuse or social isolation. Equal numbers of staff respondents had and had not experienced distress, isolation and depression on 'coming out'. Similar experiences of depression and insecurity were reported by the students, including one who had contemplated suicide. Another said, tellingly: 'to be gay is going to take more confidence than I feel I have'.

Their ratings of the university on a 'gay-friendly/homophobic' scale varied widely, possibly reflecting divergent experiences of organizational subcultures in different faculties and as a student or a member of staff. Several felt that the institutional climate had improved in recent years, to the point that the overt expression of homophobic sentiments by members of staff was regarded as unacceptable. The report of this study provides useful suggestions for improving the institutional climate for gay, lesbian and bisexual students and staff. The university's Equal Opportunities Advisory Group deserves commendation for having undertaken this project. The next part of this chapter picks up some of the themes from this report, to explore what action can be taken to address homophobia and discrimination on the grounds of sexual orientation.

Challenging homophobia

This is arguably the most important single measure in addressing the demonization of homosexuality. Over the past twenty years the academy has been forced to acknowledge that women, members of minority ethnic communities and individuals with disabilities are people too. Sexist and racist jokes and examples used in class to explain concepts which draw on sexist or racist stereotypes are now widely (if not yet universally) regarded as unacceptable: it should be possible to establish an institutional ethos, backed by mandatory staff development, in which the same applies to homophobia. This entails address-ing both the formal, specified curriculum but also the 'hidden curriculum' of messages conveyed through the way in which information is presented, and the privileging of certain ideas over others. Years ago I used to be invited by the all-male team who taught social theory in the place where I then worked to do a one-hour guest spot on feminist theory, which invariably fell on the final week of the autumn term, the morning after the Christmas disco. The messages con-veyed by that timetabling decision about the topic and the importance accorded to it formed part of the 'hidden curriculum'. Munt (1997) asserts that the same applies to so-called minority issues ('race', class and lesbianism) within Women's Studies courses.

Course committees and students' evaluations can be used to monitor nega-tive references to lesbian and gay issues, both within the formal curriculum and in informal interactions between staff and students, but the relevant questions need to be posed explicitly, and the assessments made by students who are well informed about the issues. Training to educate staff will need to be accompan-ied by awareness training for students, ideally undertaken by the students' union so that evaluation and 'policing' is not left to a few activists.

Challenging homophobia is not just a matter for the classroom, however. Institutional procedures must be developed and publicized, which specify the way to report homophobic incidents and harassment, and the penalties for being found responsible. Common examples include Lesbian and Gay Society posters being defaced or removed; homophobic graffiti; and the harassment of students in halls of residence or public places around the university. One recent conference presentation reported an example of harassment in residential stu-dent accommodation:

'every meal, breakfast and dinner, we would be standing in the queue and you would hear something being muttered behind – 'fucking lesbian' – and you turn round and you wouldn't see who it was that had said it. It would just be this sea of blank faces. And this is what I mean: there was this core of people that actually did it but all the others in the hall just stood by and let it happen . . . We were really scared most of the time. We would be sat at a table and we would be jumping every time a tray was dropped. Your behaviour changes when you are in a position where you are always frightened to death for your life. You do become very sensitive. Sarah had tears in her eyes most of the time as well, we had mega bags under our eyes that week. We went for sleeping pills to the doctor's . . . [The perpetrators were] this sort of neo-nazi group – there was a group of about ten core lads. But the majority of people in the halls would just turn their back on it and ignore it. There were about 200 people in this hall . . . and if the other 190 people did actually turn round and say collectively 'that's enough', we would have had them, but they didn't, you know. So it was allowed to go on and it escalated . . .'

(Carter *et al.*, 1996)

Making the invisible visible

There are few 'out' lesbian and gay staff to provide role models for students, but those who are take their responsibilities seriously. Munt (a lecturer at the University of East Anglia who describes herself as a working-class butch lesbian) writes:

I believe that romantic precept that education is one proven way to dissipate prejudice. I get such a kick out of standing in front of 200 18-year-olds, and being able to tell them about lesbian history, women's history. I know that, for significant numbers of them, this is the first time they have knowingly encountered a real live lesbian . . . For the one or two gay or lesbian-looking students out there, my lecture is for them. I love the way, sooner or later, they all make it to my office. We pass in the corridors and smile. The way we recognize our need for that acknowledgement is a statement of community.

(Munt, 1997: 98)

Far too much teaching assumes, in its content and examples, that the world is heterosexual, that everybody is part of a family, and that the nuclear family is the norm. More and more students are finding that one or more of these assumptions does not apply to them, making them feel marginalized and excluded. Again, staff development can help to identify approaches or topics which address this. Instead of relying on hackneyed, stereotyped themes and images, teaching and learning can be brought up to date by (say) designing a hostel for abused women in architecture; contrasting the experience of being gay in an urban and a rural area, and evaluating the services provided in each community, in health and community studies, rural and urban studies, geography, sport and leisure studies, etc; analysing the value of the 'pink pound' in economics; examining the history, art and literature on same-sex friendships; and so on.

Making the stigmatized acceptable

Staff members' and students' ignorance, as well as their homophobia, must be addressed and the classroom is probably the most appropriate site for this transformation. (I am taking it for granted that institutions will have policies in place to control the display of offensive images, but discriminatory oral presentations such as debates and presentations by external speakers may need particular consideration.) Some people will feel that their homophobic values are entirely acceptable (for example, those with certain religious convictions). Social work staff, who are highly experienced at educating students for non-discriminatory professional practice, may be willing themselves, or with their students, to provide sessions for other groups of students and staff to address this. Staff members must be educated in their responsibility not only to monitor their own speech and behaviour, but also to challenge homophobic comments by students, in the interests of creating an intellectual environment where all can flourish. Not to do so is to condone discriminatory and prejudiced behaviour, which will undermine the confidence of lesbian and gay students, and threaten their sense of being fully valued members of the academic community.

Marigold Rogers studied lesbians' experiences in a mixed comprehensive school for her MA dissertation, finding that many of her informants felt ignored and isolated (Rogers, 1994). The same is true in higher education.

> 'I think the worst aspect of my schooldays was the complete and utter absence of any mention – at school, at home, in literature, in the media – of lesbians and gay men. I felt, to use the cliché, as if I was the only person in the world to love other women. This is not to say that there was no mention of lesbian and gay issues anywhere in the media but there wasn't any in what I read, listened to, watched.'
>
> ('Helen' quoted in Rogers, 1994: 38)

Rogers quotes Julia Melia as saying, 'These young people are quite clear about what they want from education: an acknowledgement of their existence and a right to a self-defined identity' (Melia, 1989: 217 cited in Rogers, 1994). This applies equally to higher education, and Marigold Rogers' recommendations to school teachers about how this can be achieved (presented here with my amendments in italics) offer plenty of ideas for us to consider:

- open discussion of homosexuality in class, where it is not treated as a problem;
- open discussion of the oppression of lesbians and gays;
- *incorporation of lesbian and gay theories, examples and perspectives into the curriculum*;
- the identification of role models (both local/actual and in course materials);
- talks by former students (or external speakers);
- critical discussion of plays, books and other materials;
- ensuring staff acceptance of their responsibility to defend students and to challenge homophobic comments and behaviour, rather than seeking to be even-handed or abdicating this responsibility;
- establishing lesbian and gay students' right to be taken seriously;
- ensuring that all tutors and providers of support services have been educated/trained to be sensitive to issues associated with students' sexual orientation, and identifying and if necessary appointing lesbian/gay members of the support staff;
- publicizing internal and external sources of support and advice for lesbian and gay students including, if necessary, supporting the establishment of student societies.

(Rogers, 1994: 46)

Some of these do not appear at first sight to constitute part of the formal curriculum, but they do merit consideration if we conceptualize the student experience as a whole, where the 'hidden curriculum' conveys its own power-ful messages, both intended and unintended, which may support or undermine formal institutional objectives. And unless we address issues in the wider envir-onment which marginalize and alienate lesbian and gay students, they will never get to the point of engaging with the curriculum.

This chapter has sought to provide some information about the experiences of gay, lesbian and bisexual students and staff in higher education. However, as this is an under-researched topic in relation to the others covered in this book, it has been necessary to draw on materials about sexual orientation in the wider society.

The members of this particular minority group are not visible unless they choose to make themselves so. This raises a series of issues for the sensitive aca-demic or manager in higher education about how to extend appropriate sup-port to enable students and colleagues to thrive. Persistent and endemic homophobia may be on the wane among liberal academics, but it is seen as legitimate and even morally right in certain political and most religious circles. Students and staff bring with them into the university the attitudes character-istic of their social networks in the wider community. Managers in higher edu-cation have a duty to challenge homophobic attitudes and discriminatory behaviour: this chapter has provided some ideas about how this might be achieved.

References

AUT and Proud Group (AUT Sexual Orientation Network) (1998) *Equal Opportunities: An LGB Perspective*. London: AUT.

Bradford, J. and Ryan, C. (1988) *The National Lesbian Health Care Survey*. Washington, DC: National Lesbian and Gay Health Foundation.

Carter, P., Hamilton, R. and Jeffs, T. (1996) Researching sexual violence in higher educa-tion: interim findings, in *Sexual Politics in Higher Education – Conference Papers*. Newcastle: University of Northumbria.

Clarke, G. (1996) Conforming and contesting with a difference: how lesbian students and teachers manage their identities, *International Studies in the Sociology of Education*, 6(2): 191–209.

Clarke, G., Jewell, T. and Sproule, L. (1997) *Results of a Survey on Sexual Orientation Discrimina-tion at the University of Southampton*. Southampton: University of Southampton.

Clift, S. M. (1989) Lesbian and gay issues in education: a study of the attitudes of first year students in a college of higher education, *British Educational Research Journal*, 14(1): 31–50.

Colgan, F. (1998) Coming out in the union: report of a NATFHE survey of lesbian, gay and bisexual members, *The Lecturer*, April: 21.

Deevey, S. and Wall, L. J. (1993) How do lesbian women develop serenity?, in P. N. Stern (ed.) *Lesbian Health: What are the Issues?* Washington, DC: Taylor & Francis.

Dykenosis (the national bi-monthly newsletter about lesbian health) (1998) Gaining control: experiences of eating disorders, *Dykenosis*, 16: 1–2 (March).

Epstein, D. (ed.) (1994) *Challenging Lesbian and Gay Inequalities in Education*. Buckingham: Open University Press.

Faderman, L. (1985) *Surpassing the Love of Men: Romantic Friendship and Love Between Women from the Renaissance to the Present.* London: The Women's Press.

Faderman, L. (1992) *Odd Girls and Twilight Lovers: A History of Lesbian Life in Twentieth Century America.* London: Penguin.

Fahey, W. S. (1993) Lesbian and gay men's experiences of peer discrimination and harassment in higher education, *Contexts*, March. Cheltenham: Cheltenham and Gloucester College of Higher Education: 7–8.

Higher Education Statistics Agency (1997) *Students in Higher Education Institutions – 1995/6.* Cheltenham: HESA.

Kinsey, A. C., Pomeroy, W. B., Martin, C. E. *et al.* (1948) *Sexual Behavior in the Human Male.* Philadelphia: W. B Saunders.

Kinsey, A. C., Pomeroy, W. B., Martin, C. E. *et al.* (1953) *Sexual Behavior in the Human Female.* Philadelphia: W. B. Saunders.

Lesbian History Group (1989) *Not a Passing Phase: Reclaiming Lesbians in History 1840–1985.* London: The Women's Press.

Melia, J. (1989) Sex education in schools: keeping to the norm, in C. Jones and P. Mahoney (eds), *Learning Our Lines: Sexuality and Social Control in Education.* London: The Women's Press.

MIND (1997) *Without Prejudice.* London: MIND.

Munt, S. R. (1997) I teach therefore I am: Lesbian Studies in the liberal academy, *Feminist Review*, 56, Summer: 85–99.

National Gay and Lesbian Survey (1992) *Wha a Lesbian Looks Like: Writings by Lesbians on their Lives and Lifestyles.* London: Routledge.

PACE (Project for Advice, Counselling and Education) (1999) *Diagnosis: Homophobic.* London: PACE.

Palmer, A. and Mason, A. (1996) *Queerbashing: A National Survey on Homophobic Violence and Harassment.* London: Stonewall.

Patrick, P. and Sanders, S.A L. (1994) Lesbian and gay issues in the curriculum, in D. Epstein (ed.), *Challenging Lesbian and Gay Inequalities in Education.* Buckingham: Open University Press.

Rogers, M. (1994) Growing up lesbian: the role of the school, in D. Epstein (ed.) *Challenging Lesbian and Gay Inequalities in Education.* Buckingham: Open University Press.

Sanders, S. A. L. and Burke, H. (1994) Are you a lesbian, Miss?, in D. Epstein (ed.), *Challenging Lesbian and Gay Inequalities in Education.* Buckingham: Open University Press.

Weeks, J. (1989) *Sex, Politics and Society: The Regulation of Sexuality Since 1800.* Harlow, Essex: Longman.

Wellings, K., Field, J., Johnson A. M. and Wadsworth, J. (1994) *Sexual Behaviour in Britain: The National Survey of Sexual Attitudes and Lifestyles.* Harmondsworth, Middlesex: Penguin.

Woodward, D. (1999) Sexual orientation: the hidden inequality, in M. Pearl and P. Singh (eds) *Equal Opportunities in the Curriculum.* Oxford: Oxford Brookes University Equal Opportunities Action Group.

Useful sources of information

United Kingdom

Association of University Teachers, United House, 9 Pembridge Road, London W11 3JY. Tel: 020 7221 4370.

Directory of Lesbian and Gay Studies, available from Ford Hickson, DOLAGS, Unit 64, Eurolink Centre, 49 Effra Road, London SW2 1BZ.

FFLAG (Families and Friends of Lesbians and Gays), PO Box 153, Manchester M60 1LP.

LAGER (Lesbian and Gay Employment Rights) – provides free confidential advice for lesbians and gay men who are having problems at work. Unit 1G, Leroy House, 436 Essex Road, London N1 3QP. Fax: 020 7704 6067.

NATFHE (National Association of Teachers in Further and Higher Education), 27 Britannia Street, London WC1X 9JP. Tel: 020 7837 3636. NATFHE has a national lesbian and gay steering group, holds an annual lesbian, gay and bisexual conference and publishes useful materials.

NUS (National Union of Students) Lesbian, Gay and Bisexual Campaign: Cath Fletcher, NUS HQ, 461 Holloway Road, London N7 6LJ. Tel: 020 7561 6517.

PACE (Project for Advice, Counselling and Education), 34 Hartham Road, London N7 9JL. Tel: 020 7700 1323. Reports cost £15 for organizations and £5 for individuals.

Stonewall, 16 Clerkenwell Close, London EC1R 0AA. Tel: 020 7336 8860; fax: 020 7336 8864; email: info@stonewall.org.uk; web site: http://www.stonewall.org.uk

The Knitting Circle – website containing extensive resources on lesbian and gay issues, especially in higher education, produced by the Lesbian and Gay Staff Association, South Bank University, London.
web site: http://www.sbu.ac.uk/~stafflag/index.html

The Pink Paper distributed free in gay pubs, clubs and other public places. Editorial number: 020 7296 6210.

United States

The Governor's Commission on Gay and Lesbian Youth, Room 111, State House, Boston, Mass. 02133, USA. Publisher of *Making Colleges and Universities Safe for Gay and Lesbian Students*, principal author: Warren J. Blumenfeld (available free from above address). Warren is founder and first director of the National Gay Student Center, now the National Queer Coalition of the United States Student Association,
email: blumenfeld@educ.umass.edu

Queer Studies List email address: qstudy-l@listserv.acsu.buffalo.edu

A useful resource

Being Lesbian and Gay in Higher Education: Our Lives as Staff and Students
Melissa Friedberg, Sheila Quaid and Tom Shakespeare

(Excerpt from notes on a workshop held at the Sexual Politics in Higher Education Conference, University of Northumbria, March 1996. Reprinted with permission.)

Our aim for the workshop was to raise some of the dilemmas and issues we face as staff and students, and to develop some strategies we could take back to our individual institutions. With this in mind we made brief presentations, had some time for a general discussion, and discussed ways in which we could take some of the issues forward. The participants were made up of staff and students. The issues we presented covered these areas:

1. Safety and visibility

Coming out, being out and staying out to staff and students. This is a continuous process with new staff joining and each new intake of students.

Safety for lesbian and gay students and staff dealing with homophobia. Looking at issues of safety in relation to our different positions.

Working in a supportive environment but being invisible. The struggle to remain visible. Making the connections with our other identities and being seen in our totality.

2. Curriculum and relationship to colleagues

Working in an academic environment such as sociology can feel a less 'dangerous' place to be out. The experience here is one of less overt homophobia than in an administrative environment.

Problems can be associated with how one's sexuality affects colleagues' attitudes towards you: one's politics or intellectual positions are sometimes trivialized in being explained with reference to one's sexuality, 'Well, she would say that, wouldn't she?'

There is tokenism which means you are the point of call for all sexuality-related issues; one is an informal consultant or seen as an expert on any issues about diverse sexualities.

When there are problems, there is often no one to talk to; one is isolated and unsupported.

3. Different ways of being out: working with and supporting students

- Students make assumptions about one's sexuality.
- Students' expectations of how lecturers are out.
- Private/personal life and professional life can become confused, especially where the scene is small and one encounters students.
- Teaching lesbian and gay issues is often complicated, especially where there are lesbian and gay students in the cohort; questions are raised about dealing with homophobia, protecting self and students and protecting confidentiality.
- Supporting individual students with problems of homophobia and heterosexism is often an issue; this is a counselling role which is unrecognized, unsupported and unvalidated.
- Colleagues and students may be suspicious of contact between lesbian and gay staff and students; mutual recognition and solidarity enables links to be made, but this perceived closeness may be problematic.

The main points raised in the discussion related to issues of safety, isolation, being viewed as the expert, visibility, pressure and vulnerability. These issues were raised by both lecturers and students. The complex nature of being out was also discussed. Being out can give us a certain status but also creates pressure and stress. Our behaviour is often explained by our sexuality and we are identified by our sexuality. There was also the question of how out to be without scaring off other lesbians and gay men. Students who were out who had lecturers who were not out found this situation hurtful. One university lecturer spoke about the coming out process. The idea that you come out once and then your sexuality is known to everyone is not the reality. She talked about the continuing process of coming out to every new cohort of students. The nature of university work means that the decision to be out to students is repeated every year and the anxiety is experienced every time. For example, if you offer the provision of specific advice and support to lesbian and gay students, the information might be part of the induction for students. There was some discussion on this, and the decision for staff to offer support for lesbian and gay students clearly had implications for lesbian and gay lecturers.

There was much discussion around being seen as the expert. Out students were focused on by straight lecturers to give their views on issues related to homosexuality, pressure was put on them to bring up issues related to sexuality, and they were looked upon to educate straight staff. Lesbians and gay men being seen as experts can lead to being undermined and made vulnerable. There is also pressure to present a unified viewpoint, leaving us no space for difference.

The notion that some departments were 'better' than others was challenged. It was more that departments were different and not necessarily safe. It was a matter of degree as there still existed covert homophobia. Some felt that it was not the matter of subject areas that was important but having other lesbians and gay men around. We came up with the following strategies to address some of the issues raised:

- the need to create a supportive environment and to be there for others;
- having lesbian-only courses in women's studies, thus creating our own space and our own learning space;
- taking a firm line on issues related to sexuality;
- though it was felt that policies were not enough, having equal opportunities policies which mentioned and related to lesbians and gay men could provide safety;
- setting up working parties to address issues of homophobia;
- having training workshops for staff;
- mentioning the lesbian and gay life in the town and the university in the prospectus;
- developing our own support networks through our student and staff unions.

8

Social Class and Mature Entrants

John Bird

Introduction

Although they are not always recognized as such, strategies to widen participation in higher education (HE) – what used to be called widening access –
form a part of those strategies embedded in equalities legislation which seek to
provide greater opportunities (for example, in employment and in education)
for those who have, historically, been disadvantaged. They are, therefore, part
of positive action strategies. As such, these strategies recognize that forms of
discrimination do exist which have excluded in the past and still continue to
exclude people from higher education. They seek to minimize the existence
and the effects of such discrimination, be it direct or indirect, individual or
institutional.

This chapter seeks, first, to look at participation in HE in order to identify
(any) inequities in participation. Second, it looks at some successful initiatives
which have been developed to widen participation. Third, it looks at the mani-
fest failure of HEIs to enhance working-class participation. Finally, it discusses
the importance of focusing on equalities issues as they affect those *in* HE, particularly those who have accessed HE as a result of successful strategies to
widen participation.

HE participation rates in the UK, 1950–99: from exclusion of the many to greater inclusion

The Higher Education Funding Council for England's Advisory Group on
Access and Participation (HEFCE, 1996) gives us a clear picture of participation rates. Compared with 1990, more women are in HE; more mature students are in HE; more students without A-levels are in HE; more part-time
students are in HE; more students from minority ethnic groups are in HE. This
picture is reinforced in the various reports of the National Committee of

Inquiry into Higher Education (NCIHE, 1997): between 1950 and 1995, the Age Participation Index rose from 3.4 per cent to 32 per cent (Robertson and Hillman, 1997: 39–40). In others words, 32 per cent of 18-year-olds were entering higher education in 1995 compared with 3.4 per cent in 1950. This expansion in participation in higher education is uncontestable and is a reason to celebrate both the success of those students and the success of many higher education institutions (HEIs), particularly the post-1992 universities. We will turn later to issues of what happens to those students when they are *in* HE and how far the student experience is one characterized by quality and equality of treatment.

HEFCE is so sure that success has arrived that it boldly asserts, 'that questions of under-representation are no longer of central concern' (1996: executive summary, point 3). As with many such bold assertions there is a rider which makes the assertion carry less weight; a rider which argues that, while recognizing that it is difficult to analyse social class participation in HE, social groups 3 and 4 (what sociologists have customarily termed 'working-class' people) participate in numbers and proportions that remain low and have been so for a very long time. In addition, students with disabilities also have low participation rates. For working-class students the reasons for such low participation lie at an 'earl[y] stage of the education process' (HEFCE, 1996: executive summary, point 3a); for students with disabilities, the reasons are associated with 'the nature of the resourcing and support required and the severity of the disability' (HEFCE, 1996: executive summary, point 3b).

HEFCE's recognition that there are still significant patterns of under-representation is clear from the subsequent attempts to measure social class participation through postcode analysis (using home address/location as a crude indicator of class position) and to enhance participation by students with special needs through various forms of funding to HEIs which, between 1993 and 1995, totalled £6 million. In addition, HEFCE has provided £1.5 million of special funding for 1998–9 for collaborative initiatives to widen participation, and is allowing additional numbers of student places – predominantly on pre-degree courses – to rise to a total of 44,925 for 1999–2000, with a similar brief to widen participation (HEFCE, 1998, 1999). We will see later in this chapter that working-class participation rates have remained obdurately low for a considerable time and have almost been unaffected by HEFCE initiatives.

The celebration of success and the simultaneous recognition that work remains to be done is a healthy thing. In addition, it is important to recognize that the sector as a whole has not always been successful. More of the successful attempts to widen participation have occurred in the post-1992 universities, although as we will see below, this does not apply to widening participation for working-class students where universities across the board have had limited success. Early analysis of postcode data (see *THES*, 16 April 1999, and below for a discussion of the utility of postcode analysis), suggests that London universities have been more successful in widening participation than those in other areas. It is unclear whether there has been wider participation *across* the sector or whether – through special initiatives, for example to recruit more minority ethnic students to teacher education – formerly under-represented groups only enter a limited part of HE provision. Finally, and perhaps requiring a little more discussion, is the fact that there seems to have been very little discussion of what is meant by equity of representation which has, of course, made debates about target setting for recruitment and an analysis of how successful the sector as a whole or individual institutions have been, difficult to even contemplate.

The clearest example of the problem here is in the context of participation by minority ethnic groups in HE. HEFCE is clear: 'minority groups appear not to be under-represented in HE, with Black African, Chinese and Asian Other groups appearing to be particularly well-represented' (HEFCE, 1996: 17). However, there is still a recognized issue: 'Two groups appear to be under-represented – young black Caribbean men, and women from Pakistani and Bangladeshi groups' (HEFCE, 1996: 17). While these conclusions *are* borne out by the available data, there is no discussion of how we decide what 'under-representation' means. What we can see is, in some discussions of participation, an assumption that there is already *over*-representation of students from some minority ethnic groups.

It only requires a little thought to realise that ways of defining 'representation' are both contentious and political. If groups are over-represented, the argument can easily end up as one which emphasizes that they have received special treatment; it is here that the language of over-representation links to a language of what is an illegality, that is, positive discrimination. If some groups are, as a result of access strategies, now over-represented – again, assuming we can have a neutral definition of representation – then we might want to ask why was the language of over-representation rarely used to describe a time when most HE students were white, male, non-disabled and middle class? Underlying the debate about fair representation are two distinct political positions: one which takes seriously past failures and past discriminations and seeks to tackle these, for example, by opening up the system to those with a variety of qualifications and also to those who, at the end of compulsory schooling, have few, if any, qualifications; and one which sees wider participation as a negative thing whereby some groups have received special treatment and are probably entering HE without the necessary qualifications to succeed. In the latter, 'dumbing down' is seen to have occurred and to be a result of opening up the system rather than, say, being the result of wider social and cultural changes which make traditional ideas of literacy considerably less relevant.

Successful strategies to widen participation: how 'positive action' works

The formulation of positive action in the 1975 Sex Discrimination Act and the 1976 Race Relations Act indicates what can and cannot be done, and can be applied fairly easily to what HEIs *can* do to widen participation. Positive action in the 1975 and 1976 legislation is largely a matter of employment opportunities.

Employers can provide training for women and for people from minority ethnic groups to enhance their employment opportunities and their opportunities for promotion once they are employed. There is a growing body of work which looks at equal opportunities policies and positive action strategies as these affect staff in HE (see Farish *et al.*, 1995; Neal, 1998); there is considerably less on such strategies as they relate to providing greater opportunities for students to enter HE.

An obvious example of a positive action strategy for student participation in higher education is access course provision for mature students who, for whatever reason, missed out on higher education the first time round. Other examples include language support in schools for children for whom English is not their first language. What makes access courses an example of positive action is fairly clear. First, they attempt to target those who are under-represented in HE – mature students, students from minority ethnic groups, those with disabilities, those from working-class communities. Second, they cater for people who lack formal qualifications and seek to enhance their ability to compete for places in HE with those who already have the qualifications. That they have been successful is also reasonably clear. We can look briefly at some of the history of the access debate.

In 1988 the Chair of the Polytechnics and Colleges Funding Council (PCFC) received a letter of guidance from the then Secretary of State for Education underlining the importance of widening participation in higher education. The mission to widen participation became central to the PCFC and it began asking HEIs to provide information on how they contributed to this mission. The 1992 document *Widening Participation in Higher Education* (PCFC) summarized the situation. Not surprisingly, the vast majority of HEIs supported wider participation and more than half had that goal as part of their strategic planning (1992: 7–8). The details of what institutions were doing now seems almost to constitute a lexicon of good practice: flexible delivery of HE programmes; access courses for mature students delivered in further education colleges or in community settings; foundation courses operating as year zero of degree programmes; franchising the first year of degree programmes to the further education sector; outreach by HE; support for students with disabilities in HE; access courses dedicated to women and to students from minority ethnic groups; monitoring of the experience and performance of mature entrants; and the development of support strategies for mature students. By 1994 there were 1,500 access courses with some 34,000 students of whom 52 per cent went on to enter HE and a significant number went directly into employment. In addition, there was a broad range of partnerships between HEIs and further education institutions (FEIs), many of which also sought to widen participation. These included forms of franchising where the early years, typically the first year, of HE degrees were taught in FE with HEIs receiving the funding and being responsible for quality assurance. In many cases, such arrangements aimed to widen participation, the rationale being that the chance to study in a local FEI would ease the transition to HE and would also minimize the financial burden on students (Abramson, Bird and Stennett, 1996).

These various initiatives indicate some of the limitations of positive action strategies. For example, students on access courses still have to manage with significant economic disadvantages and also, as with other mature students, often have demanding family responsibilities. The problem of financial support for mature students has been a complex one. The introduction of student loans in 1989 and the more recent requirement for students to pay fees have both had an impact on mature applicants and entrants to HE. On 26 June 1998, *THES* reported concern from the Universities and Colleges Admissions Services (UCAS) and the Committee of Vice-Chancellors and Principals (CVCP) that applications for entry to HE by mature students – those 21 years old and over – had seen a significant fall of between 11 and 15 per cent. The complexities of the benefits system which required that mature students on access courses should also be available for work similarly acted as a disincentive for study. These were all problems which PCFC had already recognized in 1988 together with a further list of continuing barriers to entry to HE: the physical environment which restricted access to disabled people; students' perceptions of the cost of embarking on an HE programme of study; the geographical location of HEIs; and HEIs' perceptions that widening participation is expensive. As we will see in the next section, some of these problems are still critical, particularly those associated with how working-class students and their families perceive the costs of HE. Finally here, we should draw attention to what Parry (see Metcalf, 1993), sees as a deep flaw in the whole enterprise of accessing more students:

> There is a basic tension or contradiction in the whole Access enterprise. What is offered is a non-traditional pathway to a traditional provision; and a student-centred preparation for a subject-centred experience.
>
> (Parry cited in Metcalf, 1993: 10–11)

In other words, while we need to celebrate the success of students in entering higher education in greater numbers we should also realize that they enter a largely producer-led system in which existing programmes are offered to more diverse groups of students, perhaps with some greater flexibility in delivery. The new entrant, particularly if he/she is a mature student from an access course, moves from an environment which is student-centred to one which, for whatever reason, is subject-centred.

The excluded: the sorry tale of working-class participation in post-16 education in the UK

The continuing problem is indicated in the following headlines from the educational press:

> 'University intake startlingly biased towards rich' (*The Guardian*, 19 April 1997)

> 'Rise and rise of the middle classes' (*THES*, 30 January 1998)

HEFCE's assertion in 1996 that 'questions of under-representation are no longer of central concern' (1996: i) did include a recognition that social class participation was still an important issue. While admitting the difficulties of analysing the link between social class and participation in higher education, HEFCE (1996) concluded, for example, that while individuals from professional and managerial groups make up 37 per cent of the population, they constitute 60 per cent of the HE population. Robertson and Hillman (1997) provide substantial evidence that working-class participation remains a significant failure of the higher education system. The enormous rise in HE participation rates since the Robbins Report (1963) has had little effect on social class participation. The conclusion is simple:

> [There are] nearly constant ratios of participation between higher and lower socio-economic groups . . . approximately 75:25 for the pre-1992 universities and 68:32 for the 1992 universities. These ratios have remained unchanged over a long period . . . [this] under representation remains significant across the sector as a whole.
>
> (Robertson and Hillman, 1997: 40, 41)

Little of this will come as a surprise to most sociologists of education; there is an enormous body of evidence that those from lower socio-economic groups have low participation rates in post-compulsory education generally (for example, the classical studies by Goldthorpe, 1980; Halsey *et al.*, 1980). Indeed, HEFCE now recognizes that, although class participation rates relate to what happens before entry to HE, HEIs can do something. A number of factors attest to HEFCE concern with the relationships between socio-economic position and HE participation rates. First, HEFCE is trying to measure social class participation through the analysis of postcodes. Building on work from the University of Liverpool, which suggested that students from postcode areas that are predominantly affluent and middle class do especially well in access to higher education, HEFCE has suggested that such an analysis should become the basis for assessing levels of participation and should guide HEIs in their recruitment strategies. HEIs could, for example, target postcode areas where there are high proportions of working-class students. This will then form the basis for a second strategy by HEFCE to allocate extra student numbers to those HEIs which effectively target students in those particular postcode districts. The attempt to assess the extent of working-class under-representation in HE is an important one, even if we also have to recognize the limitations of postcode analysis including the likelihood that an affluent postcode district may contain small pockets of underprivilege which will not be revealed if only the first part of the postcode is included in the analysis.

If we investigate this long-standing under-representation of working-class students in HE, what will we learn about *how* to widen representation and about the limits of positive action? How do we address working-class under-representation without losing focus on the extent to which patterns of participation in HE are also still racialized and gendered? We can start this discussion by looking at the work of Lynch and O'Riordan (1998) which indicates some of the difficulties in tackling this form of non-participation. In a study based on detailed interviews, they indicate the nature and the obdurateness of barriers to access and participation where barriers are a mixture of the economic and structural, the social and cultural, and the educational.

What is most interesting in Lynch and O'Riordan's study is the extent to which the reasons for low staying-on rates among post-16-year-olds, and for difficulties in schooling pre-16-year-olds, remain as factors affecting participation in HE. The constraints on entry to HE include *economic ones*: poverty, lack of a place to study, pressure to leave school at 16, inability to access the private sector of education, the need to work while at school, and awareness that funding for students in HE is inadequate; and *social and cultural ones*: teachers' views that working-class children have a cultural deficit, lack of information, fear of isolation in HE; fears of being an outsider, worries among students that they would have to live in two worlds; and *educational ones*: a feeling that teachers are middle class and see working-class pupils as lacking something, a belief that schools with middle-class students provide a better education, high teacher turnover in working-class schools, and poorer resources in such schools.

Lynch and O'Riordan come to a number of conclusions which, if read with a pessimistic eye, suggest significant problems should the sector wish to increase working-class participation. First, they argue that economic constraints are the most important ones affecting post-16 education. Second, identifying what the 'real' problem is, is contested. Whereas many working-class students and parents see the problem as a combination of economic constraints and teacher attitudes and expectations, teachers more often prefer to see the problem as disinterest and alienation. Third, hidden in the idea that school makes a difference is the problem that there are significant differences between schools, for example, in resources, which means that some schools can make more of a difference than others. Finally, economic, social and cultural and educational constraints are not separate; lack of resources leads to feelings of alienation and powerlessness which means that HE is rarely seen as a realistic goal.

If higher education has, as HEFCE now seems to believe, a role to play in promoting inclusion, then the lessons from Lynch and O'Riordan's work – lessons consistently given by sociologists of education for the last 40 years – are important. If economic constraints are the most important, then greater participation for working-class students is going to: (a) take a long time to achieve; and (b) be *expensive*. It will be expensive because of the need for a realistic form of student maintenance, and long term because social, cultural and educational disadvantages are not dealt with in one or two years. In essence, economic and other constraints are intertwined; social and cultural barriers overlie economic ones. Even if systems of student maintenance were effective in tackling economic barriers, then long-standing social and cultural barriers would not automatically fall. Depending on when aspirations for education and work are set – in primary school, between the ages of 11 and 16, and after 16 – the task for HEIs is either large or very large. If working-class students are turned off post-16 education and hence higher education early in their school careers, then the task of expanding aspirations and opportunities is a long-term one.

In the context of the present government's policies on social exclusion, there seems to be a contradiction at work. As Ruth Levitas (1999) has argued, 'New Labour' has significantly reduced the categories of people who are recognized as excluded. No longer, for example, is the whole working class excluded but only the most disaffected working-class boys. By implication, little needs to be done for the majority of the working class and, of course, the resources needed to tackle the 'really' excluded are likely to be less than those required to tackle wider forms of exclusion. The lesson of the Lynch and O'Riordan study may, in this context, be going unlearned. If the majority of the working class are not 'really' excluded, then little needs to be done to deal with economic disadvantage; all that is required is encouragement to change attitudes and to take advantage of the available opportunities in HE. The really excluded are, of course, nothing to do with HE and, at least in the short term, can have no aspirations to HE. This redefinition of who is excluded – the marginalization of positive action to the 'really' excluded – means that issues of student funding and the move from grants to loans/ fees, will not be seen as a major disincentive to enter HE.

Getting them in and keeping them there: the problem of equality assurance

Successfully widening participation in HE is only part of an equal opportunities agenda and, as we have seen above, has been only partly successful. It is also important to recognize that HEIs may have difficulties in accommodating diverse groups of students and that, in the extreme, there may be forms of institutional discrimination in HE. This is what Andrew Dorn (1991) asks us to contemplate in the following: 'for too long HE has been the victim of its own ideology. Discrimination has been rendered invisible by a liberal ethos that makes it difficult even to discuss the possibility of unequal treatment.'

HEFCE itself recognizes that, in the case of students from minority ethnic groups, 'there is growing interest in their experience both in HE and in their entry to the labour market' (HEFCE, 1996: 18). Studies by Bird (1996) and others indicate that what is involved here is some significantly negative experiences of being a black person in the higher education system. Brennan and McGeevor (1987, 1990) and Jenkins (1986), for example, further indicate that these experiences are carried into the labour market and into experiences of direct and indirect discrimination.

If this is the case then the possibility that HEIs are institutionally racist should be taken very seriously. The inquiry report into the handling of the Stephen Lawrence case (the Macpherson Report, discussed in more detail in Chapter 5) includes a definition of institutional racism which has received much attention. In the context of Dorn's quote above, unintended discrimination is a possibility (Home Office, 1999). What has received less attention is the Report's recommendations for education's role in tackling racial exclusion (Home Office, 1999: 334–5). We can put this in the form of a number of questions:

- Does your HEI value cultural diversity and prevent racism (para 67)?
- Does your HEI record, publish details of, and act on all racist incidents (para 68)?
- Did HEFCE (or will the Quality Assurance Agency) examine success in the above (para 69)?

The answers to these questions will be critical in identifying whether quality is being delivered or whether forms of institutional racism are happening. The Commission for Racial Equality (CRE), in a discussion on how to eliminate racial discrimination in education, indicates the possibilities for indirect discrimination in FE and HE (CRE, 1989). Two examples from the *Code of Practice for the Elimination of Racial Discrimination in Education*, both concerning admissions criteria, will suffice. First:

> 36. Requiring academic attainment that is in excess of the particular knowledge and skills needed to undertake the course would be indirectly discriminatory if this had the effect of excluding a considerably high proportion of students from particular racial groups and these requirements could not be shown to be justifiable on education grounds.
>
> (CRE, 1989: 16.17)

Modood and Shiner (1994) have already raised the issue of the extent to which the reliance on A-level scores for entry to HE might constitute indirect discrimination on the grounds that: (a) it is not clear that such scores measure the attainment necessary to succeed in higher education; and (b) that some 'racial' groups are disadvantaged in access to A-levels which is, in itself, a consequence of earlier exclusions operating in compulsory and post-16 education. Second:

> 37. The application of non-academic criteria in determining admissions, particularly where courses are over-subscribed and there is a supply of well-qualified candidates, may have the effect of excluding disproportionately high numbers of candidates from articulate racial groups who are otherwise academically suitable. Where they do so they would constitute unlawful indirect discrimination if they could not be shown to be justified.
>
> (CRE, 1989: 17)

The examples given include reference to hobbies, cultural interests, attitudes, sporting interests, appearance and communication skills. What is interesting here is not just whether such discriminatory admissions procedures occur, but how close these issues are to the studies of employment practice carried out by Jenkins (1986). Jenkins finds employers using suitability criteria – skills and qualification – but also using criteria relating to 'acceptability' – what does someone look like? will they fit in? what is the manager's gut feeling? It is in the context of acceptability that discrimination is most likely to occur and be most difficult to detect. The subjective criteria identified by the CRE are precisely related to whether a student is acceptable and how far judgments about acceptability override those associated with qualifications. Although Jenkins' study focuses on 'race' issues, ideas about acceptability (culture, dress, language, fitting in) are also likely to affect those who have not, traditionally, entered HE. Although anecdotes do not provide evidence, there is a telling anecdote about a mature working-class man studying on an access course for entry to HE. Part of his experience was as we would expect of someone who left school at 16 with no qualifications – lack of confidence and self-esteem, lack of academic skills – but he also carried other disadvantages, for example, his friends taking bets on when he would leave the course.

The recommendations coming from the Macpherson Report on education relate closely to what the Runnymede Trust (1993) calls 'equality assurance': high quality education in an environment which supports the development of cultural and personal identity and prepares people for full participation in society. If the diversity of social backgrounds is not reflected in participation rates in HE and if students from diverse backgrounds are experiencing discrimination, then equality is not being assured. Identifying whether or not this is the case requires comprehensive monitoring of the student experience – quantitative and qualitative monitoring – as well as explicit mechanisms to tackle exclusion from HE.

Conclusion

We can conclude and, hopefully, bring some clarity to the debate, by identifying two distinct models of access-related strategies. As Bargh *et al.* argue (1994 cited in HEFCE, 1996), there are two models. First, a sponsorship model which seeks either to sponsor those who have the qualifications but do not, at present, apply to HE or to help those who do not have standard qualifications, for example, by recognizing those with GNVQs. Second, an open or social justice model, which recognizes the effects of sustained disadvantage. This is where positive action strategies – for example, access courses for mature students – fit in. As Bargh *et al.* argue, there is a need also for HEIs to modify their programmes and their modes of delivery in order to accommodate such students.

The former strategy is easier and less costly but is unlikely to widen participation significantly. A long history of disadvantage is likely to result in many young people leaving school at 16, with little chance to be sponsored and this is significant beyond the debate about widening participation in HE. As we have seen, the present government's narrow definition of social exclusion – working-class white boys and African Caribbean boys who are excluded from school, for example – suggests that the problem is also narrow. If, however, the majority of the working class continues to be excluded from post-16 education, then the job for HE is a big one and the job is not just the responsibility of higher education.

Karen Ross (Chapter 5) has already outlined some of the strategies which can enhance participation by students from minority ethnic groups. Those strategies – community outreach, mentoring, links between HEIs and schools – are also likely to be successful for working-class students. They also suggest the importance of genuine partnerships between HEIs, providers of compulsory and post-16 education and communities. Equally, the things that will enhance the quality of the student experience – effective and comprehensive monitoring of students, flexible delivery of programmes, programmes that meet the needs of new groups of students – are also likely to provide a quality experience for all students. These strategies, therefore, constitute best practice for widening participation and give some guarantee that the quality of the student experience will be assured. They also constitute a basic set of strategies which can form the centre of institutional planning for wider participation and equality assurance.

We can finish with a question: are we to be liberals or radicals as far as equalizing opportunities is concerned? This is a distinction discussed by Jewson and Mason (1986). Liberal approaches emphasize the importance of free competition for positions between individuals and see equal opportunities policies as helping to ensure, through the right structures and systems of training, fairer competition between individuals. Positive action measures are an essential part of ensuring greater fairness and will ensure that *procedures* are just. Radical approaches are more structural and place much less of an emphasis on individuals. Fairness and the lack of it is a *group* phenomenon and fairness is assessed by looking at *outcomes* as well as procedures. For radicals, fair procedures can have unfair outcomes, that is, the commitment to fairness for individuals embedded within equal opportunities policies may have little effect on structures of inequality.

The point of the distinction drawn by Mason and Jewson is a lack of consistency in how people and organizations actually deal with unfairness. There seems to be an assumption – probably held by many in higher education who are concerned with wider participation – that the procedures favoured by a liberal approach will deliver the outcomes favoured by a radical approach.

References

Abramson, M., Bird, J. and Stennett, A. (1996) *Further and Higher Education Partnerships: The Future for Collaboration*. Buckingham: Society for Research into Higher Education and Open University Press.

Bargh, C., Scott, P. and Smith, D. (1994) Access and consolidation: the impact of reduced student intake on opportunities for non-standard applicants. Unpublished report to HEFCE. Leeds: University of Leeds.

Bird, J. F. (1996) *Black Students in Higher Education: Rhetorics and Realities*. Buckingham: Society for Research into Higher Education and Open University Press.

Brennan, J. and McGeevor, P. (1987) *The Employment of Graduates from Ethnic Minorities*. London: Commission for Racial Equality (CRE).

Brennan, J. and McGeevor, P. (1990) *Ethnic Minorities and the Graduate Labour Market*. London: CRE.

Commission for Racial Equality (1989) *Code of Practice for the Elimination of Racial Discrimination in Education*. London: CRE.

Committee on Higher Education (the Robbins Report) (1963) *Committee on Higher Education Report*, Cmnd. 2145. London: HMSO.

Dorn, A. (1991) Notes on ethnic minority participation in HE. Unpublished paper presented to the Widening Participation in HE Conference (organized by the Polytechnics and Colleges Funding Council), London, March.

Farish, M., McPake, J., Powney, J. and Weiner, G. (1995) *Equal Opportunities in Colleges and Universities: Towards Better Practice*. Buckingham: Society for Research into Higher Education and Open University Press.

Goldthorpe, J. (1980) *Social Mobility and Class Structure in Modern Britain*. Oxford: Clarendon Press.

Halsey, A., Heath, A. and Ridge, J. (1980) *Origins and Destinations*. Oxford: Clarendon Press.

Higher Education Funding Council for England (1996) *Widening Participation in Higher Education*. A report by the HEFCE's Advisory Group on Access and Participation. Bristol: HEFCE M 9/96.

Higher Education Funding Council for England (1998) *Consultation: Widening Participation Funding Proposals*. Bristol: HEFCE 98/39.

Higher Education Funding Council for England (1999) *Widening Participation: Special Funding Programme, 1998–1999*. Bristol: HEFCE 99/07.

Home Office (1999) *The Stephen Lawrence Inquiry* (the Macpherson Report). Cmnd. CM 4262–1, London: HMSO.

Jewson, N. and Mason, D. (1986) The theory and practice of equal opportunities: liberal and radical approaches, *Sociological Review*, 34(2): 307–34.

Jewson, N., Mason, D., Drewett, A. and Rossiter, W. (1995*)* *Formal Equal Opportunities Policies and Employment Best Practice*. London: Department for Education and Employment (DfEE), Research Series no. 69.

Jenkins, R. (1986) *Racism and Recruitment*. Cambridge: Cambridge University Press.

Levitas, R. (1999) *The Inclusive Society: New Labour and Social Exclusion*. London: Polity Press.

Lynch, K. and O'Riordan, C. (1998) Inequality in Higher Education: a study of class barriers, *British Journal of Sociology of Education*, 19(4): 445–78.

Metcalf, H. (1993) *Non-Traditional Students' Experience of HE: A Review of the Literature*. London: CVCP.

Modood, T. and Shiner, L. (1994) *Ethnic Minorities and Higher Education*. London: Policy Studies Institute.

Neal, S. (1998) *The Making of Equal Opportunities Policies in Higher Education*. Buckingham: Society for Research into Higher Education and Open University Press.

Parry, G. and Wake, C. (1990) *Access and Alternative Futures for Higher Education*. London: Hodder and Stoughton.

Polytechnics and Colleges Funding Council (PCFC) (1992) *Widening Participation in Higher Education: Report of a Study of Polytechnics and Colleges of Higher Education in England*. Bristol: PCFC.

Robertson, D. and Hillman, J. (1997) Widening participation in HE for students from lower socio-economic groups and students with disabilities, in *National Commission of Inquiry into Higher Education (the Dearing Report) Higher Education in the Learning Society*, Report 6: 32–68. Norwich: HMSO.

Runnymede Trust (1993) *Equality Assurance in Schools*. London: Trentham Books.

Part 3

Institutional Measures to
Promote Equality of Opportunity

9

The Role of Senior Management

Diana Woodward

Introduction

It is the responsibility of the most senior tier of staff in a university or college to establish long-term strategic goals for the institution's development or survival, and to take appropriate action in the short- and medium-term in order to move towards these goals, in anticipation of and in response to changing external and internal factors. Managing a large enterprise such as a university or college, many of which are now among the largest employers within their local communities, is not unlike steering an ocean liner. Within the five or ten years' tenure typical of vice-chancellors it may be possible to develop the organization in a new direction to the extent of (at most) merging with a smaller local institution, or more typically constructing a new building or two, or restructuring the organization's configuration of departments, or achieving modest improvements in the average grades awarded to subjects through the external scrutiny of teaching and learning or research. It has become all too evident in recent years that vice-chancellors also have the capacity to inflict serious damage on their organization through financial impropriety or the reckless pursuit of policies which jeopardize the quality of the education provided or the institution's reputation. However, apart from a few headline-catching cases, the typical vice-chancellor's period at the helm (to continue the nautical analogy) is generally too short, and the time-lag in changing a university's image for the outside world is too great to implement a fundamental change in its ethos, identity and character. This is a particularly difficult situation to manage when external funding is static or contracting, and there are no subsidized schemes to promote early retirement, which make it virtually impossible to appoint significant numbers of new staff who might be expected to bring with them a fresh approach (or can be selected in order to achieve a dramatic shift in the staffing profile or organizational culture, for example by age, qualifications and research capability). It may take a generation to achieve a major enhancement in the public perception of an institution.

An anecdote illustrates this. Soon after the UK's former polytechnics received university designation following the Further and Higher Education Act (1992), an audience of academics at a conference was asked to give their names and to identify their institutions when putting questions to the speaker. When one questioner identified his institution as the newly designated Teesside University, several delegates behind him struggled to suppress their scornful laughter at the notion of the former Teesside Polytechnic now being a university. However, when asked which institution they represented they proudly answered 'Brunel', without any conception that exactly the same interchange might have taken place in the mid-1960s, but this time with them as the butt of the laughter. Following the publication of the Robbins Report in 1963, nine English colleges of advanced technology became universities, including Brunel, which moved from Acton to a larger site at Uxbridge. With their heavy concentration on engineering and the applied sciences, close industrial links, commitment to sandwich courses, and teaching staff who were typically less well-qualified academically than university staff were then (Halsey and Trow, 1971), these institutions were for many years held in rather low esteem by the academic community of the then 'old' universities. This is itself ironic, since many of them had experienced a similar elevation not so many years earlier from being university colleges offering London University external degrees. Leicester University only achieved this status in 1957 and when I studied there a decade later some of the staff offices were in 'temporary' buildings which reputedly had been part of the lunatic asylum which formerly occupied the site. And so the cycle continues of institutions' admission to the league of major players, followed by the slow and grudging acceptance of their right to belong by virtue of the standards of their entering students, their calibre and employability at graduation, and the quality of staff members' research.

My point is that universities acquire over a period of many years a reputation for having a certain character, which may or may not be accurate and well founded. In most cases it will be somewhat out-of-date, as parents and other graduates disseminate views based on their own student experiences, often years earlier. It may also be based on partial information, particularly in relation to applicants from homes with no tradition of university education. A study by Lesley Pugsley, of the School of Education at the University of Wales, Cardiff, of 700 sixth-formers and their families in south-east Wales, found that middle-class parents were, not surprisingly, much more discriminating and better informed in their aspirations for their children's higher education (reported in *THES*, 21 August 1998). This was particularly true in relation to 'the rhetoric of equality surrounding the former polytechnics', where the middle-class parents 'decoded' the implications for entry to the labour market, whereas some of the young people from working-class homes made ill-informed choices about A-level subjects (the principal qualifications used as entry criteria for a place at a university or college of higher education), type of course and selection of relevant university, with unfortunate consequences.

The decision to signal a commitment to equal opportunities, where no such aim already exists, must therefore be handled judiciously if this claim is to carry sufficient credibility to lead to changed perceptions and behaviour in the wider community (such as greater willingness for members of certain social groups to apply for posts or student places). It is unlikely to be successful if it diverges too far from the institution's existing profile and priorities. Furthermore, this is not the kind of institutional change which can successfully be achieved by top-down imposition, without genuine commitment from both middle managers and the staff who will be responsible for implementing real change at the inter-faces with potential applicants and actual students.

For example, a newly appointed Master of Trinity College, Cambridge, or Balliol College, Oxford, might wish to recruit a higher proportion of mature student entrants from access courses at deprived inner-city further education colleges, possibly in response to political or financial pressures to broaden their university's recruitment base. He (or even she?) might find this to be a chal-lenging task, given the well-established reputation of Oxbridge in general, and these colleges in particular, for recruiting terrifyingly intelligent school leavers from privileged backgrounds, with a clutch of A-level passes at grade A, who may well find themselves tutored on an individual basis within the college by Nobel prize winners or Fellows of the Royal Society. Before embarking on such an initiative, the Master should ensure that appropriate support mechanisms exist to enable students from radically different social groups to feel that they have someone approachable on whose services they can call, who understands both the college's and the university's norms, expectations and requirements. Many institutions have chaplains to meet the needs of students from different religious affiliations, and have international officers to support overseas stu-dents. Others have 'buddy' systems to pair up experienced students with novices. Formal and informal measures of this kind are needed to ensure that students who lack the 'cultural capital' to feel confident in higher education, for whatever reasons, have easy access to the kinds of advice and support they need to help them to thrive.

Few of these potential recruits will know the exact proportion of Trinity or Balliol students who have come from state schools or who are mature students, but their initial attitudes to any overtures from the college will be based upon their image of a typical Oxbridge college, which may well be out-of-date or inaccurate in other respects. Likewise, the inner London former polytechnics are perceived as places which typically recruit local students seeking to acquire, often on a part-time basis, the qualifications and skills which will help them to enter or to progress in their chosen careers. For one of these universities to develop a reputation for high-level scholarship in, say, classics (as an avoca-tional discipline taught more in fee-paying schools than in the state sector) might be an uphill struggle, given its lack of consonance with the institution's current missions and the character of its students and staff.

To overcome the perception of the intended recruits, whether staff or stu-dents, that 'this is not somewhere where I would expect to feel comfortable, and where I will be able to find other people like me' will require assiduous, well-planned effort. This next section is intended to suggest why vice-chancellors and other senior managers might want to make this kind of effort to change the status quo and external perceptions of their institutions, and how this can be achieved. The issues to be addressed are: the institutional image; the establishment of an institutional policy which includes an explicit commitment in the mission statement; implementation of the mission, in both quantitative and qualitative terms; and, finally, embedding equal opportunities in the normal functioning of the institution.

Institutional image

Fairly well-developed, if stereotyped, images of the character of major higher education institutions have long existed, at least within the academic community itself, if less so in the outside world. Now that higher education has become a mass concern which impinges on a far higher proportion of the population than a generation ago, either directly as students themselves or as the parents or partners of students, these perceptions may be more widely held and possibly better informed, thanks to the publication of authoritative/official and scurrilous/informal guides to aid the initial choice of a place to study. Effective marketing requires a strong 'brand image', with identified selling points chosen to differentiate between the many universities, which are promulgated in prospectuses and recruitment advertising targeted at both staff and students. Senior managers need to ask themselves some direct questions, and to arrive at some honest answers, about the character of their own institutions, and market research is needed to test how far the wider public shares these perceptions.

Potential students and members of staff, whether recruited locally or nationally, will have their perceptions of the institution influenced by the image presented in undergraduate and postgraduate prospectuses and in recruitment advertising, both for courses and for posts. These materials represent the character of the institution, as its senior managers see it. Is there a prominent heraldic badge in press advertisements, perhaps with a Latin inscription? If so, this signifies tradition, elitism and social exclusion, as does the use of a classic font for the written material. Or are the graphics more modern and lively? This could, to the kind of sophisticated middle-class parents studied by Lesley Pugsley (*THES*, 21 August 1998), denote a university which does not have an academic tradition to boast about! Does the prospectus mainly show images of young, white school-leavers, with sport and alcohol-related leisure activities prominently represented? Is the crèche mentioned, with information about its location, cost and waiting list? Are there profiles of successful students and graduates who represent a diversity of age, ethnicity and entry qualifications? Every institution claims to be friendly, but do the images presented clearly demonstrate social diversity, so that potential applicants can identify with the students and staff members shown in these recruitment materials? Is the text aimed at a particular segment of the market, or will a range of potential applicants see these materials as emanating from a university with an ethos with which they are likely to feel comfortable?

The establishment of institutional policy

Having established the current character and image of an institution, it is then necessary to determine what kind of place the staff want their university to be. What does it stand for? What are its long-term aims? What values do its members hold dear? Does its history provide a basis for its contemporary values and objectives? How is it regarded externally? Does it have a regional, national or international reputation? For what achievements does it have an external reputation? A decade ago many academics would have reacted in horror at the notion of having to devise a Mission Statement, as something that American-owned fast food chains or computer software firms might have, but which were anathema to universities. In the short time since the introduction of a national process for assessing the quality of students' learning experience, all universities and colleges have now devised formal, stated missions, not least because it is required within the self-assessment document which sets the agenda for the assessment visit. Discussions about mission at university level have been echoed by a similar debate within departments to identify their distinctive goals, aims and objectives within the broader framework set for the institution as a whole. Many academics have, somewhat to their surprise, found these debates to be illuminating and useful in helping to forge an explicit shared vision for their departments, whereas hitherto there may have been few opportunities to review or discuss fundamental issues of this kind. It is clearly important to base an institutional mission statement on broad consultation, involving both 'top-down' and 'bottom-up' communication, as well as debates within the appropriate committees, to ensure that the points identified as its distinctive characteristics and the values identified as paramount receive wide endorsement.

At all levels within institutional hierarchies these statements of mission or aims and objectives must be grounded in reality, building upon a core of achievements which can be identified and publicized. The same point applies to recruitment materials, if students and staff are to feel that their own values accord with those of the institution. Wherever possible, these claims should mesh with the external reputation of the university or department, assuming that this perception is both positive and well founded, to avoid the need for intensive publicity to modify an inappropriate public image. Adverse publicity, especially concerning academic standards or financial probity, is likely to have a swift but enduring damaging effect on an institution's reputation. Most universities and colleges will wish to claim that they strive to achieve excellence in their teaching and research as justification for the investment of public money which maintains them, and as justification for the quality of their academic work. Others have in recent years additionally identified a commitment to widening access to higher education, or to the promotion of equal opportunities.

The Quality Assessment Division of the Higher Education Funding Council for England gathered policy statements on equal opportunities from HEIs in 1996. Kingston University, for example, had an explicit policy which commits the university to equality of treatment regardless of gender, age, disablement, colour, race, ethnic or national origin (all monitored) and class, sexual orientation, mental status, family responsibilities, religion or political beliefs. The University of Kent had a policy pertaining to staff and students covering harassment, publicity and recruitment, admissions, curriculum, teaching and assessment, support services, accommodation and access, staff/student relations and monitoring. Cranfield University offered merely an employment code of practice and the Royal Academy of Music had only a draft policy on equal opportunities in employment at that time.

If the consultation exercise leading to the production of the mission statement has involved dialogue throughout the university, drawing in staff in all departments through departmental meetings, discussion within the appropriate committees, and in other contexts, then all staff will feel that they have had an opportunity to contribute to its development. Then, if the agreed mission is publicized internally within the institution through a newsletter or whatever, they will learn of the outcome and will be expecting to hear how its aims are to be achieved. It should inform strategic planning by seeking to translate general aims into specific objectives, with targets identified towards their attainment. We will return to this later. The mission statement should be widely disseminated within materials generated for external consumption, such as undergraduate and postgraduate prospectuses, and the annual report, to inform their readership about the institution's values and aims.

Graham Upton, Vice-Chancellor of Oxford Brookes University, explained earlier in Chapter 2 why he sees a commitment to promoting equality of opportunity as an institutional priority. This is not a new theme in tertiary education; the mechanics institutes' movement which spread through Britain in the first half of the nineteenth century was set up to provide education for young industrial workers who, at that time, had no hope of entering university. The redoubtable Henry Sidgwick of the University of Cambridge was not only a pioneer of the Oxford and Cambridge Extension movement which sought to make university education available in provincial cities, but he was also a leading figure in the struggle for women's access to higher education (Halsey and Trow, 1971; McWilliams-Tullberg, 1975). For many vice-chancellors, a modern version of the same set of values justifies their university's place in the community and provides a moral template for developing policies and making management decisions. Where this goal coincides with other institutional priorities, so much the better. Also, there is growing encouragement at national level for regional collaborations which link higher education institutions with each other and with local industry and commerce.

To give an example, the development of close links with a 'feeder' further education college which specializes in supporting hearing-impaired students, who would be expected to move on to the university after taking the first year of their degree courses in the college, will incur development costs. These might include installing technical aids such as hearing-induction loops in classrooms and the provision of vibrating alarm clocks to resident students, and investment in staff development. However, by ensuring that these students will receive the best possible technical and personal support, the university will gain a reputation within regional and national networks for providing a good service to hearing-impaired students, which may well attract able students from further afield. Also, the improvements in the delivery of teaching arising from the staff training (such as improved diction and lecture presentation, and the production of handouts summarising the main points of each class) are likely to benefit *all* students.

Any drive to promote equal opportunities needs to take into account, as a starting point, the current profile of the institution and its stage of development towards attaining parity of opportunity and achievement for students and staff from all social groups. It is immoral and ultimately self-defeating to launch a campaign to recruit more students from minority backgrounds, for example, unless an institution's senior staff are confident that these students can be adequately supported and encouraged during their studies. If there are virtually no minority ethnic academic staff, and no attempt is made to adapt staff attitudes, or to establish student support systems to enable the needs of this new group to be identified and met, then their subsequent progression is likely to be affected, leading to higher rates of withdrawal and academic failure. It is well known that students tend to approach people with whom they feel comfortable (rather than their formally designated academic tutor or student welfare officer) to discuss any difficulties with their work or personal lives, so if they are unable to identify members of staff whom they regard as sympathetic and understanding, they may well not see their courses through to successful completion.

Implementation of the mission: 1 Achieving quantitative change

Having determined that the university's mission should include a commitment to broadening opportunity to social groups beyond the traditional narrow confines of the children of the middle classes, the next stage is to develop an equal opportunities policy which is both consonant with it and which will help to promote institutional aims. This will involve devising policies, seeking to implement them, supporting them through staff development, and evaluating and monitoring progress, followed by the periodic review of both the policies and their implementation. As with other aspects of the manager's role, the promotion of equal opportunities is most easily handled when it is embedded within the standard systems and procedures of the institution, rather than being separate from and outside of these regular arrangements. The appropriate procedures for devising an equal opportunities policy are likely to be similar to those employed within the institution to draft the institutional mission together with departments' own missions. Whether this is done by a committee, a working party or an executive group, together with appropriate consultation to promote 'ownership', the same consonance must be achieved between central and local objectives, backed by local implementation.

The most suitable over-arching mechanism within which to address equal opportunities issues is the development and implementation of the strategic plan. At institutional level, targets can be set which arise from the mission, and these can be adopted and adapted to fit local circumstances by departments and courses in setting their own objectives and reporting on progress towards their attainment. These targets will differentiate between departments and units concerned with student or with staffing matters, but the same principles apply. As with other matters of institutional policy, there needs to be effective dialogue between central managers and local managers responsible for implementation to ensure that the targets set are sufficiently ambitious to bring about real change within a reasonable time-frame, but yet are achievable, given sufficient impetus.

At the present time a plethora of initiatives is being developed and implemented, at regional, national and even international level (through European funding), to expand recruitment to higher education and to broaden the social profile of those admitted. Some of the major programmes are mentioned within this volume, but the fast-changing nature of this aspect of higher education means that it is not possible to cover them all, and any attempt to do so would quickly become dated. Senior managers need to establish measures to ensure that funding opportunities of this kind are identified as they arise, and that high-level scrutiny takes place to ensure that those which fit the institution's mission are pursued, while at the same time avoiding the 'promiscuous opportunism' to which universities have become prey, in their unremitting search for additional funding. Most institutions will have established processes, probably based in registries or strategic planning departments, for managing responses to initiatives and identifying which initiatives are worth pursuing, in terms of the likely benefits and the opportunity costs of preparing bids. It is also important to operate an internal system for funnelling information and bids through a senior 'gatekeeper' to ensure that staff time is not wasted on preparing competing bids and that only the strongest bids, which have received institutional endorsement, are submitted. Once again, any initiatives relating to equal opportunities ideally should not be handled any differently from other kinds of development. Rather, they should be processed within standard institutional systems and procedures, as far as is appropriate, with the input of specialist expertise being managed along the same lines as would any other kind of application for external funding.

National or regional peer networks are invaluable for sharing intelligence and ideas about funding opportunities and initiatives. The growing impetus for partnerships between higher education institutions, which was endorsed by the Dearing Report (NCIHE, 1997), can contribute to this process. Bids from regional consortia or institutions, or from broader networks united by discipline or other common characteristic (such as professional concern for people with a specific kind of disability), will shorten the odds of submitting a successful bid by reducing the number of competing bids, and will strengthen partnerships which may subsequently be mobilized for other purposes. Once the senior or middle-management staff from a group of educational institutions or other organizations have established good working relationships and mutual understanding of each others' institutions, a basis then exists for other kinds of collaboration in terms of inter-personal trust and possibly formal memoranda of co-operation. Future co-operative ventures then become more easily achieved, whether they are matters associated with institutions' strategic plans (which are under their control and take place at a time-scale of their own choice) or rapid responses to externally driven initiatives.

Within the institution there will almost certainly be groups of colleagues or individuals who are knowledgeable and committed to the principle and practice of equal opportunities, whether as a global concept or a particular aspect of it. Their expertise and energies represent a valuable resource, which may be mobilized to advise on the formulation of local plans and their implementation, or they could be brought together on a cross-institution basis to look at equal opportunities across the board or issue by issue. If they are appointed to short-life working parties, for example to advise on setting and implementing the first round of central and local targets for equal opportunities, then again the outcomes when agreed should be embedded in the institution's standard systems. Some mechanism needs to be found which harmonizes with these systems, but which enables this expert knowledge to inform the management of departments and units. If the newly devised mission involves a shift from the status quo, then the heads of the departments or units at the level where change is to occur need to be motivated to support this innovation; to be able to call on expert advice to help them to set realistic targets; and to achieve changes in the institution's culture and practices which will bring them about. Leicester and Lovell (1994) found that most higher education institutions mentioned equal opportunities in their mission statements or had explicit policies on equal opportunities. However, less than 10 per cent of the departments they surveyed in pre-1992 universities had similar policies and just 2 per cent had a formal policy on women, even though the recruitment of both students and staff mainly takes place at this level. Clearly incentives, staff training and policies need to be targeted at this level.

Quantitative data already collected for other purposes may provide useful information for setting targets, a process which is often called 'benchmarking'. To give an example: if an analysis of the student profile for the whole institution or for departments, disciplines or courses within it indicates that it is significantly different from that of other institutions with a similar catchment area or recruitment base, or that a certain group within the local community is seriously under-represented (if the mission is geared to local recruitment), then this needs to be addressed. What would be appropriate targets to set ? Over what period might they realistically be achieved? Why is X University succeeding where we are failing in the recruitment of students from a specific social group? Comparative data should be available nationally which throw light on a number of relevant issues: in the UK, sources such as HEFCE Institutional Profiles or information produced from institutions' returns to the Higher Education Statistics Agency (HESA) could be used. Such data will enable institutions to compare their own performance in a number of respects with other similar institutions. Also, certain commercial consultancy firms which have devised effective systems for benchmarking in further education colleges are now seeking clients in higher education, and are keen to improve the bases of their comparisons by extending the range of institutions on which they hold data.

Internally generated quantitative data will enable similar comparisons to be made between departments or courses or student cohorts. Once again, the more that this exercise is based on standard practices, the easier it will be to undertake these comparisons and to review them annually. For this reason it is essential to have data collected within the institution using exactly the same conventions and categorizations, and preferably on the same basis as, say, the HESA data. This will facilitate both internal and external comparisons, with the capacity to interrogate them in relation to a whole series of variables associated with equal opportunities. The same point applies to data on staffing, although national comparisons are difficult except for some fairly basic issues such as the profile of teaching staff in general and specific grades like the professoriate, in terms of gender and ethnic origin. Where such data are not routinely or reliably collected within an institution, and it seems unlikely that they can be within the current configuration of systems, it may be worth undertaking a one-off survey to establish the current situation. Depending on the scale and complexity of this task, it could be carried out across the institution, or sampling techniques could be used to provide illustrative comparisons. However this exercise is done, it must be capable of generating the data that managers need in order to identify whether they have an issue in their own area which needs to be addressed. Managers may find it useful to have a regular statistical bulletin issued, covering a range of useful information which indicates how well their own area is performing in relation to others within the institution.

The details of how change might be implemented at local level towards the attainment of institutional objectives follows later. At university level, arrangements can be established to check on progress through the annual updating of strategic plans, when heads of units are required to report on action taken and achievements in relation to the previous year's plan, at the same time as specifying targets for the current year. Their reports will be informed by other cyclical processes such as student recruitment and course monitoring, so their timing should be synchronized to follow them.

Implementation of the mission: 2   Achieving qualitative change

Having set a mission which incorporates a commitment to equal opportunities, and then establishing strategic objectives which reflect this commitment, backed up by the specification of quantitative targets, the next task is to promote greater knowledge and awareness in the staff who are expected to achieve these objectives. The culture of the organization may need fairly radical change, in terms of modifying the way that staff members interact with students and their expectations of them in relation to a range of issues. It is likely that the staff in some departments already have well-considered systems, practices and codes to support students from disadvantaged groups, whose expertise can be mobilized to provide development sessions for other staff. Over the past decade, staff in British university departments of social work, for example, have been required by their professional course validation agency to address issues of anti-discriminatory practice within the curriculum. They are therefore likely to have the technical knowledge, the sensitivity and the pedagogic capacity to be able to offer effective training to other staff. Great skill and diplomacy may be needed to achieve a shift in prevailing practice; each person feels that their views and behaviour are reasonable and rational, but where a departmental culture or an individual's behaviour is experienced by students or other members of staff as patronizing or overbearing, it needs to be challenged. To achieve this effectively it may be helpful to use external trainers, perhaps chosen on the advice of colleagues in social work or staff development departments, if it is thought that these hard messages are unlikely to be well received from internal colleagues.

This kind of staff development needs to cover experiential issues about discrimination and prejudice, about mutual respect and valuing diversity, about sexual harassment and bullying behaviour, about body language and styles of speech, and about cultural variations in attitudes, customs and behaviour. It also needs to cover the need to review the curriculum and its delivery and assessment, adapting it where necessary to meet the needs of new student groups. A whole series of technical issues should also be addressed, such as legal issues in hiring and promoting staff and available sources of expert advice, as well as issues about promoting good practice. These might include improving and adapting support mechanisms, for example by establishing peer support groups with departmental support, and actively seeking to shift the staffing profile by encouraging suitably qualified staff from under-represented groups to apply. Appropriate wording in job advertisements might include:

> 'The University of X is an Equal Opportunities Employer and welcomes applications from all sections of the community.'

> 'We particularly welcome applications from black people and members of other minority ethnic groups and disabled people who are under-represented in the workforce; all applications are considered on merit.'

> 'We are seeking to appoint a lecturer with experience of teaching, research publications and commercial consultancy in Soil Mechanics, who will also be able to take responsibility for the department's school link initiative to encourage young women to consider studying engineering.'

The final one is a fictional example designed to show how the way in which a post is described can help the department to achieve broader objectives, by encouraging members of under-represented groups to apply, and providing signals that their minority status will be positively valued. The usual way of seeking to fill a gap in the staff profile has been addressed (namely, in terms of sub-disciplinary expertise), but this advertisement conveys the additional implicit message that, all other things being equal, the appointment of a woman would be preferred. However, this approach is only likely to work where the pool of applicants is likely to be sufficiently large to permit this level of selectivity to be exercised. In very esoteric fields or where posts are hard to fill, it may not be feasible. University personnel departments will offer technical advice about the legality of recruitment advertisements.

Staff development and training on equal opportunities are of the utmost importance in persuading staff, who are the key to improving the student experience, of the need to review their practice and also in offering them the means to do so. It is therefore vital that the most senior staff of the institution demonstrate publicly their own commitment to this task by attending training sessions themselves, for the whole session, and showing by their attentive involvement that this is an institutional priority.

A further issue requiring early attention is the development and dissemination of an institutional code of practice (or perhaps several of them, tailored to specific groups within the academic community) concerning discriminatory behaviour or harassment, with specified sanctions and procedures for investigating any violation of its code. Once again, the expertise of knowledgeable individuals will be invaluable here. They might be invited to join a working party, together with representatives from each of the major areas of the institution, to discuss, consult, explain and champion the code (or codes) with their colleagues. To have such a document available and its existence publicized is to proclaim a commitment to protecting the rights of students and staff from all social groups. The specification of what constitutes unacceptable behaviour, in this form, provides a means by which students or members of staff can make a complaint if they feel that these rights have been violated.

Embedding equal opportunities

The preceding sections have dealt with some 'first order' issues to be faced by institutions seeking to promote equality of opportunity, starting from a fairly low base of awareness and commitment at senior level. However, many institutions have progressed in recent years much further down the road towards equality of opportunity. Many of them have developed effective arrangements for shifting their recruitment profile for both students and staff, and for promoting parity of esteem and opportunity within the organization for all its members. One simple device is to help to establish homogeneous peer networks, capable of providing mentoring and informal support. Examples include a women managers' network, or a black social work students' group (with a regular timetable slot and administrative support if its members want it). Also, a steady number of guides and reports have been issued in recent years to offer guidance on good practice. Staff and student unions in higher education have an exemplary record of disseminating useful information on equal opportunities issues, and these are regularly updated or reissued. Some useful publications are listed below. The state of knowledge is such that it is impossible here to cover the whole field in depth for those unfamiliar with this literature. However, information can be given on what kind of issues senior managers should be considering and advice offered on appropriate sources of information.

One extremely comprehensive and useful publication for those with managerial responsibility for equal opportunities in higher education is *Higher Education and Equality: A Guide* (Powney *et al.*, 1997), which was jointly sponsored by the Commission for Racial Equality, the Equal Opportunities Commission and the Committee of Vice-Chancellors and Principals. This handbook begins with a section which explains the rationale for equality in higher education, introduces the legal issues, and provides checklists of items which should be included in equal opportunities policies, practices and performance indicators. The main part of the booklet addresses each of the principal activities and functions of the university in turn, and poses questions about how equal opportunities policies might be pursued and implemented. It concludes with examples of good practice and lists of sources of further information.

References

Halsey, A. H. and Trow, M. (1971) *The British Academics*. London: Faber.

Leicester, M. and Lovell, T. (1994) Equal opportunities and university practice. Race, gender and disability: a comparative perspective, *Journal of Further and Higher Education*, 18(2): 43–51.

McWilliams-Tullberg, R. (1975) *Women at Cambridge: A Men's University, Though of a Mixed Type*. London: Gollancz.

National Committee of Inquiry into Higher Education (the Dearing Report) (1997). *Higher Education in the Learning Society*. Norwich: HMSO.

Powncy, J., Hamilton, S. and Weiner, G. (1997) *Higher Education and Equality: A Guide*. London: Commission for Racial Equality, Equal Opportunities Commission and the Committee of Vice-Chancellors and Principals.

Quality Assessment Division (1996) *Institutional Policy Statements on Equal Opportunities*. Bristol: Higher Education Funding Council for England.

Useful sources of information

The Equal Opportunities Commission, Overseas House, Quay Street, Manchester M3 3HN. Tel: 0161 833 9244
  Equal Opportunities: A Guide for Employers to the Sex Discrimination Acts, 1975 and 1986
  Sexual Harassment: What You Can Do about It
  Part-time Workers, Not Second Class Citizens: Guidance to Employers on the Employment of Part-time Staff
The Association of University Teachers, United House, 9 Pembridge Road, London W11 3JY. Tel: 020 7221 4370
  Equal Opportunities, Employment and Domestic Responsibilities
  Dealing with Harassment: A Guide to Handling Complaints

The National Association of Teachers in Further and Higher Education, 27 Britannia Street, London WC1X 9JP. Tel: 020 7837 3636

Race Equality in Further and Higher Education
Fighting Extremist Homophobia
Lesbian and Gay Rights at Work: An Issue for NATFHE Branches
Advice on Consensual Relations between Staff and Students
Age Discrimination: A Discussion and Policy Document
Equal Opportunities: A Best Practice Guide for Negotiators
Equal Opportunities in Staff Appraisal and Development
Harassment at Work: How to Deal with It

10

The Role of Middle Management

Diana Woodward

Introduction

The preceding chapter explored the ways in which senior managers in a university or college can shift the ethos of the institutions they manage, and, if they are serious in their commitment to equal opportunities, the kind of measures they need to take to promote real organizational changes for their staff and students. This chapter addresses similar issues, but for staff in management roles below directorate level. The matters discussed here should provide both an awareness of the main issues and some ideas about appropriate initiatives for such people as deans and heads of departments or schools. This is addressed mainly to managers in academic areas, but also to those in generic 'support' functional areas where service delivery may benefit from being reviewed in the light of a changing student profile. It is beyond the scope of this book to deal with those university-wide specialist roles where the implementation of equal opportunities is an inherent part of the job, such as student counsellors or personnel staff. Their incumbents will already have extensive technical knowledge of these matters, coupled with an appropriate awareness of local circumstances. Their expertise provides a useful resource for managers in seeking to bring about changes in the organization's policies and practices.

Some of the points which follow deal with the work of admissions tutors, personal tutors and other staff at the interface between student and university. Although these are not strictly management roles, academic managers do need to have some understanding of the work of these people in order to be able to promote change in an informed way.

As in other chapters, distinctions are made between issues concerning students and those concerning members of staff. However, here the distinction is not such a clear-cut conceptual matter as it is in other chapters, as the promotion of equal opportunities in relation to staff in academic and support departments will have a direct and beneficial impact on the student experience. As mentioned in the previous chapter, a useful handbook for managers seeking practical guidance on the implementation of equal opportunities policies and practices is *Higher Education and Equality: A Guide* (Powney *et al.*, 1997), which is jointly published by the Equal Opportunities Commission, the Commission for Racial Equality and the Committee of Vice-Chancellors and Principals of the Universities of the UK.

The impetus for changing the student experience: 'top-down' and local initiatives

Change towards the more assiduous promotion of equal opportunities within academic faculties and departments may be precipitated by a range of factors. First, the institution's mission may have undergone review, leading to pressures for change coming from the highest level of management. This may be the case when a new vice-chancellor is appointed, who may wish to shift the university's ethos. Alternatively, there may be a strategic shift in direction, again set at this senior level, in response to changing external conditions such as an opportunity (for example, a funding council initiative offering additional income or extra funded student places) or a problem (for example, a downturn in student applications and recruitment from the customary social groups for that institution).

Where change is initiated in a 'top-down' way, clear messages are likely to be forthcoming about the desired direction of any change, together with specific guidance about the outcomes sought, for example as a series of targets for achievement over a specified period of time. There may be less guidance provided about the 'how' of implementation – what steps to take to move from the status quo to the desired position – either because this is left to departments to address in ways which are appropriate for them, or because the culture of the organization emphasizes local management autonomy coupled with accountability. If clear direction about both targets and strategy is forthcoming from the most senior level of management, then the middle manager's task in implementing them is made easier, at least in the sense that they are not expected to devise their own strategy. If this is not the case, and the level of collegiality permits it, it may be worth seeking to set up an informal meeting of peers from within middle management to share thinking and, if possible, to devise a common approach. This will provide an opportunity to reflect on the issues in the company of informed peers, and will also provide reassurance for individual managers that their own approach will not be too far out of line when they are held accountable for the progress made in their area at some future time.

Managers in the UK's 'post-1992' universities are familiar with this centralized approach to strategic planning. This form of explicit centralized executive authority is less common in the 'old' universities, where decision-making is ostensibly made by large committees such as Senate, and middle managers see themselves as academics first and managers second (if at all, and even so, any management roles are likely to be temporary fixed-term distractions from the 'real job' of writing for publication). Changing circumstances are bringing with them stronger central planning in the 'old' universities. 'Central planning' is probably a more acceptable label in this context than 'hierarchical management', and in practice power may be wielded by the registrar rather than the vice-chancellor. At the same time, perversely, in the 'new' universities greater local autonomy has passed from the vice-chancellor or director to faculties and schools since the former polytechnics' incorporation as independent businesses, freed from local authority control. Massive increases in the size of these universities mean that faculties may now have thousands of students – as many as whole universities had, a generation ago – making it impossible to exercise the kind of close centralized scrutiny and hands-on management of even minor issues which prevailed as recently as ten or fifteen years ago. These large units within the organization have therefore been accorded substantial freedom to pursue their own academic and financial objectives, within a framework of centrally-set objectives and procedures. In these circumstances, deans and heads of department in both pre- and post-1992 universities now enjoy considerable latitude to pursue policies of their own choosing, as long as they are financially viable and can be justified in terms of the organization's mission.

A couple of case studies, one actual and one hypothetical, may serve to illustrate the kinds of problems currently facing senior and middle managers in relation to the promotion of equal opportunities. These both raise issues of institutional responsiveness to external factors, and require collaborative endeavour by managers at various levels in the hierarchy. First, the case of undergraduate students at the universities of Oxford and Cambridge, which have recently been put on the defensive by national political concerns and which require sophisticated handling. Its colleges are currently under public scrutiny for both quantitative and qualitative reasons. Quantitatively, their recruitment profile is far out of line with that of other higher education institutions and with the national profile for secondary education in terms of the proportion of students who come from fee-paying schools (cited in *The Guardian*, 24 May 1999). This implies a social class skew, but there is also a significant distortion in the proportion of mature students recruited (which receives far less public attention). The standard Oxbridge entry requirement is three grade As at GCSE A-level. Seventy per cent of those who achieve this nationally do so at state schools. Over half of Oxbridge entrants have been privately educated, although fewer than 10 per cent of the nation's pupils are. This admissions profile has barely changed in over two decades, even though the state school students' performance is better in final degree examinations, and both universities have set up initiatives to encourage applications from members of under-represented groups. The blockage appears to lie in the perceptions of Oxbridge held by potential applicants from state schools, who think they may not fit in there, or in the interview process, which may confer advantage on public school pupils who are able to mobilize 'cultural capital' (including confidence and eloquence in presenting themselves), derived from their educational advantage.

Qualitatively, there are concerns about the experiences of women students at the University of Cambridge, given its well-documented history of misogyny and the continuing dearth of senior women academic staff who provide both role models and tutors for women students (see, for example, McWilliams-Tullberg, 1975; Hansard Society Commission, 1990; Dyhouse, 1995; Eagle,

1998). This issue has been highlighted in recent years in reports alleging high levels of harassment and 'institutional sexism' affecting women students, media accounts of the humiliating interview experienced by a female applicant from Essex, and a case of alleged sex discrimination in the University's promotion procedures which has been erupting periodically for several years. Given the advantaged position of Oxbridge, where funding council monies at relatively generous levels are received at both university and college level (although the fees paid to colleges are now being reduced), there are political pressures on their senior staff to demonstrate that equity and value for money are being achieved.

Taking a second, fictionalized, example: the senior staff of an institution in a rural area which has traditionally recruited school-leavers from middle-class urban families might have major worries about the sustainability of this position. The cost of fees and rising living costs may be encouraging many potential entrants from this socio-economic group to find a university place within daily travelling distance from home, to reduce living costs and possibly in order to keep on their part-time jobs. Universities in localities with low population density cannot compensate for a decline in applications for full-time places by substantially increasing their provision of part-time courses, at undergraduate or postgraduate level, because their catchment areas are unlikely to be able to sustain this growth. The senior managers at this institution realise that radical steps are required now.

Both of these examples show the pressures facing institutions which probably need to be addressed initially at the most senior level, but which carry implications for other staff, and which are likely to bring changes in equal opportunities policy and practice. In the Oxbridge case, the substantive position needs to be changed in the direction of actively and successfully shifting recruitment towards students from under-represented social groups. If this is deemed impossible, a cynical and pragmatic response to the situation would be to defend the status quo, presenting it in a way which justifies it in terms of national political priorities and values (such as an unabashed defence of privilege and elitism). In the case of the rural university, the maintenance of the income represented by student enrolments requires either assiduous effort to sustain recruitment from the customary social groups (through more effective marketing to increase market share, or the development of innovative payment arrangements, or a restructuring of the academic year to enable students to have more time for short-term employment and to release accommodation for vacation-time short courses or holiday letting) or the attraction of new kinds of student (for example, an emergent reputation for the effective support of students with a specific type of disability could be built upon, backed by a targeted recruitment campaign). If these measures are not realistic possibilities, then development of new income streams is required to compensate for this shortfall. One solution might be the provision of new kinds of 'academic product' based on sound market research, such as the development of distance learning materials, or of residential short courses for niche markets, or modular part-time course provision delivered in blocks for local or national organizations. In both these case studies, a real shift in the direction of equality of opportunity can address these current problems.

Where there is no strong central direction in relation to equal opportunities, middle managers are likely to have wide discretion. This leaves them the same kind of latitude as is described above in relation to vice-chancellors, either to pursue policies which reflect their own values or to devise initiatives which accord with wider considerations, based on moral or financial considerations or both, insofar as they are pertinent for the disciplines, professions or activities of their unit. Wherever possible, new directions in policy and practice should seek to integrate personal and institutional values with identified opportunities, gaps or niches in provision, to maximize their likely success. As the previous chapter emphasized, innovation should wherever possible quickly be embedded within the routine practices of the unit in order to sustain it. The promiscuous opportunism of chasing short-term funding sources can be very wasteful of staff time and leads to what has recently been termed by the Committee of Vice-Chancellors and Principals 'initiative fatigue'. Well-managed faculties and departments offer a sense of stable, directed progress towards clearly defined appropriate goals, which inspires confidence in its management from service users and staff alike. Of course, it is usually advisable to test the water by means of a small-scale pilot before launching an innovation, especially where it will involve the commitment of more than marginal resources, or where the projected outcomes will have a substantial impact on present operations. The establishment of effective monitoring arrangements, so that the impact of the initiative can properly be assessed, is another priority. A review of the effects of an initiative, after an agreed period, will show whether it warrants permanent incorporation into the unit's routine operations.

For the middle manager who wishes to initiate change, and has the latitude to determine locally what direction it might take, these are some of the questions to be asked in seeking to identify its likely success. These are mainstream issues for managers, the answers to which may have implications for equal opportunities. For most managers, this represents a more realistic approach than starting from a visceral commitment to equal opportunities, which then has to be packaged as a mainstream initiative in order to secure wide-ranging commitment from staff.

- What are the institution's values, as expressed in the mission statement? Where, in particular, do my own values overlap with them? What are the prevailing values of my staff team?
- What are the current and prospective problems for my unit, in terms of its capacity to sustain and expand its core activities (such as to recruit students of the right quality and in sufficient numbers)? To what extent can they be addressed through a broadening of opportunity to under-represented groups within the population?
- How can we keep our courses attractive in content, structure, cost, mode of delivery, and promote the employability of our graduates or their capacity to proceed to further study?

- Can we continue to attract able staff with appropriate qualifications and experience, to teach and to administer our services or courses ? Should we be thinking of new ways to recruit and retain staff?
- Can we continue to provide appropriate resources to underpin our provision or courses (including accommodation, equipment including library and information technology facilities, staff time and student support mechanisms)? Can we find better or more cost-effective ways of maintaining or improving provision?
- Can we continue to provide sufficient high quality placement opportunities?
- What scope is there for the development of partnerships with external agencies for recruiting additional or different types of student, for delivering courses in different ways, or for sharing resources?
- Can we develop partnerships within the institution to support these collaborations (with other academic or support departments)?
- How can I mobilize the commitment of my staff to certain core values and agreed objectives, and their expertise, to achieve the changes needed for my unit to prosper and to meet corporate objectives?

Assuming for the moment that the unit in question is an academic one which derives most of its income from providing award-bearing courses, many answers to these questions will have equal opportunities implications. Where the recruitment of suitably qualified applicants from traditional socio-economic groups is declining, or not increasing at the rate required to meet recruitment targets or to maintain income, then the targeted marketing of current products (such as courses) to new groups might be productive. However, first it is necessary to review how far these products themselves and the way they are made available actually meet the needs of these new groups. If there are no problems, then why has this group been hitherto under-represented within the student intake? It is more likely that aspects of their delivery will need to be changed to make them more attractive to a new group, or that the products themselves will need to be changed. It is often part of the scrutiny process when new courses are being developed to ask whether market research has indicated their attractiveness to target groups. Invariably the proposers assert that these projected courses have been acclaimed by their intended audiences, but all too frequently no hard evidence is put forward to substantiate such claims.

These are some of the equal opportunities issues which need to be considered by the manager of an academic unit when seeking to manage change in relation to the kinds of questions outlined above. As ever, the intention is to analyse the present position, to identify areas for development, to set targets and monitor progress towards them (either as pilot projects which are then reviewed, or as mainstream changes, where there is substantial evidence of their likely success) and to embed these developments in the standard operations of the unit or institution. The ideal situation would be to have reliable management information collected centrally, on a regular basis, to inform these processes. If this does not exist, and cannot readily be established, then it may be necessary to gather such information at local level and to share it with peers elsewhere, to provide benchmarks indicating the status quo, to inform target-setting and to assess progress towards targets.

Recruiting and retaining prospective students from under-represented groups

If a course or disciplinary field already has a substantial proportion of applicants, entrants and successful completers from certain social groups, it is worth reviewing how they are recruited and their socio-demographic profile. If you are already recruiting well from certain quarters, you could build on these achievements. If there are gaps, then greater recruitment activity could help fill them. This will involve an assessment of the mechanisms through which applicants select your course. For example, if you recruit strongly to certain courses from school-leavers in certain schools within your region, then it could be a good investment of effort to focus on recruiting still further from this pool by developing links with additional schools and further education colleges. This may be more cost-effective than trying to develop recruitment from areas and groups where you have no established reputation. Personal connections count. Satisfied clients are your best ambassadors, who may persuade their friends, colleagues and other family members to apply to your institution or course, or who may be recruited to stay on for further study.

You may not need to set up your own faculty or departmental links with schools or colleges if effective institutional links already exist. However, these link-people need to be well-informed about the details of your recruitment criteria and course provision, and you need to receive the intelligence information which they gather in the course of their work. Careers events and other opportunities to present your wares to large numbers of prospective recruits (for example, by having a stand at county shows or other mass events) might represent a good use of staff time. Again, the people who are seeking to sell your product must be sufficiently well-informed to be able to answer questions accurately and to pass on queries for a prompt and informed response.

Ask yourself what media these potential applicants see, distinguishing between the various socio-demographic groups which have been identified as worth seeking to attract. A cinema advert may help attract local people, and the use of the internet and CD-ROMs which include recruitment materials such as the undergraduate prospectus are likely to become major recruitment tools for the IT-literate younger generation. They may not be appropriate for mature students and will fail to reach those who do not use these media. Newspaper advertisements and fliers inserted in local papers may prove to be an expensive broad-brush means to attract a small number of applicants, although they will heighten the local profile of the institution. Your marketing and publicity department may have useful information to inform these decisions, for example analyses of the recent responses to such advertising, which can be used to predict the likely return on the financial cost and the cost of staff time invested in using them.

Promotion of your achievements as a faculty or at university level may be an invaluable long-term marketing device. Again, your marketing and publicity department can help to present information in an appropriate way to secure positive media coverage. Take a leaf out of your local MP's book by aiming to secure favourable coverage in the local paper at least once per week. Can you run events open to the public or to school pupils and college students, or get media coverage for specialist events, which draw attention to staff members' research achievements?

Many people from sections of the population which have no family history of participation in higher education see universities as alien and 'not for people like them'. These barriers need to be dismantled before such people will feel able to apply. Whenever possible, think what steps can be taken to bring them onto the campus or to promote the university as a community resource. Consider what symbols or features might be off-putting, including its physical location or symbolic representation. These might include the display of heraldic crests as part of the institution's 'branding', or heavy security at its entrances, intimidating architecture and high walls which appear to keep 'them' out, or the use of esoteric language to describe everyday phenomena such as 'buttery' or 'refectory' for 'dining room'. Devices to bring in people for short bursts of learning such as day conferences or exhibitions or concerts or short extra-mural courses or prize-givings for courses delivered locally, by the university or by others, will help to overcome these feelings of exclusion and alienation. However, it is all too easy for academics' customary habits of thinking in terms of exclusion rather than inclusion to leach out into these initiatives in ways which implicitly undermine their intent. For example, one red-brick university's web-site provides information on undergraduate and postgraduate courses and 'courses for the public', thereby demarcating them as 'other', and not part of the academic community, which is implicitly inward-looking.

Another form of exclusion relates to transport. City-based universities and colleges may not have this problem if they are well served by public transport, but poor transport links and inadequate or unsafe parking can be major deterrents, especially to part-time students. The numbers of people who daily attend university and college campuses, as students, members of staff and visitors, run into thousands on many sites. It may well be possible to negotiate for better public transport links, or, if necessary, even for the university to provide dedicated services in the morning and evening rush hours to link campuses to local bus and rail stations. This will need to be addressed at senior level within the university, but the impetus for such an initiative could come from local units if they can demonstrate that recruitment is being adversely affected.

If central services are not being delivered in ways which meet current and prospective students' needs, or if the university is missing opportunities to improve its service delivery, then critical feedback from local units is required, voicing actual and prospective students' concerns. University finance offices are often the target of critical comment, perhaps because its staff are more likely to have been recruited from outside education and so may lack the capacity to assess the operation of their systems from the student's perspective. Are payment arrangements for fees sufficiently flexible to meet students' needs? Is accurate and accessible information on payment arrangements easily available to prospective students? Are queries dealt with politely and promptly? The need for responsiveness applies to other support departments and services of various kinds. Does the university have an employment agency for helping to identify temporary and part-time jobs for students? Do term dates and assessment schedules fit students' domestic, religious and other personal circumstances? Can students submit work or get access to library information electronically, via home modems? If there is a centrally organized timetable, could it be restructured to require full-time students to attend only on two or three days per week? With students' fast-growing ownership of home computers and modems, far-reaching changes can be made quickly in relation to attendance, access to information and even to fellow students and staff, and in assessment practices. However, their potential knock-on effects need careful consideration. If there is a shift from class-based learning towards home-based learning using information technology, this may make it easier to find a parking place on campus, but will reduce expenditure in catering facilities. The deployment of staff in learning resources departments will need to shift away from stacking returned books and towards information technology support. These developments could reduce absolute demand for places in halls of residence, or could shift demand to a couple of midweek nights, rather than a full week. Would this release accommodation for weekend and vacation use by students doing postgraduate courses such as an MBA or a taught doctorate in education through blocks of study? So should halls become more like hotels and, if so, how can the needs, financial resources and living habits typical of young full-time students be reconciled with some older part-time employed students' desire to have en-suite bathrooms and peace after 11pm? How far can it be assumed that all students have access to information technology at home? Does this assumption tend to exclude students from less affluent households, or older students who fear computer technology?

Alongside tackling these generic university-wide barriers to participation, staff in certain faculties or departments might address the issue of whether they wish to recruit actively from certain selected under-represented groups rather than others. The motives for doing so have been covered earlier. This should be a matter for widespread debate, in order to think through the implications collectively as fully as possible, and to ensure the broadest possible commitment to this objective. The recruitment of school-leavers from middle-class households is a relatively straightforward and inexpensive matter, using well-oiled mechanisms such as the undergraduate prospectus and open days. It becomes much more expensive in terms of both staff time and additional resources to achieve good results from work with 'hard-to-reach' groups, and the mechanisms involved will need to vary depending on which groups are identified and what they are being offered.

For certain groups, notably mature students, a tried-and-tested approach has been to study for GCSE A-levels or to take an access to higher education course provided locally, usually in a college of further education. This might be on a part-time of full-time basis and is likely to lead to an interview or (pending successful performance on their course of study) the offer of a place to study at a local university or college. Many FE colleges offer the first year or all of a programme of study leading to a higher education qualification such as an HND or HNC or degree, usually franchised from a university and therefore bringing its award. The advantage of these arrangements is that the student never needs to leave their home area to obtain their award. A mid-way point is provided by colleges or other agencies which may offer the first level of a higher education award, successful completion of which enables the student to transfer to the 'parent' university to complete the higher levels of their study programme. One example of this is the provision of a restricted choice of first-level modules in the humanities and social sciences to mature women students at Castleford Women's Centre, in West Yorkshire, after which they study for the rest of their degree at Leeds Metropolitan University, travelling daily to Leeds city centre to do so. Students come to the Women's Centre in the town centre one day a week to study in small groups with a tutor who gets to know them well. The limited curricular choice and restricted range of library resources need to be set against the high level of peer and tutor support, which provides constant encouragement to overcome the inevitable setbacks. Having successfully completed their Level 1 modules, the students then have the confidence to move on to advanced study, in the previously daunting setting of a large city-centre university. Similar schemes in other parts of the UK likewise are based on universities located in the region, and might involve Level 1 study at community centres or in schools, often using information technology. Where distance is a barrier, relocation to the university might be necessary for further study at higher level, or students can switch to Open University study, having established the skills and confidence needed to succeed as independent learners.

Now that over half of all university students are mature on entry (defined as aged 21 and over on entry to undergraduate courses and 25 and over for postgraduates), older students need no longer fear being a member of a conspicuous minority (HESA, 1997: 16). However, there are major differences by subject and institution. Combined studies courses, education and subjects allied to medicine attract a higher proportion of students aged over 25 than do medicine and dentistry, the physical sciences and languages (HESA, 1997: 17). There is some evidence that mature students' employment rates on graduation are lower than those for younger students. This may be because they are less geographically mobile or are constrained by continuing child-care or domestic commitments, or they may suffer from employers' ageism. There are clear implications here of matters which admissions tutors, personal tutors and managers need to consider in asking themselves whether their courses are likely to provide a positive and ultimately successful university education for members of these groups. Can tuition be provided within a daily timetable which enables mature students to travel daily from their homes to study, possibly by public transport, and does it take account of any domestic commitments? This might mean fitting lectures and small group sessions into an abbreviated working day of 10am to 3pm, and ideally only requiring attendance on certain days, but this has implications for the staff who teach them, for other students (whose groups are then more likely to be timetabled for off-peak times) and for the efficient usage of teaching accommodation. Does the university have a nursery, and if so, does it have a long waiting list? Are its charges affordable for students and what are its opening hours? How are mature students with child-care responsibilities expected to cope with school half-term holidays? Does the university provide a temporary child-care scheme for these times? Are assignment deadlines and examinations timed to mesh with these commitments (for example, with no early or late examinations, or deadlines immediately after school holidays)?

Students from non-traditional groups need to feel well supported by their personal tutors, who will carry the main duty of providing encouragement and guidance during the students' courses. If such informed, empathetic support is not forthcoming, students risk failing to meet course requirements and will have correspondingly higher rates of failure and withdrawal. This represents a personal tragedy for the student concerned, as well as a wasted opportunity for them and the department. It is therefore vital that a sufficiently large 'critical mass' of non-standard students is admitted so that they can provide effective peer support and will feel sufficiently confident to articulate their needs. It is equally important that identifiable role models exist on the staff, who have insight into these students' situation and so can provide effective mediation, interpretation and representation services on their behalf. Departments need to have the wisdom to interpret course requirements with some flexibility where they conflict with students' other commitments. Where student numbers are large, as in many institutions, it is vital for each student to feel that their personal tutor understands their circumstances and is prepared to champion their interests. This is why it matters to have a diverse staff profile in academic departments. However well-intentioned they might be, the white, male middle-aged members of staff who predominate in many departments, especially in declining subjects such as science and engineering, are unlikely to be perceived as empathetic by young women students who fear they might be pregnant, or who worry that an outbreak of cystitis will interfere with their exam performance. Who can an overseas student turn to for help, when his exam failure is making him suicidal at the thought of the shame involved in returning to his family without the successful outcome to his studies which he sought? If a young Asian woman student is finding it almost impossible to reconcile the cultural expectations from her 'traditional' family with her own desire to study, what does she do? A male mature student from a stable working-class community is finding the adjustment to study difficult, not only in financial terms but also in reconciling the new ideas to which he is being exposed with the values of his family and community. A young man who thinks he may be gay is being bullied in his hall of residence, and this is affecting his capacity to work. Whatever formal arrangements for student support are set up locally, within academic departments, and centrally in student welfare offices, it is well known that students in trouble will approach members of staff whom they know and perceive as likely to be sympathetic. Without planned, structured contact with a diverse range of staff from an early point in students' programmes and continuity with one personal tutor, who gains their trust, the likelihood grows that students who encounter problems will withdraw, either because they feel unable to continue or because their academic performance falls below an acceptable level. The wasted investment of time, money and reputation which this failure represents, for both the student and the university, provides evidence in support of 'the business case' for equal opportunities.

The examples given above of tensions between the standard model of university education and non-standard students' circumstances indicates the range of individuals, from various social groupings, who may feel marginalized, poorly supported or excluded from the academic community. It is important for managers and academic and support staff who have direct contact with students to develop the necessary insight and sensitivity to be able to provide them with the kind of support which they require, if they are to thrive within the university system. Gender is certainly one important variable to consider, and not only in conjunction with 'maturity', with or without the added constraints arising from caring responsibilities. The chapter on gender in relation to students discusses the marginality experienced by some women in male-dominated disciplines. Other variables which can bring marginalization in the academy (either in its formal academic guise or in informal peer networks) are ethnic minority status (whether such students are 'home grown' or from overseas), being a part-time student, social class and 'cultural capital', and regional origin. Additional characteristics which may be used by students to distinguish between in-groups ('us') and out-groups ('them') include religious or political affiliation, sexual orientation, lack of interest in sport and alcohol, and other criteria which might not matter in the outside world but which can be the basis of painful social exclusion, harassment or even bullying in halls of residence or other informal groups.

In a widely read handbook written for research students, Phillips and Pugh (1994) include a chapter called 'How to survive in a predominantly British, white, male, full-time academic environment'. It begins:

> University departments in Britain are largely staffed by British white male full-time academics. Less than a quarter of academics are women and the majority of those are in junior posts, often on short-term contracts. There are even fewer black academics and part-time academic staff are also rare in this country. What does this mean for research students who are not members of the majority group?
>
> (Phillips and Pugh, 1994: 113)

Some of the problems which they identify (based on their extensive experience and data gathered for research projects) are likely to apply equally to students on other kinds of course, especially those which involve extensive contact with staff in one-to-one or small group settings, such as tutorials or the supervision of lab work, projects or dissertations. One not uncommon difficulty experienced by women when they are numerically very much in the minority within the student group is being patronized or over-protected by male tutors, out of misguided chivalry. Far from helping the women who experience this gentlemanly treatment, it may make it difficult for them to acquire confidence in their own abilities and to learn by doing, even if that involves making mistakes. Phillips and Pugh also describe the problems encountered by women students in informal settings when interacting with male academics or students who, because they are not used to treating women as professional peers and colleagues, lack the repertoire of social skills required to do so. Although these days this situation is almost unimaginable for social science and humanities specialists, where the proportion of women students (if not staff) is over half, there are still disciplines and university departments where women are very much in the minority. And it is not only women who may experience exclusion or discomfort from their peers; the 'othering' of members of minorities based on a range of criteria (such as ethnicity or sexual orientation) leads to similar outcomes.

The lack of role models is also noted. The presence of 'someone like you' in a department provides a basis for shared experience which can make all the difference between thriving and failure. They can effectively represent your case and champion your position where necessary (for example in exam boards, if a student's progress is marginal, by putting the case for discretion to be exercised). In addition, they provide a visible manifestation of career success as an academic, whose contacts and advice can help sponsor the first steps in a graduate's career by lifting ambitions and helping to identify opportunities in employment or for further study. The under-representation of women, people from minority ethnic backgrounds, visibly disabled people and members of other minorities in positions of power in universities reduces the scope for sponsorship of this kind, which serves to perpetuate inequality. How many PhD holders can assert that they had no guidance from a mentor or sponsor to encourage them to start a research degree?

Various studies have identified the prevalence of sexual harassment and non-peer sexual relationships, usually between male academics and female students, although in many institutions, the main trade unions and the National Union of Students now have codes which proscribe or discourage it (although one recent report described it as being perceived by some male academics as virtually 'a perk of the job'). Staff members may be required to record such relationships, and steps are usually taken to prevent their involvement in the assessment of the student concerned. There is anecdotal evidence of the high incidence of physical harassment in places such as university libraries, where the staff are mainly female. Although when the early reports were published it was argued by some that relationships which take place between staff and students involve consenting adults and so should not be regulated, there is clear evidence that this is a form of sexualized dominance. As such, it threatens to undermine the confidence of the less powerful parties who experience it. There is much less documentation on other forms of harassment, such as racial abuse, within higher education, so its extent is uncharted although it undoubtedly does take place. Managers have a clear responsibility to deal with harassment and affairs between staff members and students, or between students and other students where this has generated a complaint, in accordance with institutional procedures, in the interests of protecting vulnerable students.

International students undertaking study in institutions away from home often complain that they are too often seen as a lucrative source of income for their 'host' universities. Many institutions with significant numbers of students from abroad have established support mechanisms such as overseas student advisors or international officers, and students may set up their own friendship networks with their compatriots. However, the problems of loneliness and cultural isolation felt by many such students, especially during vacation times, may require particular measures to address them, at local or university-wide level. Teaching staff may need to have awareness training to sensitize them to cultural differences which could, through their ignorance, jeopardize international students' progress. Examples include differences in norms about original work and plagiarism and the excessively high expectations (in relation to British norms) held by families about their children's academic performance which can make suicide seem preferable to failure. Some international students in the UK report that their tutors display patronizing or paternalistic benevolence towards them. Many universities have sorry tales to tell of research students funded by government grants who fail to appreciate or to meet local expectations about doctoral study, leading to delayed submission of their thesis, referral or outright failure. Again, these issues are to some extent foreseeable and therefore, with effective management intervention, become amenable to resolution. Disparaging attitudes from staff can also affect students from minority ethnic backgrounds and Phillips and Pugh (1994: 129) describe the very careful process of selecting a university for postgraduate study undertaken by some minority students to find somewhere with a congenial and empathetic institutional culture and some role models.

There are various strategies which can be used by managers at departmental level to secure feedback from students to ensure that their department's provision is meeting their needs. Institutions and departments with effective quality assurance arrangements will have these measures in place, and can demonstrate responsiveness to constructive criticism within this framework. Starting from the individual student's viewpoint, the existence of effective peer support networks is a vital aid to successful study. Departments of social work, who have for over a decade now been expected to build their students' experiences around anti-discriminatory practice, have long recognized the value of establishing homogeneous student groups to provide support for each other during their course. Often these relationships will develop informally, in the form of peer friendships within the student group. Ideally, supportive and amicable relationships will also flourish between staff and students. They should not transgress the boundary between the kind of relationship appropriate where one party is engaged in the formal assessment of the other, into a situation where the necessary social distance cannot be maintained, or a romantic or sexual relationship develops. The establishment of cordial staff/ student working relationships is facilitated where students are mainly taught by the department's own staff, without the presence of other students in the class, and the buildings' architecture and departmental practices can also contribute. Where departments enjoy the luxury of exclusive use of a space (whether a Victorian house or a floor of a larger modern building) and above all if they have dedicated social accommodation which is used by most students and staff such as a cafeteria or common room, these facilities will foster a sense of identity with the community. Minor matters can be dealt with quickly and informally, before they accrue the magnitude of a major problem, and without students needing to sum up the personal resources required to make an appointment with a tutor or adviser.

Of course, modular programmes, large heterogeneous student groups and university-wide timetables for accommodation use all militate against the kind of cosy collegiality that we think of when harking back to the golden age of academe which we imagine existed some ten years before any of us were students. (We will gloss over the white, male, middle-class character of this mythical community of scholars, and ignore its notorious intrigues and competitive individualism.) In these circumstances, formal systems need to replace the informal concern with individuals' progress and welfare which can exist in small communities. Partly as a result of national quality review programmes, most institutions now have regular arrangements for eliciting student feedback on modules and courses, using questionnaires and committee meetings where staff meet student representatives and provide minuted responses to issues raised. Good management practice involves the peer review of teaching and the use of the results of this and formal evaluations to inform staff members' annual performance reviews. In addition to these formal mechanisms, the progressive head of department or course leader may encourage the establishment of semi-formal student support groups, such as the Black Students' Group for a social work course. As the fluid membership of such groups poses problems of continuity, a sensitive head of department will initially ensure that the students wish for such a group to be established, and then will book a room for a regular programme of meetings and (if the students want) provide a minuting secretary or 'friend', so that the issues raised can be passed on to the appropriate person or committee. As it is important that any messages are heard and understood by someone with sufficient authority to be able to progress them effectively, the students may wish for a trusted member of the academic staff to serve as the link person.

In many cases students may prefer to seek peer support networks at institutional rather than local level, through the students' union. Most universities have mature student groups, LGB (lesbian, gay and bisexual) groups, societies for Muslim students and/or international students, and other networks which bring together like-minded students. It will probably pay dividends to ensure that students are made aware of these groups in their induction programme, or through notices in the public areas in the department.

A generation ago, disciplines were taught in higher education according to a canon which left no space for political or personal concerns. The politicization of the higher education curriculum has brought sexism, racism, ethical and ecological concerns into the teaching of many subjects over the past couple of decades. However, there is ample evidence that in many institutions the ostensible pluralism and diversity of the documented curriculum is not matched by a genuine commitment on the part of all staff. The powerful messages of liberalism and challenge implied by the formal curriculum may be no more than a sophisticated veneer presented by those who can speak the language of equal opportunities, but who use it as a cloak to deflect real change and to preserve their own positions. The work by Phillips and Pugh (1994) cited earlier describes the struggle of some postgraduate students to have their choice of topic and approach accepted as legitimate by those committees which decide such things. Feminist and 'personal' topics are still in some quarters seen as biased or not representing proper scholarship. Members of multidisciplinary research degrees committees (which will almost invariably be male-dominated, due to the low proportion of women academics in senior positions) feel free to pass ill-informed judgmental comments on proposals in areas such as social science, education and cultural studies, when they would not think about doing so for topics from other fields. Many female academics in the social sciences can recount tales of how male colleagues who are reluctant to give up their control of prestigious courses such as theory and research methods pander to the need to address feminist issues by offering a female colleague a 'guest spot'. In subjects where the majority of students are women, there is usually great interest in feminist theory and perspectives, raising the further problem that the guest lecturer's proffered essay topic or examination question elicits a massive response and a disproportionate share of the marking! A similar issue is the continuing popularity of courses in women's studies, but they often suffer from marginality and consequent under-resourcing, in relation to other emergent fields of study. A comparison with other 'new' courses is instructive in this respect, such as sports studies and materials science, where the gender profile of students is rather different and the subject matter is seen as less challenging in terms of institutional politics.

The main message which should have come from this preceding section is that students need to feel that they belong within the academic community in which they have chosen to study. When higher education was an elite system in which departments selected promising students, the expectation that the students would conform to the ethos of the department was perhaps just about defensible. The balance of power between departments seeking to recruit students and the student selecting a course has shifted somewhat, and clearly there is now far greater diversity between institutions than the Robbins Committee would have found in the early 1960s when it set about a thorough review of the higher education sector in the UK. There is more emphasis on the student as customer or client, exemplified by the shift towards the direct payment of tuition fees, and there is a higher expectation in the UK at least, for higher education to account for the £4 billion of public money which it receives annually. The business case for equal opportunities meshes with these pressures to promote concern about achieving a successful outcome for each student, partly as a moral imperative but also to demonstrate the effectiveness of the course team, the department and the institution, as judged by performance indicators.

Equal opportunities matters concerning staff

The preceding discussion has largely concerned middle managers' responsibilities for equal opportunities issues in relation to students' experiences. However, it should have become abundantly clear that their staff constitute an
important element in the partnership to provide students with a positive
experience. It is a truism that organizations are only as good as their staff. In
the context of higher education, the calibre of academic staff has traditionally
been assessed in terms of the proportion with PhDs and their record of research
publications. This position is unlikely to change in the short term, given the
symbolic and financial significance of the United Kingdom's Research Assessment Exercise and the international significance of a person's or a department's record of winning research grants and citations. However, the growing
national concern with other performance indicators such as the quality of
teaching and learning (as assessed by quality review scores in the UK), student
withdrawal rates and graduates' destination data are legitimating the achievements of departments in areas other than research outputs. The incorporation
of equal opportunities measures into the pantheon of performance indicators
validates the efforts of staff in certain departments and institutions to cater for
students from a diverse array of backgrounds, and to gain public recognition
(and possibly to win additional funding) for their success in doing so.

The preceding section, concerning the student experience, has addressed
certain important management issues concerning staff. These include the need
to shift the staff profile in the direction of reflecting the student intake, in socio-
demographic terms, and the need for formal and informal mechanisms for
student support and for responding to issues that they raise about their experiences. Advice about the latter can be obtained from the university's specialist
staff for student support and quality assurance. Management of the staffing
profile is clearly a more protracted matter, given the duration of the average
academic's career and the low opportunities to appoint new staff in most
departments, as a result of the long-standing decline in the 'unit of resource'
(that is, expenditure per student). The few areas where growth in student numbers has so outstripped this decline that new staff have been recruited include
subjects such as business studies, information technology and sports studies.

There is a certain amount of technical information, especially in relation to
legislation, which managers need to consider in making academic appointments. Equal opportunities legislation concerning gender, disability and ethnicity will apply to the recruitment process. This includes the wording of
both the advertisement and the contract, and the use of 'closed recruiting'
where only members of a specific population category may apply. The relevant
expertise to guide managers should be available from staff in the personnel
department, and basic information may be covered in a personnel handbook.
All staff involved in recruitment and selection interviewing should have had
training in equal opportunities. This should seek to ensure that they operate in
a legally defensible way (for example, by not asking women applicants about
child-care arrangements if they do not also ask men) but should also cover

cultural concerns about fair recruitment procedures. The use of formal person specifications and job specifications in appointment procedures (which set out, in advance of the recruitment process, the essential and desirable characteristics of the ideal appointee and the nature of the post) has become commonplace, partly arising from employers' concerns about subsequent challenges through the industrial tribunal system. They can help to crystallize the characteristics being sought in a way which promotes rational criteria-based selection, as opposed to panels' well-documented predilection to perpetuate the status quo by seeking to appoint people with whom they feel at ease socially.

The point about seeking not only to recruit but also to retain students from under-represented groups by providing them with an environment within which they feel well supported applies equally to staff. Engineering departments which wished to promote the recruitment of women students have often tried, in a well-intentioned way, to support this by appointing a woman member of staff. However, one lone female lecturer among 50 or 90 male colleagues is unlikely to feel at ease. She will be expected to shoulder a disproportionate share of administrative and pastoral duties as the 'token woman' on appointment panels and personal tutor to all women students, and at the same time her academic record as a researcher and lecturer is under public scrutiny because of her conspicuous difference by virtue of her sex. During one professional visit I made to a very male-dominated faculty, one such young woman lecturer described her feelings of being terribly over-burdened by these responsibilities and expectations, but said that she felt unable to voice her concerns. The appointment of mentors for newly appointed staff (which, in such cases, should be an experienced woman colleague from another department) is good practice anyway, but is particularly desirable under these circumstances.

Rather than seeking to appoint a woman member of staff only if she ranks highest according to the usual criteria such as qualifications and research record (which is statistically unlikely in many fields because of major historic gender imbalances in the ratio of postgraduate and research students), managers may wish to operate in a more subtle way to effect change. Instead of seeking to appoint someone with a particular technical specialism, it is worth considering whether a recruitment advert could be worded in a more open-ended way about the exact teaching or research expertise sought, and linked with a specified duty such as tutor to women or international students or students with a disability (see pages 141–2). This sends out clear signals about the characteristics of the person being sought. Likewise, the medium chosen for a recruitment advertisement carries messages about the recruiter's intentions. Even if it is unlikely that many applicants will arise from an advertisement in newspapers serving minority ethnic or gay and lesbian communities, to advertise here is to make a public statement about the values of the department and institution.

The culture of the department is an important factor in promoting feelings of belonging, for staff and students. Once again, there is evidence of problems from departments where almost all students and teaching and technical staff have historically been male, and where there have been few appointments of younger staff who may bring different, less traditional attitudes. 'Laddish' culture, where banter is commonplace, is likely to be experienced as alienating and exclusionary by women and other minority groups, and although objective evidence is hard to get, it seems that reports of sexual harassment are more common from such milieux. In part this may be because of a culture clash, where behaviour which has been regarded as commonplace is experienced as harassment by entrants from different social groups. However, there is ample evidence from male-dominated occupational settings outside higher education of the deliberate use of verbal or physical harassment as a tactic to drive out such incomers (see for example Martin, 1988).

The tone of a departmental culture is established by its head, and can change as the incumbent changes. It is important in public settings such as meetings to set a tone of mutual respect and acknowledgement of diversity through the use of language, including body language, and the conduct of meetings. Heads of department should try to emulate good role models, and may wish to ask for equal opportunities training to help identify issues which may not otherwise have occurred to them. If staff who are members of under-represented minorities feel conspicuous representatives of their sex or ethnic group, they may be reluctant to raise issues which draw attention to their position or which look like special pleading. It can take great sensitivity and awareness to intuit people's needs. For example, few women staff will feel able to withdraw from a meeting in progress to collect their child from a nursery, or to miss an appointment in order to stay at home to let the washing machine mechanic in, whereas many of their male colleagues feel that they earn special praise and credibility as a 'new man' by doing exactly the same thing. If it is asking the impossible to expect a manager to divine what problems their staff may be encountering, then a climate should be established in which it becomes acceptable to raise such issues, in private if not in public.

The annual staff review meeting can provide an important opportunity for the two-way exchange of views between the manager and the staff member from a minority group. This will supplement the routine interchange of information which takes place both informally and formally throughout the year. If a member of staff is experiencing alienation within the department, then it is likely that students do, too, and the departure of students and staff for this reason represents a waste of human potential and institutional resources.

University-wide opportunities for staff to work together provide for the cross-fertilization of ideas about good practice, in many areas including equal opportunities. Committee meetings, working parties and staff development events expose staff to the routine practices and style of other parts of the institution. If there appear to be difficulties, for example if some people's personal styles or their use of language or their sense of humour cause offence, it may be worth setting up staff development sessions. These matters could be confronted directly, or a session could draw attention to best practice in the guise of working on another matter, such as 'dealing with difficult colleagues' or 'handling meetings effectively'.

The injection of sound advice from external peers elsewhere in the university, or from colleagues within similar departments in other institutions, is invaluable to the concerned manager. These advisers will be familiar with the organizational culture of the university and with the discipline-based culture of the subject, which cross-cut at departmental level. Few problems are unique to one department, and colleagues elsewhere may be able to offer guidance based on their own experience. If certain issues are exercising someone in a management role, the chances are that their peers are facing similar issues. In this case, it may be worth setting up a working party or internal staff development event, to bring to bear a pool of relevant expertise, or even of organizing a regional or national conference, which could bring in additional income, as well as enhancing the institution's reputation! Many of the issues identified as problems in this book are the result, at least in part, of out-dated perceptions, stereotypes and attitudes which will disappear in due course as new generations of staff and of increasingly articulate students arrive in the academy. However, this pace of change is too slow. Students and members of staff who are here now deserve to be treated with consideration and respect. The best advice to the manager who seeks to improve his/her practice is to listen and take heed of constructive criticism, whether from students or members of staff, and to establish an ethos of mutual respect and consideration within which members of this community feel able to voice their concerns and have confidence that they will be addressed.

References

Dyhouse, C. (1995) *No Distinction of Sex? Women in British Universities 1870–1939*. London: UCL Press.

Eagle, M. (1998) She was one pupil in 450, *THES*, 13 March.

Hansard Society Commission (1990) *Women at the Top*. London: The Hansard Society for Parliamentary Government.

McWilliams-Tullberg, R. (1975) *Women at Cambridge: A Men's University, Though of a Mixed Type*. London: Gollancz.

Martin, M. (ed.) (1988) *Hard-Hatted Women: Stories of Struggle and Success in the Trades*. Seattle: Seal Press.

Phillips, E. and Pugh, D. S. (1994) *How to Get a PhD: A Handbook for Students and their Supervisors*, 2nd edn. Buckingham: Open University Press.

Powney, J., Hamilton, S. and Weiner, G. (1997) *Higher Education and Equality: A Guide*. London: Equal Opportunities Commission, Commission for Racial Equality and Committee of Vice-Chancellors and Principals of the Universities of the UK.

11

Conclusion

Karen Ross

As the material contained in this book demonstrates, the business of managing equal opportunities in order to maximize the potential of staff and students and therefore the institution as a whole, is complex and complicated but *can* be done and done effectively. But equal opportunities strategies are too often products of a 'quick fix' rhetoric which sees the production of a policy as an end in itself, where the document stands as proxy for action. In the UK, while one government-funded enquiry after another (see previous chapters) supports what has become commonly 'known' about the 'problem' of *un*equal opportunities in terms of access to higher education, the moral and ethical arguments which are brought to bear on the debate are supplemented, increasingly, by an altogether more pragmatic imperative to get more students, including more non-traditional ones, through the door. So strategies which deliver widened participation are not only good for the corporate soul but also good for the corporate bank balance.

And it's not as if examples of good practice are hiding under their own modest bushel: any number of seminars, workshops and conferences on the theme are bulging with excellent examples of successful strategies to, say, involve more women in science, make lecture theatres more accessible to students with physical disabilities, nurture and mentor young women lecturers, support specific student communities such as Asian or gay students, and so on. But still the sector persists in asking itself the same hoary old questions to which we all, surely, now know the answers. At a recent workshop on gender and higher education hosted by a reasonably 'progressive' university, one key strategy to emerge from the day's deliberations was that of peer support, but do we really have to spend yet another day of group activities to generate the 'new' idea that women in the academy should be supporting each other more? It sometimes seems that the principle of lifelong learning which we exhort our students to embrace mysteriously disappears when we think about our own modus operandi where too many of us feel uncomfortable without a wheel to reinvent. The Royal Economic Society wanted to find out why women are not taking up academic economics and its study showed, among other things, that women students are anxious about the lack of women role models in the academic discipline, a fear borne out entirely by those few women in the academy who *are* doing economics and who say they feel lonely and isolated (Propper, 1998). As Professor of Economics at the University of Bristol, Propper has cause to know but, refreshingly, at least has a couple of suggestions to make about countervailing this tendency, i.e. women-only awards/prizes (such as the Orange prize for literature) and encouraging men to promote (in all senses of the word) their women colleagues.

Do we need to carry out more gender audits, more satisfaction surveys, more accessibility studies, other than to provide empirical evidence to support what we know anecdotally about unfair and unequal practices? What we need to *do*, as managers in higher education institutions, is start taking action and we can make that start by finding out what else is going on and examining how those other strategies in other places are faring and how transplantable they are to our own HEI. That is why this book is important, because it provides a number of useful and usable illustrations of work-in-progress which can be selectively sampled at will.

An interesting study was recently funded jointly by CVCP, the Council for Industry and Higher Education, the Funding Councils for England, Scotland and Wales, the Committee of Scottish Higher Education Principals and the Standing Conference of Principals to identify good practice in widening participation to higher education to young people from low socio-economic backgrounds. The research project was eventually reported on in the document *From Elitism to Inclusion* (Woodrow, 1998) and, together with an earlier dissemination conference, highlighted a number of strategies for working towards an inclusive higher education. This is essential reading for managers of equal opportunities in the sector, both in terms of the guiding principles which it lays out carefully and thoughtfully, including some thought-provoking questions of the, 'but how much will it cost me?' variety, but also for the very practical case studies which it discusses.

The funding/policy context is increasingly informed by an equal opportunities agenda and crucially, in the British context, HEFCE's new funding arrangements for 1999–2000 give a strong steer to institutions to adopt a strategic approach to widening participation, marking a very clear shift from the 'traditional' knee-jerk reactive approach towards one which is mainstream and embedded in the culture and ethos of the institution itself. After significant consultation with higher education institutions during 1998 on its proposals for encouraging wider participation, HEFCE launched its *Widening Participation: Special Funding Programme 1998–9: Outcome of Bids* document (HEFCE 99/07) in February 1999 in which it detailed the projects it would be funding from its first tranche of monies it had made available under the general rubric of widening participation, some £1.5 million. One of HEFCE's stated aims for the programme was to encourage institutions to 'increase the participation of underrepresented groups and to ensure that such students succeed. We will also encourage collaboration between higher education institutions (HEIs) and other education sectors, to tackle the problems of poor progression rates' (HEFCE, 1998: 1). The amount of money mentioned in early consultative documents was a not insignificant £30 million.

In January 1999 HEFCE produced its guidance on base-level provision for disabled students in higher education institutions (HEFCE 99/04). The guidance specifically describes what a 'base level' of provision looks like with regard to this diverse student group, aiming to offer a benchmark against which both students and institutions can evaluate the provision currently offered and thus determine what still (if anything) needs to be put in place. HEFCE's document makes it clear that not only should staff with a specific remit for 'disability' issues be involved in this process, but that all staff might develop a consciousness around disability issues, including senior managers and learning resources staff. The document itself provides useful commentary on a number of topics associated with disability and higher education, including why students with disabilities are an issue for HEIs, the range of disabilities which students disclose and the various strategies which HEIs can develop to support them and a self-completion questionnaire for HEIs to use to determine where they are in relation to the minimum base-level provision suggested by HEFCE. While HEFCE's guidance is just that, guidance rather than legislation, the government itself is beginning to recognize the importance of disability issues in higher education, particularly the fact that the current legislation which 'protects' the rights of people with disabilities – the Disability Discrimination Act 1995 – does not apply to students and it is likely to close this loophole in the near future (Newell, 1999). This will mean, among other things, that staff in the sector will need to be much more knowledgeable about the rights of disabled students and the institution's obligations.

The desirability for a more strategic and considered approach to the whole issue of managing equal opportunities is echoed in Neal's recent work, looking at the actuality of equal opportunity policies and practices (and the rhetoric which underpins them) across the higher education sector (Neal, 1998). Neal advises caution when developing a new strategy since she fears that 'to become bound up in searching for practical (possible) solutions can circumvent the more fundamental question that exists around the ability of equal opportunities discourse itself . . . to make a meaningful difference to equality issues' (Neal, 1998: 117).

While, clearly, some of the dysfunctional aspects of a poorly conceived approach to managing equal opportunities – lack of knowledge about policy, lack of consultation with staff and students, lack of rigorous monitoring and evaluation, lack of ownership, top-down implementation – are being addressed by many HEIs, as the abundance of good practice described throughout this book will testify, it is important to question the extent to which this self-examination is driven by intrinsic rather than extrinsic factors. In the end, perhaps the locus or driver of the action does not matter and outcome is everything, though this is probably a bit simplistic. Pragmatic 'solutions' to the problem of *un*equal opportunities, such as awareness-raising sessions for staff on issues such as recruitment, on-site childcare provision, flexible working, advice lines for lesbian and gay students and developing multicultural curricula are important first steps and are useful in demonstrating that 'something' is being done, but they are not enough in the medium or longer term. Such strategies will not, by themselves, challenge the racism, sexism, homophobia, elitism (and all the other 'isms') which perpetuate inequalities of access, opportunity and experience in higher education since the emphasis needs to be as much on the cause as the effect. If we are not to fall into the trap of seeing the widening out of access to and participation in higher education as a 'special measure', with all the attendant patronizing assumptions with which they are accompanied, then we need to grasp the ideological and attitudinal nettle and ask *ourselves* a few hard questions. As Srivastava argues, 'widening access requires not only action at the point of access . . . but also responsibility to improve pathways to courses. It is a process requiring commitment and understanding of equal opportunities' (1997: 35).

While we are doing that, we might remember that individual HEI's efforts finally to do something proactive about *un*equal opportunities in higher education are part of a much wider (perhaps even global) agenda. For example, the European Access Network was launched in 1994 as part of the European Union's Action IV Programme and exists as the only non-governmental, European-wide organization which sets out to extend access to higher education (see Chapter 6 for further details, including contact information). Its public 'mission', taken from its (undated) promotional literature, is to 'encourage wider access to HE in all European countries for those who are currently under-represented, whether for reasons of gender, ethnic origin, nationality, age, disability, employment status, income level, family background, vocational training, geographic location or earlier educational disadvantage'. Such an inclusive and exhaustive list makes the few 'isms' which most usually constitute the British perspective on equal opportunities appear a little narrow and old-fashioned and we would do well to rethink the scope of widening participation strategies so as to avoid perpetuating the very thing we are trying to challenge.

References

Higher Education Funding Council for England (1998) *Widening Participation in Higher Education: Funding Proposals, Ref 98/39*. Bristol: HEFCE.
Higher Education Funding Council for England (1999a) *Widening Participation in Higher Education: Special Funding Programme 1998–9. Outcome of Bids, Ref 98/39*. Bristol: HEFCE.
Higher Education Funding Council for England (1999b) *Guidance on Base-Level Provision For Disabled Students in Higher Education Institutions, Ref 99/04*. Bristol: HEFCE.
Neal, S. (1998) *The Making of Equal Opportunities Policies in Universities*. Buckingham. Society for Research into Higher Education and Open University Press.
Newell, A. (1999) Enabling technologies, *THES*, 16 April.
Propper, C. (1998) An equal opportunity cost, *THES*, 17 April.

Srivastava, A. (1997) Gender, education and access to professions: tensions between equal opportunities and professional culture investigated through the case of construction courses in higher education. *ISPRU Occasional Paper no. 4*. Leeds: International Social Policy Research Unit, Leeds Metropolitan University.

Woodrow, M. (1998) *From Elitism to Inclusion: Good Practice in Widening Access to Higher Education*. London: CVCP.

Index

The Society for Research into Higher Education

The Society for Research into Higher Education (SRHE) exists to stimulate and coordinate research into all aspects of higher education. It aims to improve the quality of higher education through the encouragement of debate and publication on issues of policy, on the organization and management of higher education institutions, and on the curriculum, teaching and learning methods.

The Society is entirely independent and receives no subsidies, although individual events often receive sponsorship from business or industry. The society is financed through corporate and individual subscriptions and has members from many parts of the world.

Under the imprint *SRHE & Open University Press*, the Society is a specialist publisher of research, having over 80 titles in print. In addition to *SRHE News*, the society's newsletter, the society publishes three journals: *Studies in Higher Education* (three issues a year), *Higher Education Quarterly* and *Research into Higher Education Abstracts* (three issues a year).

The society runs frequent conferences, consultations, seminars and other events. The annual conference in December is organized at and with a higher education institution. There are a growing number of networks which focus on particular areas of interest, including:

Access	Learning Environment
Assessment	Legal Education
Consultants	Managing Innovation
Curriculum Development	New Technology for Learning
Eastern European	Postgraduate Issues
Educational Development Research	Quantitative Studies
FE/HE	Student Development
Funding	Vocational Qualifications
Graduate Employment	

Benefits to Members

Individual

- The opportunity to participate in the Society's networks

- Reduced rates for the annual conferences
- Free copies of *Research into Higher Education Abstracts*
- Reduced rates for *Studies in Higher Education*
- Reduced rates for *Higher Education Quarterly*
- Free copy of *Register of Members' Research Interests* – includes valuable reference material on research being pursued by the Society's members
- Free copy of occasional in-house publications, e.g. *The Thirtieth Anniversary Seminars Presented by the Vice-Presidents*
- Free copies of *SRHE News* which informs members of the Society's activities and provides a calendar of events, with additional material provided in regular mailings
- A 35 per cent discount on all SRHE/Open University Press books
- Access to HESA statistics for student members
- The opportunity for you to apply for the annual research grants
- Inclusion of your research in the *Register of Members' Research Interests*

Corporate

- Reduced rates for the annual conferences
- The opportunity for members of the Institution to attend SRHE's network events at reduced rates
- Free copies of *Research into Higher Education Abstracts*
- Free copies of *Studies in Higher Education*
- Free copies of *Register of Members' Research Interests* - includes valuable reference material on research being pursued by the Society's members
- Free copy of occasional in-house publications
- Free copies of *SRHE News*
- A 35 per cent discount on all SRHE/Open University Press books
- Access to HESA statistics for research for students of the Institution
- The opportunity for members of the Institution to submit applications for the Society's research grants
- The opportunity to work with the Society and co-host conferences
- The opportunity to include in the *Register of Members' Research Interests* your Institution's research into aspects of higher education

Membership details: SRHE, 3 Devonshire Street, London W1N 2BA, UK. Tel: 020 7637 2766. Fax: 020 7637 2781. email: srhe@mailbox.ulcc.ac.uk world wide web: http://www.srhe.ac.uk./srhe/ *Catalogue*: SRHE & Open University Press, Celtic Court, 22 Ballmoor, Buckingham MK18 1XW. Tel: 01280 823388. Fax: 01280 823233. email: enquiries@openup.co.uk

BLACK STUDENTS AND HIGHER EDUCATION
RHETORICS AND REALITIES

John Bird

Black students in the UK have done relatively well in gaining access to higher education but, once they are at university or college, their experiences are often difficult, and characterized by isolation and discrimination. This book examines black access to, and progression in, higher education and is illustrated throughout by quotations from black students. It asks:

* what is the experience of black students in higher education?
* how can institutions act to enhance both black access to and experience of higher education?
* how can both quality and equity be assured?

John Bird considers, for example, working with schools and black communities, staff and curriculum development, ethnic monitoring, the development of black support groups, and the black experience of the labour market after higher education.

This is an important book for higher education policy-makers and for academic staff.

Contents

144pp   0 335 19626 8 (Paperback)   0 335 19627 6 (Hardback)

EQUAL OPPORTUNITIES IN COLLEGES AND UNIVERSITIES
TOWARDS BETTER PRACTICES

Maureen Farish, Joanna McPake, Janet Powney and Gaby Weiner

This book is the *first* attempt to consider the effectiveness of equal opportunities policies for staff (in colleges and universities) after the policies have been passed and implemented. It suggests future strategies for policy-makers and equal opportunities 'activists' in the light of the findings which concern structure, policy coherence and policy contradiction.

It provides an account, through the detailed case-studies of three educational institutions (one further education college, one 'new' and one 'old' university) of how equal opportunities policy-making has developed over the last decade and what gains have been made. It also examines the complexity of trying to judge the effectiveness of such policies by viewing policy from a number of standpoints including those of managers and policy-makers, those charged with implementing the policies (for instance, equal opportunities or women's officers), and those at the receiving end. In trying to unravel the complexity, what emerges is the importance of institutional history and context as well as policy structure and content.

Contents

Setting the context of equal opportunities in educational organizations – Brorough college incorporated: case study – Town university: case study – Metropolitan university: case study – Critical moments and illuminative insights – Codifying policy and practice – Contrasting contexts – Shared themes – Munro bagging: towards better practices – Appendix: research methodology – Bibliography – Index.

224pp   0 335 19416 8 (Paperback)   0 335 19417 6 (Hardback)

MAKING EQUAL OPPORTUNITIES POLICIES IN UNIVERSITIES
Sarah Neal

This book explores how higher education in contemporary Britain has responded to questions of equal opportunities (particularly questions of race), what types of responses have been made, and how effective they have been. It analyses the political character of equal opportunities policies, the processes of their formation, and the structures put in place to implement them. Foregrounding research dilemmas, Sarah Neal draws upon four university case studies, using both equal opportunities documents and interviews with key personnel. She focuses upon the institutional discourses which surround equal opportunities in the universities. She is concerned not only with their treatment of the issues but also with the positions taken up by academic trade unions.

This important book contextualizes and tells the story of equal opportunities policies in the everyday world of higher education. It reveals the contradictions and ambiguities that lie at the heart of the relationships between universities and equal opportunities policies.

Contents

176pp   0 335 19807 4 (Paperback)   0 335 19808 2 (Hardback)